The Economy of Late Achaemenid and Seleucid Babylonia

In this book Reinhard Pirngruber provides a full reassessment of the economic structures and market performance in Late Achaemenid and Seleucid Babylonia. His approach is informed by the theoretical insights of New Institutional Economics and draws heavily on archival cuneiform documents as well as providing the first exhaustive contextualisation of the price data contained in the Babylonian Astronomical Diaries. Historical information gleaned from the accounts of both Babylonian scholars and Greek authors shows the impact of imperial politics on prices in form of exogenous shocks affecting supply and demand. Attention is also paid to the amount of money in circulation. Moreover, the use of regression analysis in modelling historical events breaks new ground in Ancient Near Eastern Studies and gives new impetus to the use of modern economic theory. The book explains the theoretical and statistical methods used so that it is accessible to the full range of historians.

REINHARD PIRNGRUBER is currently a postdoctoral researcher at the University of Vienna working on a project dedicated to the diplomatics and palaeography of Neo- and Late-Babylonian archival documents.

The Economy of Late Achaemenid and Seleucid Babylonia

REINHARD PIRNGRUBER

CAMBRIDGE
UNIVERSITY PRESS

CAMBRIDGE
UNIVERSITY PRESS

University Printing House, Cambridge CB2 8BS, United Kingdom

One Liberty Plaza, 20th Floor, New York, NY 10006, USA

477 Williamstown Road, Port Melbourne, VIC 3207, Australia

4843/24, 2nd Floor, Ansari Road, Daryaganj, Delhi - 110002, India

79 Anson Road, #06-04/06, Singapore 079906

Cambridge University Press is part of the University of Cambridge.

It furthers the University's mission by disseminating knowledge in the pursuit of education, learning, and research at the highest international levels of excellence.

www.cambridge.org

Information on this title: www.cambridge.org/9781107106062

DOI: 10.1017/9781316226766

First published 2017

Printed in the United States of America by Sheridan Books, Inc.

A catalogue record for this publication is available from the British Library.

ISBN 978-1-107-10606-2 Hardback

To Micaela, Arianna and David

Contents

Figures

Tables

Preface

This book is the revised version of a doctoral thesis defended at the VU University Amsterdam in March 2012, which was written within the framework of the interdisciplinary research project 'On the Efficiency of Markets for Agricultural Products in Pre-industrial Societies: The Case of Babylonia *c.* 400–*c.* 60 BC', financed by the Netherlands Organization for Scientific Research (NWO). Throughout the process of writing and revising the thesis, I greatly benefited from the assistance, advice and encouragement of many colleagues. In the first place, special thanks are owed to Bert van der Spek for including me in the exciting project he had devised. Bert was an exemplary supervisor, who, while granting me a maximum amount of freedom to carry out my research, followed my efforts over the years with greatest interest. His valuable criticisms and suggestions much improved the quality of this book. I also would like to acknowledge the inspiring conversations over the years with fellow project members Joost Huijs and Bas van Leeuwen. In particular, the latter's wisdom in all things economic was of great help in the process of coming to terms with the price data contained in the Astronomical Diaries. I also would like to thank the members of the doctoral committee for their comments and suggestions, Bas van Bavel, Jan-Gerrit Dercksen, Michael Jursa, Kristin Kleber and Jan-Luiten van Zanden, as well as the two anonymous readers for Cambridge University Press. Michael Jursa is further to be thanked for enabling me to revise the dissertation during my tenure as post-doctoral researcher in the National Research Network '*Imperium* and *Officium* – Comparative Studies in Ancient Bureaucracy and Officialdom', funded by the FWF – Fonds zur Förderung der wissenschaftlichen Forschung (Vienna), under his direction. Chapter 3, 'Land, Labour and Capital: The Factors of Production', was written in its entirety during that period. I am indebted to several other scholars who have supported me in one way or another with their advice, by making accessible yet-unpublished papers, or otherwise. Among them, I would like to mention Heather D. Baker, Johannes Hackl, Yuval Levavi, Julien Monerie, Martina Schmidl, Marten Stol, Sven Tost, Caroline Waerzeggers and the participants of the seminar 'Economics for Ancient Historians' organised by William V. Harris and Peter Temin at Columbia

University in spring 2009. Jen Hicks corrected the most glaring faults and infelicities of the English text; she should of course not be held responsible for any remaining deficiencies. Daniel Hammer helped with the preparation of the graphs. Finally, I would like to thank Michael Sharp and his staff at Cambridge University Press and Christopher Feeney, copy-editor for Out of House Publishing, for their patience and supportiveness in preparing the final manuscript.

Abbreviations

Abbreviations follow the conventions of the *Archiv für Orientforschung*, available at http://orientalistik.univie.ac.at/forschung/publikationen/ archiv-fuer-orientforschung/#other sub Liste 1 (last accessed 28 December 2016). Additionally:

AD + number: text published in Hunger and Sachs 1988, 1989 and 1996
DN: divine name
EE + number: text published in Stolper 1985
GN: geographic name
IMT + number: text published in Stolper and Donbaz 1997
RN: river name
S/W + number: text published in Slotsky and Wallenfels 2009.

PART I

Introduction

1 | The Economy of Late Achaemenid and Seleucid Babylonia: State of the Problem, Methodology and Sources

Introduction

The division of this book into two key parts – structure and performance – takes its cue from a 1978 paper by Nobel laureate Douglass C. North, 'Structure and Performance: The Task of Economic History'. The fact that the latter part clearly outweighs the former in this volume does not imply a postulated precedence of economic performance over structures as key determinant of an economy's potential for growth or the welfare of a society. Nor should it be taken as indicative of a research strategy focussing on the quantification of data to the detriment of qualitative historical analysis. Rather, it reflects the state of sources for an economic history of Late Achaemenid and Seleucid Babylonia. On the one hand, we have at our disposal a remarkable series of commodity prices contained in a text genre known as the Astronomical Diaries, which allows for unmatched sophistication in the analysis of an ancient economy. On the other, the dearth of archival material from this period means that many aspects of the background to these prices can be elucidated only rudimentarily and by recourse to parallel situations both within and beyond the Seleucid Empire.

The Babylonian Astronomical Diaries (henceforth ADs, or diaries) are a set of cuneiform tablets recording a variety of observed celestial, climatic, ecological and economic phenomena, as well as giving accounts of historical events.[1] They comprise one of the largest collections of observational data available from the Ancient World, consisting of hundreds of tablets dating from *c.* 650 to 60.[2] The reason for taking the turn of the fifth to the fourth century as the starting point for our analysis is the increasing

---

[1] The Astronomical Diaries (ADs) have been published in several volumes by H. Hunger and A. Sachs (Astronomical Diaries and Related Texts = ADART). Relevant for this investigation are ADART I (1988), ADART II (1989) and ADART III (1996). The tablets from these volumes are quoted with the siglum 'AD (astronomical year recorded)'. See Clancier 2009, especially 159–63, 169–72, 185–95 and 212–13 on the provenance of the diaries and their collection history in the British Museum.

[2] All dates are BCE unless otherwise specified. This interest in the collection of data, for the purpose of establishing an empirical basis for both astronomical and astrological prediction, differed markedly from Greek science, see Rochberg 2004: 147–51.

availability of price data after *c.* 400, as for the fifth century only three diary fragments containing prices are extant (and even fewer for the earlier years).[3]

The better part of the information contained in the Astronomical Diaries relates to astronomical observations, and in particular the position of the moon in the ecliptic during each night of a given (Babylonian lunar) month. However, the ADs are at the same time the single most important source for the political history of Late Achaemenid and Seleucid Babylonia. Among the historical accounts, the quite extensive report of the battle of Gaugamela and Alexander the Great's subsequent entry into the city of Babylon (Kuhrt 1990 and van der Spek 2003) has attracted particular attention, as has the description of preparatory measures preceding the First Syrian War between the Ptolemaic and the Seleucid Empires in 274/3 (see Will 1979[2]: 146–50). At this point, it has to be emphasised that the somewhat misleading term 'Astronomical Diaries' was coined in 1948 by their later editor, A. Sachs, who was mainly interested in the astronomical content of the tablets. The more neutral Babylonian designation was *naṣāru ša ginê*, meaning 'regular observation'.

Furthermore, with a total of more than 2,000 observations of the silver equivalents of six different commodities, among which are the staple foods barley and dates, the ADs together with a handful of Late Babylonian Commodity Price Lists provide us with one of the largest economic datasets for any pre-industrial society in world history.[4] This wealth of material has not failed to elicit scientific interest, and two monographs as well as several shorter articles have already been dedicated to an analysis of the price equivalents of the ADs. The first systematic investigation of this price series was A. Slotsky's *The Bourse of Babylon* (1997a), which was followed in 2001 by *A History of Babylonian Prices in the First Millennium BC. I, Prices of Basic Commodities* by P. Vargyas. The former certainly chose a more innovative approach. A trained economist, Slotsky attempted a statistical examination of the long-term trends in the datasets of the individual commodities by means of a regression analysis. Vargyas on the other hand provided a discussion of both short-term and long-term fluctuations, but employed a much cruder methodology and restricted himself mainly to simple discussions of changes in the monthly equivalents and of centennial averages.

---

[3] A synoptic overview of the available data on commodity prices from Babylonia during the fifth and fourth centuries is provided by Hackl and Pirngruber 2015: see 118–20 for the price data culled from the diaries -461, -453 and -418.

[4] The Commodity Price Lists have been published by Slotsky and Wallenfels 2009; the texts are quoted with the siglum S/W (number of text).

However, both of these investigations have met with severe criticism. An important review of both studies by van der Spek and Mandemakers (2003) found fault in particular with the failure of both authors to convert the silver equivalents into genuine prices prior to analysis, which in both cases lead to several errors in the interpretation, and with their non-consideration of the impact of political history on commodity prices. An elaboration of the first point is provided in the above-mentioned review (especially 523–4 and 535–7), and we shall thus confine ourselves to a brief example. Between February and April 278, the equivalent of barley rose from 156 to 198 litres for 1 shekel of silver. This rise was in all probability caused by an improved supply situation as the barley harvest in Babylonia took place in April. The difference of 42 litres corresponds to a relative increase of 27 per cent in the equivalent; however, the decrease in the actual price (shekels per ton or *kurru* of barley) amounts to only 21 per cent.[5] Hence, sticking to equivalents conveys a flawed idea of the magnitude of actual price increases or decreases. Furthermore, a conversion of the equivalents of the ADs into genuine prices will also facilitate comparisons with other historical periods, from Mesopotamia or other regions.[6]

It is thus the main aim of this book to add a historical perspective to the price data contained in the Astronomical Diaries and the Commodity Price Lists. Rather than providing a mere statistical description[7] of the data, it will attempt to explain the general trends found in commodity prices as well as the deviations thereof. Particular attention will be paid to exogenous shocks, defined as historical events which had tangible repercussions in the price data. To be sure, there have already been first assessments of the impact of political history and ecological phenomena on the Babylonian commodity prices. Pertinent examples are several papers by van der Spek on the impact of warfare and royal policy (especially 2000), a study by Müller (1999/ 2000) on the influence of climate as visible in the changing river level of the Euphrates or a contribution by the present author on the detrimental effect

[5] This principle emerges even more clearly by means of a fictitious example of a decrease in the equivalent from, say 60 to 30 litres per shekel, which is a halving (−50 per cent) of the equivalent but a doubling (+100 per cent) of the price. Also, note that as opposed to modern price quotations the Babylonian way of recording prices tends to emphasise particularly low prices in graphic representations, see Müller 1995/6: 164.
[6] Throughout this book, shekels (8.33 grams) of silver per *kurru* (180 litres) of a given commodity have been chosen as price unit in order to facilitate comparison with the price data from the Neo-Babylonian period analysed by Jursa 2010, which is the most obvious reference point.
[7] See the criticism of Slotsky 1997a by van der Spek and Mandemakers 2003: 523.

of locust invasions (Pirngruber 2014).[8] The following analysis of the price data seeks to advance our knowledge of the impact of exogenous shocks by investigating in a systematic manner which types of events influenced commodity prices and to what extent in Late Achaemenid, Early Hellenistic and Seleucid Babylonia. Rather than discussing a single type of potential impact or one particular period only, and in order to avoid oversimplifying mono-causal attempts at explanation, we shall opt for a comprehensive approach and attempt to integrate as much information as possible. To this end, hitherto uncharted methodological territory in Ancient Near Eastern studies, namely regression analysis employing dummy variables, will be employed alongside a more traditional historical investigation of the price data in order to integrate historical events in a formal statistical model. This part of the analysis will thus allow us not only to trace developments in prices for basic goods during the Late Achaemenid and Seleucid periods, but also to see which types of exogenous shocks – comprising such different events as warfare on an imperial scale and more localised natural disasters – have an impact on commodity prices in Babylonia and to quantify them. Furthermore, it enables us to make qualified statements about the performance of the economy, which in this context can be succinctly defined as 'the capability of markets to adapt to exogenous shocks'.[9]

Such an analysis of any group of commodity price data is, however, necessarily incomplete without due consideration of the general socio-economic and political fabric into which it is embedded: in short, the realm of what North famously called an economy's institutional framework: 'the underlying determinant of the long-run performance of economies'.[10] In this section of the book, which will by logic precede the price analysis, the focus will be *inter alia* on the existing patterns of land tenure and storage practices: Not only do these two aspects fundamentally impact price formation, but the former in particular also sheds light on the close ties between

---

[8]   Other important articles dealing in one way or another with the price data include Vargyas 1997 and the response Slotsky 1997b; Zaccagnini 1997 (especially 375–7); Grainger 1999; van der Spek 2000a, 2006b and 2014; Temin 2002; Földvári and van Leeuwen 2011; van der Spek and van Leeuwen 2014; Huijs, Pirngruber and van Leeuwen 2015; van der Spek, Földvári and van Leeuwen 2015.

[9]   Van der Spek, van Leeuwen and van Zanden 2015b: 3.

[10]   The classic formulation is North 1990: 3: 'Institutions are the rules of the game in a society or, more formally, are the humanly devised constraints that shape human interaction'; the quotation in the text: 107. A convenient fuller definition is provided by Menard and Shirley 2008: 1, according to whom institutions 'include (i) written rules and agreements that govern contractual relations and corporate governance, (ii) constitutions, laws and rules that govern politics, government, finance, and society more broadly, and (iii) unwritten codes of conduct, norms of behavior, and beliefs'.

the political and the economic. Moreover, it brings us into the sphere of another key determinant of the efficiency of commodity markets, that of the factors of production – land, labour and capital – and the ways they are deployed by those who wield power over them.

By jointly analysing aspects of the structure and performance of the Babylonian economy in the Late Achaemenid and Seleucid periods, rather than by considering the price data of the Astronomical Diaries in isolation (as is the case in both Slotsky 1997a and Vargyas 2001), I hope to achieve a piece of genuine 'economic history with economy', to take up the challenge posed by Manning and Morris.[11]

Structure of this Book

In what follows, recent trends in the debate concerning the nature of ancient economies will be discussed. In particular, the potential contribution of New Institutional Economics to shed new light on ancient economies will be pointed out. The remainder of this introductory chapter will then give a description of the sources drawn upon in this assessment of the structure and the performance of the Babylonian economy. Chapter 2 discusses the overall historical and socio-political framework into which the price data of the Astronomical Diaries is embedded. Emphasis will be laid on the question of continuities and breaks with the preceding and exceptionally well documented Neo-Babylonian and Early Achaemenid period. Chapter 3 then takes the above-average price volatility during the Late Achaemenid period as its point of departure. An analysis of the distribution of the main factors of production – land, labour and capital (assets) – sheds new light on the prevailing institutional framework that can be shown to be not at all conducive to economic stability or even growth. Chapter 4 tries to contextualise the Babylonian price records by analysing the extent of inter-annual storage (or carry-over) of the basic foodstuffs barley and dates in Hellenistic Babylon. Such an assessment of a strategy of risk aversion is particularly relevant for the question of price volatility.

Chapter 5 proceeds to a price history of Late Achaemenid and Seleucid Babylonia. This chapter is partly descriptive in that it traces the development of the prices of the various commodities over time. The basic characteristics of the dataset of prices, in the main the mean price and the average deviations thereof, are also discussed. The price data was organised according

---

[11] Morris and Manning 2005: 3.

to four different periods (Late Achaemenid, Early Hellenistic, Early and Late Seleucid), which each exhibit a different structural background. In addition to the descriptive part, each subchapter on the different historical periods also includes analytical sections. I have first sought to explain the overall movement of prices in terms of variations in the three major price-determining factors, namely supply, demand and amount of money in circulation. The historical background will be shown to have exerted a strong influence on the price data. I will pay due attention to outliers, hence particularly high or low prices, and their relationship to political history. Peak and trough prices visible in the graphs in this chapter are explained in the light of available historical information from the ADs and other sources. The Hellenistic period, for example, was characterised by continuous warfare within but also beyond Babylonia, and a high level of monetisation made possible by the capture of the treasures of the Achaemenid kings. It is thus not unexpected that prices during these three decades are significantly higher compared to the preceding and subsequent periods, a fact that needs to be duly accounted for in any assessment of the long-term development of prices in Babylonia. Also, in the section of this chapter headed 'The Late Achaemenid Period: The Issue of Price Volatility', which deals with the price data from the Late Achaemenid period, some basic comments on statistical description and the pitfalls encountered are made. Economic terminology that the historian may be unfamiliar with is briefly explained in the form of a glossary at the end of the book.

Chapter 6 then goes deeper into the issue of price developments under the impact of historical events. In the methodologically most innovative part of this book, a regression analysis was run on the Babylonian price data, with the information on political history modelled in the form of dummy variables. Two different approaches were pursued – one summarising the historical data in the form of political episodes, the other focussing on the basic factors underlying price oscillations – and their results compared, also to the findings of the preceding chapters. The repercussions of certain categories of historical events in the price data can thus also be shown in a formal way.

The brief conclusion will summarise the results obtained and consider the Late Achaemenid and Seleucid price data in a comparative context. I close this book with the question of conceptualising research on the ancient (or perhaps better pre-industrial) economies beyond the by now sterile debate between primitivists and substantivists versus modernists and formalists, and the fruitful integration of new theoretical approaches provided by recent research in Institutional Economics.

Prices, Markets and the Ancient Economy

The prices in the diaries, which will be at the centre of this investigation, are – typically for Mesopotamia – quoted as price equivalents, thus as amount of the commodity which can be purchased for one fixed unit of silver, namely 1 shekel (8.33 grams) of silver.[12] The commodities at issue are barley, dates, sesame, cress, cuscuta – a parasitical plant used mainly to season date beer in the first millennium – and wool, almost invariably in this sequence.[13] The precise nature of these price notations has occasionally been questioned and the possibility of their treatment in economic terms doubted,[14] but by now, it can be considered a given that we are dealing with historical prices, the formation of which is owed to market forces. To the impressive array of empirical arguments collected by van der Spek 2000a (295–6), one can add the econometric analyses of Temin 2002 and Földvári and van Leeuwen 2011, both confirming that the behaviour of these commodity prices, and in particular their unpredictable oscillations, is exactly as expected in a market situation. We would like to explicitly emphasise at this point that we consider the prices to be observed entities just like all other events recorded in the diaries (with the exception of a few predicted astronomical phenomena).

This occasionally voiced scepticism concerning the veracity, or rather even the reality, of the Babylonian price data is of course rooted in the debate on whether something like a 'market' – both as a physical entity and as an institutionalised process – actually existed in Ancient Babylonia. The starting point for this debate was an essay by the economist Karl Polanyi entitled 'Marketless Trading in Hammurabi's Time' (1957). Polanyi distinguished between three forms of economic exchange, reciprocity, redistribution and the market. In his view, the latter played at best only a very marginal role in pre-industrial societies, where economic activities were strongly embedded in their social environment. His conceptualisation proved to be influential

---

[12] Slotskya 1997a: 8–11 provides numerous references to this particular manner of formulating commodity prices from the late third to the late first millennium.

[13] See Slotsky 1997a: 23–42 for an extensive discussion of the commodities. Curiously enough, Slotsky and Wallenfels (2009: 13) cast doubt on the identifications of *kasû* with cuscuta, *sahlû* with cress and of *samaššammû* with sesame. However, they do not provide any kind of justification for their revisionist reasoning. Suffice it to briefly mention Bedigian 1985 and Stol 1983/4 and 1994 (all referred to in Slotsky 1997a) for the well-established and overall accepted interpretations of *sahlû* and *samaššammû*, only the identification of *kasû* with cuscuta (Stol 1994) is still occasionally doubted, e.g. by Geller 2000.

[14] Zaccagnini 1997: 375–6, and Joannès 1997: 315.

in the field of Ancient Near Eastern studies, but also provoked a great deal of (justified) criticism.[15]

The antipode to Polanyi are scholars like M. Silver and D. Warburton, who apply concepts borrowed from modern, i.e. neo-classical, economics rather uncritically and often with a scarce command of the primary evidence – as was the case with Polanyi, too – to ancient societies (e.g. Silver 2004). This approach likewise results in a rather distorted portrait, subordinating livelihood to the rationality of an abstract *homo oeconomicus*, whose motivations and needs/wants are supposed not to have changed throughout the course of history.

In recent years, however, this unhelpful dichotomy between primitivism/substantivism versus modernism/formalism[16] has increasingly been replaced by a different and more fruitful approach. It is, then, no coincidence that the name of Douglass C. North was already mentioned at the very beginning of this introductory chapter, as it is the strand of research associated chiefly with his name, the New Institutional Economics (NIE), that has started to gain a foothold in Ancient (Near Eastern) history. The towering monument attesting to this trend is the *Cambridge Economic History of the Greco-Roman World* (Scheidel, Morris and Saller 2007), which contains two sections dealing with the periods and regions under discussion in the present book. P. Bedford, in his chapter on the Achaemenid Near East,[17] dedicates a significant amount of analysis to the legal framework within which economic activities took place, and the impact of the prevailing socio-political constellations. R. van der Spek's (2007) account of the Hellenistic Near East focuses *inter alia* on increasing monetisation of the Babylonian economy after the conquest of Alexander the Great, and the effect of Seleucid policies on the local economy.

Some of the latest works on aspects of the economy in the field of Ancient Near Eastern studies follow the above-mentioned research trend, albeit

---

[15] Polanyi's writings have generated a vast literature, see, e.g., North 1977 and the contributions in Clancier, Joannès, Ruoillard and Tenu 2005. Veenhof 1972: 351–7 provides an early rebuttal of the theory of a marketless society on the basis of Old Assyrian material. For Polanyi's influence in the field of Ancient Near Eastern studies see succinctly van de Mieroop 1999: 116–18.

[16] This debate is succinctly summarised from an Ancient Near Eastern perspective by van de Mieroop 1999: 108–23; see also Garfinkle 2012: 5–17 with a focus on the Ur III period in the late third millennium. A valuable take on current approaches to the economy of the Ancient Near East is found in Jursa 2010: 13–25. For the Mediterranean World see, e.g., Morris, Saller and Scheidel 2007; the essays collected in Scheidel and von Reden 2002 provide a convenient overview of research on the ancient economy from the 1980s and 1990s CE.

[17] Bedford 2007. The pertinent data culled from cuneiform tablets from Babylonia plays an important role in his account, as the region is one of the better-documented areas of the Achaemenid Empire.

often without explicit reference to theory. S. Garfinkle (2012), for example, in his study of the archives of important merchant families from the Ur III state in the late third millennium, puts forward a striking criticism of the alleged dichotomy of private versus state economy. Instead of engaging in this (rather sterile) debate, he convincingly reinterprets these entrepreneurs to have been facilitators of different types of economic transactions, from money lending to commercialisation of agricultural produce to long-distance trade. Although they acted upon their own initiative, the state and its agents relied upon their activities to such an extent 'that the efficient operation of the economy by the central administration of the Ur III state was dependent upon the existence of entrepreneurs whose activities were not controlled by the state'.[18] This focus on an institution perceived as economically efficient is of course reminiscent of much NIE research, not least of North's earlier work (e.g. North 1977; but see now Ogilvie 2007 for a critical assessment of this approach), and Garfinkle stresses this point in several passages of his concluding chapter. Moreover, he discusses the presence of features associated with market exchange such as competitive and profit-orientated actors in the peculiar setting, or institutional framework, of the Ur III period.[19] In this regard, he follows the assessment of Wilcke, who characterises the economy of that time as a 'System gewinnorientiert wirtschaftender Pfründen', albeit one with strong redistributive elements (Wilcke 2007: 114). In the latter article, the motive of pursuit of profit is thus extended from merchants and other entrepreneurs to state officials, the holders of the allotments/prebends Wilcke refers to.

Closer to the period dealt with in the present book, and with a detailed discussion of the theoretical framework employed, is L. Graslin-Thomé's (2009) monograph dedicated to long-distance exchange in the Ancient Near East in the first millennium. The influence of North is clearly discernible (and explicitly accounted for); a central part of the book is dedicated to the question of transaction costs, a key concept in the NIE.[20] On the one hand, she analyses the ways in which long-distance trade, especially during the Neo-Assyrian period, was facilitated by means of various measures taken by the state. Agreements between rulers – mainly the Neo-Assyrian king and the petty kings in the empire's orbit – and the imposition of a

---

[18] Garfinkle 2012: 137 and *passim*.

[19] For example, Garfinkle 2012: 14 reiterates that 'the presence of entrepreneurial households allowed for greater efficiency in managing the institutional economies'. The competitive elements in the economy of the Ur III are acknowledged *ibid.*: 150.

[20] Graslin-Thomé 2009: 343–79; see also 120–3. On transaction costs see, e.g., North 1990: 27–35.

unified system of measures and weights within in the empire are discussed, as is the question of monetisation. On the other, state interventions to its own benefit but hampering mercantile activity (taxation, trade restrictions, monopolies, etc.) also receive due attention.

However, the question of the market as a 'form of (economic) integration', to use Karl Polanyi's terminology, and in particular the performance of local commodity markets, is tackled only peripherally in all these contributions. The lone exception here who tackles the impressive amount of quantifiable data in the cuneiform documentation is Jursa 2010. This sweeping study of 'economic geography, economic mentalities, agriculture, the use of money and the problem of economic growth' (thus the book's subtitle) of Babylonia in the long sixth century is based on a corpus of about 20,000 archival records both from institutional and private archives. Its results will be presented in more detail in the following chapter, as the transformation of economic structures in the period investigated by Jursa lingers on into the Late Achaemenid and Seleucid periods. Suffice it here to note that performance of the economy constitutes a key aspect in his treatment of the question of economic growth in Babylonia (Jursa 2010: 745–53 and 783–800, especially 793–4).

The overall focus on structure and almost complete neglect of performance in most treatments is all the more regrettable, as NIE provides scholarship with a helpful definition of the market, which makes this rather elusive concept, which too often is taken for granted, very amenable to historical research. In the definition of Furubotn and Richter, there are two crucial aspects of the market to consider. First, the market constitutes 'a social arrangement to facilitate repeated exchange among a plurality of parties (as opposed to occasional exchange between individuals)'.[21] This focus on concrete social contexts to transactions dispenses with the obstructive assumption of the unbounded (instrumental) rationality of the elusive *homo oeconomicus*[22] and allows for the integration of differing economic mentalities into an economic order that may still exhibit – or even be determined by – market forces.

---

[21] Furubotn and Richter 2005: 314. In the words of one economic historian of the Ancient World, 'the market as an instituted process however (that is as learned behavior, as opposed to the abstract market of neo-classical economics) is a social construct that reflects the specific cultural settings in which it develops' (Verboven 2014: 139)

[22] In the definition of Black, Hashimzade and Myles 2009: 130 (s.v. economic man) the concept of the *homo oeconomicus* 'achieves generality by placing no restrictions on the nature of preferences or on constraint upon choice'. The Weberian distinction between instrumental rationality (*Zweckrationalität*) and value rationality (*Wertrationalität*) is pertinent here, as any aspect of the latter, that is, 'the conscious belief in the value for its own sake of some ethical, aesthetic, religious or other form of behavior, independently of its prospects of success' (Weber 1978: 24–5), is absent in this definition. See on this point also (and more exhaustively) Bresson 2016: 9. Criticisms of the concept of a perfectly rational *homo oeconomicus* are found

Second, and this addendum is particular to the NIE, a market is also 'an order or governance structure governing the transactions between individual actors'. Consequently, a market is not simply an immutable given, but it is 'produced' by certain social actors.[23] Ogilvie elaborated one consequence of this interplay between the political and the economic in her brilliant analysis of the development of institutions. Rather than ascribing the rise and persistence of a given institution to its efficiency in responding to an economic need, she points to the role of distributional conflicts in shaping institutional frameworks and to a 'rent-seeking agreement between political authorities and economic interest groups'.[24] In view of the generally close relationship between ownership of land and access to political power in pre-industrial agrarian societies, this aspect is particularly relevant when it comes to factor markets.

Hence, instead of uncritically accepting an alleged superiority of markets as 'probably the most efficient means of distributing a limited number of goods' (Warburton 2003: 361), the NIE approach invites us here to focus on the socio-economic configurations in the background. In particular, the manipulations of the institutional framework by major economic actors with the political potential to do so – in Babylonia, temples and crown as well as their protégés immediately spring to mind – to garner as big a slice of the economic pie as possible emerge more clearly. It is thus one important ramification of this approach that it enables us to focus on such interferences and disturbances of an economic system, which was shaped to a significant extent (as will be shown in greater detail below) by market forces, rather than downplaying the relevance of the latter.[25]

Sources

For this investigation into the economy of Late Achaemenid and Seleucid Babylonia, both the Classical sources and the cuneiform evidence have been scoured for relevant facts. Before going *in medias res* it is therefore apposite

---

throughout a vast array of NIE literature, e.g., Furubotn and Richter 2005: 21; North 2005: 23–4; Menard and Shipley 2008; and Bresson 2016: 16–24.

[23] Furubotn and Richter 2005: 350.

[24] Ogilvie 2007: 664; note that the same concept of 'rent-seeking elites' looms large in North, Wallis and Weingast 2009.

[25] For example, Bedford 2007: 325: 'Market transactions certainly took place, but it was not the exclusive means of exchange; indeed, it was arguably not the main form of exchange.' Cf. Liverani 1988: 896, who was already aware of the greater relevance of a *mercato libero* compared to redistribution and similar mechanisms during the Neo-Babylonian and Achaemenid periods.

to briefly discuss the most fruitful sources. In the first place, obviously, the Astronomical Diaries have to be mentioned. Not only do they contain the bulk of the price data, their historical sections equally provide us with precious information on a wide variety of events that occurred in Babylonia in the second half of the first millennium. They are by far the richest source at our disposal, although often in a very fragmentary state, and constitute the backbone of any investigation into the history of Babylonia during the Late Achaemenid, Hellenistic and Seleucid and Parthian periods.[26] They often contain information that can be integrated with what is known from later texts written in different languages and from an outside perspective (e.g. the works of Greek and Roman historiographers), but in at least equal measure they record events that were hitherto unknown to historians. To give just one brief example, the local unrests occurring in and around Babylon during the 230s and in the late 140s are not known from other sources, but can reasonably be expected (and in fact will be shown) to influence the prices of the basic commodities. The present work has greatly benefited from the excellent *editio princeps* by Hunger and Sachs of the Astronomical Diaries (Hunger and Sachs 1988, 1989, 1996), without which this investigation could not have taken place in the present form. The commented edition of the historical sections of the ADs by Del Monte 1997 (which alas does not contain the diaries from the Late Achaemenid period) also deserves to be mentioned here.

As the diaries are at the very heart of this study, they shall be introduced in some detail and by means of a rather extensive example text, the reverse of AD -158B recording observations for month V of year 153 SE (July–August 159):[27]

1 […] …

2 [… Night of the 12th, beginning of the night, the moon was] 2 cubits [in front of γ Capri]corni, [it stood] 1½ cubits behind Saturn

3 [… Night of the 13th, beginning of the night, the moon was] 2½ cubits [behind] δ Capricorni; the north wind blew. The 13th, moonset to moonrise: 10°.

---

[26] For their relevance as historical sources see, e.g., van der Spek 1993a and 1997/8. The historical sections of the ADs have been discussed in several articles on Late Babylonian history, see, e.g., van der Spek 1998a and 2003. The reconstruction of the political history of Late Achaemenid and Hellenistic Babylonia by Boiy 2004: 99–192 also draws heavily upon the information provided by the ADs. Del Monte 1997 provides an edition with minimal historical commentary on the historical passages from 331 – the account of Alexander the Great's conquest of Babylon – onwards.

[27] Hunger and Sachs 1996: 46–51 and plate 174.

4 [… sunrise to moonset: x]+1°, measured (despite) mist; the north wind blew. Night of the 15th, sunset to moonrise: 8°; the north wind blew.

5 [… Venus was] 1 cubit [above] α Virginis. [Around the 15th], Mercury's last appearance in the east in Leo; the north wind blew. Night of the 16th (and) the 16th, the north wind blew. Night of the 17th, the north wind blew;

6 [last part of the night, the moon was] 3½ cubits [in fro]nt of η Piscium, the moon being 4½ cubits low to the south, ½ cubit below Mars, the moon being ½ cubit back to the west. The 17th, the north wind blew.

7 [Night of the 18th], the north wind blew; last part of the night, the moon was 5 cubits below β Arietis, the moon being ½ cubit back to the west. Night of the 19th (and) the 19th, the north wind blew. Night of the 20th, the north wind blew;

8 [last part of the night, the mo]on was 4 cubits below η Tauri, the moon having passed a little to the east. The 20th, the north wind blew. Night of the 21st, the north wind blew; last part of the night, the moon was ½ cubit above α Tauri, the moon having passed ½ cubit to

9 the east. The 21st, the north wind blew. Night of the 22nd, the north wind blew; last part of the night, the moon was 1½ cubits below ζ Tauri. The 22nd, the north wind blew. Night of the 23rd, the north wind blew;

10 [last part of the] night, the moon was above γ Geminorum, the moon being ½ cubit back to the west, 1 cubit below Jupiter. The <23rd>, the north wind blew. Night of the 24th, the north wind blew; last part of the night, the moon was

11 4½ cubits below α Geminorum, the moon having passed ½ cubit to the east. The 24th, the north wind blew. Night of the 25th, the north wind blew; last part of the night, the moon was 1½ cubits in front of δ Cancri,

12 the moon being 1½ cubits high to the north. The 25th, the north wind blew. Night of the 26th, the north wind blew; last part of the night, the moon was 4 cubits below ε Leonis. The 26th, the north wind blew. Night of the 27th, the north wind blew;

13 last part of the night, the moon was 2 cubits behind α Leonis, the moon being 1 cubit high to the north. The 27th, moonrise to sunrise: 22°, measured. The north wind blew. Night of the 28th (and) the 28th, the north wind blew. Night of the 29th (and) the 29th, the north wind blew.

14 That month, the equivalent was: barley, in the beginning of the month, 2 *pān* 3 *sūt*, in the middle of the month 2 *pān* 4? *sūt* 2? *qa*, at the end of the month, 2 *pān* 4 *sūt*; dates, 2 *pān* 4 *sūt*; cuscuta, 3 kur;

15 cress, 5 *sūt*; sesame, 2 *sūt* 3 *qa*, at the end of the month 2 *sūt* 2 *qa*; wool, 3 minas. At that time, Jupiter was in Gemini;

16 Venus, until the middle of the month, was in Virgo, until the end of
    the month, in Libra; Mercury, in the beginning of the month, was in
    Cancer; around the 15th, Mercury's last appearance in the east in Leo;
    Saturn was in Capricorn;

17 Mars was in Pisces. That month, the river level receded 8 fingers,
    total: 30 was the *na* (gauge). That month, the satrap of Babylonia from
    Seleucia,

18 [which is on] the Tigris, entered Babylon. On the 9th day, merrymaking
    took place everywhere. The administrator of Esangil

19 [...] the *dudê* [gate] of Esangil opposite the Lamassu-rabi gate, the rep-
    resentative of the administrator of Esangil

20 [...] they went. On the 17th day, offerings at the entering of Madānu
    and the entering of Bēltiya of the gate [...]

21 [...] because of their injustices. The *nindabû*-offering did not take place.
    That month, [...]

22 [...] made ... On the 19th, the satrap of Babylonia

Upper Edge   went out [from Babylon] to Seleucia which is on the Tigris.

2   [Month VI,] (the 1st of which was identical with) the 30th (of the
    preceding month), sunset to moonset: 12°?, measured (despite) mist; it
    was high to the sun.

More than half of this report (lines 1–13) is dedicated to astronomical
observations, with a clear focus on the position of the moon in the ecliptic
and the positions of the planets, which are also summarised in lines 15–
17.[28] Additionally, the diary contains references to the prevailing weather;
the recurring utterance 'the north wind blew' (twenty-seven times!) conveys a good idea of the repetitiveness of some ADs.[29]

Lines 14 and 15 contain then the observations of the price equivalents for
the period in question. The Akkadian term for price equivalent is *mahīru*,
usually written by means of the Sumerogram KI.LAM; the word derives
from the verb *mahāru*, with the basic meaning 'to receive', 'to accept' (valuables, staples, etc.). Commodities are quoted in the diaries in the traditional
capacity measures of *kurru* (180 litres), *pānu* (thirty-six litres), *sūtu* (six
litres) and *qû* (one litre), except for wool, which is weighed in minas (a unit
corresponding to half a kilogram). The sequence of the commodities seems
to be at least partly dictated by their relevance in daily life, as barley and
dates – the two mainstays of the Babylonian diet, counting for more than

---

[28] For more detailed descriptions of the contents of the Astronomical Diaries see Hunger and
    Sachs 1988: 11–38 and Hunger and Pingree 1999: 139–59 (with a strong focus on astronomy).
[29] The meteorological observations have been discussed in detail by Graßhoff 2010.

two-thirds of daily caloric intake (see Jursa 2010: 50) – are always listed first and price indications for these two goods tend to be more detailed. Indeed, AD -158B quotes two different prices for barley at the middle and the end of the month.

The fact that these prices are observed, rather than the results of actual transactions, may give rise to the question of their context and their representability. Regarding the former, the level of volatility clearly indicates that the prices recorded in the ADs were not administered by the temple, nor can they be considered as representing conversion rates internal to the temple economy.[30] The observations are, it has to be emphasised, genuine market prices, but we do not know whether the notations of the ADs were the prices the temple got for its disposable surplus in the city's commercial areas,[31] which is the most attractive solution, or paid for its needs, or whether they stem from a randomly chosen merchant, or similar. The question of the representability of these prices seems to be less of a problem, as anthropological research shows that markets for basic foodstuffs in pre-industrial societies tend to exhibit a rather low level of dispersion.[32]

The rationale for the inclusion of the price quotations in this text corpus has been discussed elsewhere in more detail (Pirngruber 2013), in response to a shortcoming addressed by Zaccagnini (1997: 375), namely the necessity to try and understand the price quotations of the diaries in their literary context. One needs to bear in mind that the ADs are a scientific text corpus, with a close relationship to both Babylonian divinatory culture and an emerging predictive science based on mathematical calculation, mainly applied to astronomical phenomena.[33] Two aspects emerge then more clearly. First, oscillations of commodity prices were an important subject in omen apodoses, just as were the two other main non-astronomical categories recorded in the ADs, meteorological phenomena and historical events. Second, just like the other phenomena recorded – the pattern of rainfall and the river level, as well as (to the Mesopotamian mind) history – prices

---

[30] See Jursa 2010: 587 for the stability of prices in temple-internal transactions during the long sixth century.

[31] On market places (most prominitly *sūqu*) in Babylonian cities see for now Jursa 2010: 641–4; a detailed investigation of the harbour area (*kāru*) in the city of Sippar is provided by Waerzeggers 2014: 75–93.

[32] Fanselow 1990: 254. His research concerns twentieth-century CE Javanese markets, but the fundamental parameters apply also to first-millennium Babylonia, namely unbranded and loosely sold goods sold in frequent and similar small-scale purchases, setting a high number of precedents for a price.

[33] Pirngruber 2013: 206. The development of Babylonian and Assyrian scientific culture is the subject of the monograph Brown 2000. On the emergence of mathematical astronomy see most recently Ossendrijver 2015.

were considered as cyclical and hence possibly predictable events. Prices are thus an ideal category for the ADs: potentially legible against a divinatory background, they are equally a suitable test case for the emerging predictive science, which underlies the corpus of the Astronomical Diaries as a whole.

As observed for the astronomical phenomena (and as holds equally true for the river level or the historical sections), and in line with the development of Mesopotamian science, more than what is strictly needed for divinatory purposes is recorded. After all, in omen apodoses only the direction of the price movement – upward or downward – rather than the exact extent of the oscillation in litres is recorded as the consequence of the birth of an *izbu* (a miscarriage), a stellar constellation, or otherwise. An example from the collection *šumma izbu* (tablet V, line 79) reads in the translation of its editor (Leichty 1970: 78): 'If a ewe gives birth to a lion and its face is covered with fatty tissue – trade values (KI.LAM/*mahīru*) will fall.'[34] An omen from *Enūma Anu Enlil* reads: 'If an eclipse occurs on the 15th day and it (the god) disappears while it is in the eclipse, and a meteor falls: Flood will devastate the land. The economy (KI.LAM/ *mahīru*) of the land will diminish.'[35]

One should furthermore note briefly that the economic interest in divinatory texts goes beyond the mere registrations of increases and decreases of the *mahīru*. For example, references to the harvest outcome of specific commodities – usually those of the diaries – are found, which in turn can be interpreted as having influenced the price equivalent. One pertinent instance reads: 'If Adad thunders, sesame and dates will not flourish.'[36] Instead of mentioning the outcome of specific commodities, the threat of a general harvest failure facing the country is encountered: 'If an eclipse occurs in *nisannu* in the middle watch, the harvest of the land will not thrive, var., there will be famine' (*Enūma Anu Enlil* 17 § I 2, Rochberg 1988: 123).

After the summary of planetary positions, the diary continues with a short remark on the level of the Euphrates, which had receded in the current month. The typical pattern is that of a peak level in spring, after the snowmelt in the Anatolian mountain region, the main source of water of

---

[34] The most recent edition is De Zorzi 2014 II: 479. Note that there are several ways of translating *mahīru* (KI.LAM), cf. CAD M I, s.v. *mahīru*: 92–8. For the omen apodoses, translators vary between meanings 2 (business activity or the economy in general) and 3 (price equivalents). As in any case falling equivalents (i.e., rising prices) can be interpreted as manifestations of a dwindling economy, either translation amounts to the same outcome. However, a translation as 'price equivalents' in these passages is more accurate in my opinion.

[35] Tablet 21, § I 2; translation Rochberg 1988: 233.

[36] *Enūma Anu Enlil* tablet 22 II §IV 2; translation Rochberg 1988: 264.

the Euphrates, and a trough in the arid summer months, before local rain-fall ameliorates the situation.[37]

The diary given as example closes with a brief historical passage, which relates a visit from the satrap from his residence in the provincial capital Seleucia-on-the-Tigris to Babylon for a sojourn of ten days. During that time, he performed some sacrifices together with local dignitaries such as the *šatammu*, the 'temple administrator', or 'bishop' in earlier literature. There seem to have been some irregularities, the nature of which cannot be specified due to a lacuna on the tablet – alas, another quite common occurrence with the tablets of the Astronomical Diaries. It has already been noted by the editors that these historical notes are centred very much on the city of Babylon (Hunger and Sachs 1988: 36). For the purpose of the present study, however, this is all the more valuable as an immediate context for the price data is provided.

A second important category of cuneiform texts, and in some way related to the ADs, is the series of Babylonian chronicles from the Hellenistic period, Babylonian Chronicles of the Hellenistic Period (BCHP), published online at www.livius.org/babylonia.html.[38] These texts bear great similarity to the historical sections of the ADs as regards terminology and composition and likewise give valuable insight into the political vicissitudes of Seleucid Babylonia. With one exception in the so-called Chronicle of the Successors or Diadochi Chronicle (BCHP 3 = ABC 10), which records the long-lasting conflict between various Greek generals in the aftermath of Alexander the Great's death in 323, these texts do not provide us with price observations. Also this text group extends into the Parthian period, although the majority of them date to the third century, with a notable peak in the crown prince-ship of Antiochus I in the 280s. The most intriguing of these chronicles, however, describes the Ptolemaic invasion of Babylonia in the course of the Third Syrian War in winter 246/5 – an event not mentioned by the (extant) Classical sources.[39]

In a similar fashion, the works of Greek and Roman authors also focus strongly on political history. The most fruitful work for our purposes is the

[37] Brown 2002 and Huijs, Pirngruber and van Leeuwen 2015:135–7 and fig. 7.7.

[38] Last accessed 1 June 2015. See also the extensive textual commentary provided on this homepage. Also Grayson 1975 and Glassner 2004 contain several of the Hellenistic chronicles. However, in recent years important new texts such as BCHP 14, describing the establishment of a Greek colony under a king Antiochus, have come to light, which are not included in these earlier editions. On the relationship between chronicles and diaries see most recently Waerzeggers 2012: 297–8 and Pirngruber 2013: 200–1.

[39] The text is preliminarily published as BCHP 11 = Ptolemy III Chronicle at livius.org. See also Clancier 2012a.

Bibliotheca historica by Diodorus of Sicily. Of particular relevance are his books XIV to XVI on Late Achaemenid history, book XVII on Alexander the Great and books XVIII and XIX on the history of the Successors, with many events taking place in Babylonia. The later books are preserved only very fragmentarily, but still contain occasionally interesting information.

The best-documented period in absolute terms is certainly that of Alexander the Great, whose feats elicited already in antiquity a wealth of literature such as Arrian's *Anabasis* (*Alexandri*) and the *Historiae Alexandri Magni* of Q. Curtius Rufus. Of course, the results of modern scholarship also need to be duly considered in any attempt to reconstruct the impact of political history on prices, especially as regards controversial subjects. A good case in point is the notoriously uncertain chronology of events during the period of warfare between the diadochi in the aftermath of Alexander the Great's death in June 323.[40]

Important reference works for the contextualisation of price data and historical information contained in the primary sources include Will 1979[2] and 1982[2]; Bosworth 1988; Green 1990; Briant 1996; Boiy 2004; and Grainger 2010.[41]

As regards the socio-economic background to the price data, the sources at our disposal are notoriously meagre. For Babylonia, and northern Babylonia in particular, 484, the second year of Xerxes, was an important watershed: the successful suppression of the rebellions of Šamaš-erība and Bēl-šimânni was followed by some sort of punitive measures against the northern Babylonian urban elites supportive of the revolts. One consequence was the so-called 'end of archives', the widespread disruption of documentary evidence in the cities involved, among which we count such important places as Borsippa, Sippar (including the large temple archive of the Ebabbar) and of course the city of Babylon itself.[42]

From the fifth and fourth centuries, there are at least four larger archives providing important information on administrative practice and thus providing context for the price data of the diaries. The Kasr archive documenting the business activities of the Achaemenid satrap Bēlšunu (Xenophon's Belesys) and the Esangila archive from the city of Babylon, as well as the

---

[40] Boiy 2000 and *passim*. Boiy 2007a provides an exhaustive discussion of the problems, as well as a convincing proposal for a solution.

[41] For the early Hellenistic period see also Schober 1981 (with a focus on Babylonia) and Anson 2014. Furthermore, the monographs Bikerman 1938; Sherwin-White and Kuhrt 1993; Capdetrey 2007; and Kosmin 2014a on various aspects of the Seleucid Empire deserve mention here.

[42] Waerzeggers 2003/4; Kessler 2004; and Baker 2008; the longer-term economic consequences of this event are discussed by Jursa 2014a; see also Pirngruber forthcoming A and B.

Brewers' archive and the Tattannu archive from Borsippa. Unfortunately, as of yet these archives have not been adequately published.[43] These texts are relevant in so far as they give us insights into economic transactions and administrative practices of the temple households (of the Esangila in Babylon and the Ezida in Borsippa) and hence shed light on the prevailing economic structures within which of the prices recorded in the ADs need to be considered.

Finally, the Murašû archive, with some 800 texts the largest archive of the Late Achaemenid period, dates to the last quarter or so of the fifth century and hence predates the price documentation of the ADs.[44] Furthermore, it stems from the southern city of Nippur, which is usually thought to constitute a less integrated rural area on the fringes of the Babylonian plain (see Jursa 2010: 405-4, for the comparative marginality of the region). However, this archive is of crucial importance in elucidating the patterns of land tenure in Late Achaemenid Babylonia, and the social structure as reflected in this archive seems to be generalisable for the whole region and period.

This archival material will be employed above all in our analysis of the structural background to the Late Achaemenid and Seleucid economy, in an attempt to integrate the price data from the ADs and Commodity Price Lists with administrative records from the ambiance of the temple and with legal documents and records from private archives. Unfortunately, this material is by no means comparable – in terms of both density and variety of aspects covered – to the documentation of the 'long sixth century' so profitably analysed by Jursa and others.[45] Not only is the outlook of the present

[43] See Jursa 2005a: 73–76 and 94–97. As regards the Esangila and Brewers' archives, the text copies in CT 49 (for which see also the important review, Oelsner 1971) constituted the bulk of published material upon which this study could draw. Additionally, several scattered text publications (Stolper 1993a; Jursa 1997 and 2002; Kessler 2000) can be added. This corpus of Late Achaemenid and Hellenistic archival texts from northern Babylonia stemming for an institutional, i.e. temple, background has now been significantly expanded by Hackl 2013, who also provides an exhaustive study of their diplomatics. CT 49 contains among other tablets also material from the smaller private archives of Murānu (third century) and Rahimesu (early first century), which are closely connected to the realm of the Esangila temple. These archives were discussed by Jursa 2006 and van der Spek 1998b, respectively. The Kasr archive is currently being studied by Andrew Dix (Chicago); tablets of this private archive of a high official have been the focus of several publications by Stolper (1987, 1995, 2004 and 2007). On the Tattannu archive see preliminarily Jursa and Stolper 2007.

[44] The archive has been the subject of the influential study Stolper 1985, see also van Driel 1989 and 2002, esp. 194–273 and Pirngruber forthcoming A.

[45] See especially Jursa 2010. Other important contributions include Jursa 1995, 2004a and b, 2005b, 2008 and 2009; Wunsch 2000; van Driel 2002; Waerzeggers 2003/4 and 2010; Baker and Jursa 2005; Janković 2008 and 2013; Kleber 2008. Jursa 2005a provides a succinct overview of the archival sources from first-millennium Babylonia.

work thus necessarily different because of the diverseness of the underlying source material, but the lack of pertinent information also means that fundamental parameters of the economy of Hellenistic Babylonia have to remain somewhat elusive. It hardly comes as a surprise, then, that investigations concerned with the structural background to the price data that have been undertaken so far, have taken a deductive approach informed by economic theory. Prominent questions include the level of market integration and trade in basic commodities within and beyond Babylonia (van der Spek and van Leeuwen 2014 and van der Spek 2014b) and developments in the level of monetisation and its impact on prices (van der Spek, Földvári and van Leeuwen 2015).

For further preliminary remarks, I refer the reader to the introductory sections to each chapter. The next chapter provides a brief introduction to Late Achaemenid and Seleucid Babylonia and elucidates the economic background of the prices recorded in the diaries

PART II

Structure

2 | Some Key Developments in First-Millennium Babylonia

Introduction

The centuries between the turn of the millennium and the establish-ment of the Neo-Babylonian dynasty by Nabopolassar in 626 are usually characterised as the 'political nadir' of Babylonia in several ways.[1] In the international sphere, the country fell under the sway of its more powerful neighbour Assyria, culminating in the quite regular accession of Assyrian kings to the throne in Babylon from the reign of Tiglath-pileser III (745–726) onwards. Internally, once prestigious cities and their institutions declined, while political power became increasingly fragmented and shared with newly arrived Aramean and Chaldean tribes.[2] It is hardly surprising, then, that Nabopolassar, the founder of the Neo-Babylonian dynasty, was himself of Chaldean descent. This state of political disarray is correlated to adverse – i.e. notably warm and arid – climatic conditions and concomitant crop failures afflicting the country, especially in the period between 1200 and 900.[3] The Epic of Erra and Išum, composed in this very period, aptly catches the bleak circumstances. The story tells how the god of pestilence and destruction, Erra, temporarily accedes to Marduk's throne and wreaks havoc over Babylonia.[4] In the god's own words:

I will strike down the mighty, I will terrorize the weak,
I will kill the commander, I will scatter the troops ...,
I will make breasts go dry so babies cannot thrive,
I will block up springs so that even little channels can bring no
   life-sustaining water,
I will make hell shake and heaven tremble,

---

[1] Brinkman 1968: 318. This still unsurpassed monograph provides the basis for any reconstruction of the history of the area down to 722; for the period of Assyrian rule see Brinkman 1984a and Frame 1992.

[2] Brinkman 1968: 246–88, and most recently Beaulieu 2013.

[3] Neumann and Parpola 1987. Brinkman 1984b: 175 sums up the textual evidence for the years between 1100 and 750 as 'scattered allusions to climatic irregularity, crop failure, famine, outbreaks of plague, and disruptive tribal incursions'.

[4] See Foster 2007: 65–7 for brief introductory remarks to this epic. A full edition is found, e.g., in Foster 2005[3]: 880–911; the passage quoted above is at 907.

I will make the planets shed their splendor,
I will hack out the tree's roots so its branches cannot burgeon,
I will wreck the wall's foundations so its top tumbles.

However, after around 900, the climatic secular trend changed, and during the remainder of the first millennium, the Near East seems to have been characterised by a colder and moister climate compared to the preceding millennia; in other words, a climate that was more conducive to a prosperous agriculture.[5] Moreover, on a smaller time scale some particularly favourable periods may be identified for roughly the first half of the fifth century and the decades between *c.* 220 and 140. It is also possible to make a case for the latter improvement in climate to have had a positive impact on Babylonian commodity prices (Huijs, Pirngruber and van Leeuwen 2015).

This overall amelioration of climatic circumstances in the first millennium was accompanied by a second trend, which started around the seventh century and continued until about the middle of the first millennium CE, namely an unprecedented growth in population. As the study of Babylonian demography is still in its infancy, especially as compared to what is known from Hellenistic and Roman Egypt, scholarship still has to rely on the groundbreaking settlement surveys carried out by Robert McC. Adams about half a century ago.[6] For the period at issue in this book, Adams observed a combination of three important developments taking place, 'extensive urbanisation, population growth, and the gradual transformation of the irrigation system in the direction of a more intensive, large-scale, artificially maintained, and regionally interdependent enterprise' (Adams 1965: 68). While this period of expansion clearly started with (or even slightly before) the Neo-Babylonian Empire, it accelerated significantly during the Seleucid and Parthian periods, reaching its peak in the subsequent Sassanian and Abbasid eras. The numbers Adams reports are unequivocal: between the beginning of the Neo-Babylonian period and the Seleucid and Parthian period, the total number of settlements increased by three, with the number of urban sites – settlements of minimum 10 hectares, in his definition – increasing disproportionately strongly, by a

---

[5] Butzer 1995: 136, see also his map 2 (133) for the flood levels of the Euphrates and Tigris between *c.* 3000 and 1000 CE. Brown 2002: 52 and Jursa 2010: 34–5 reach the same conclusions.

[6] Adams 1965 and 1981, and Adams and Nissen 1972. For Egypt, see, e.g., Scheidel 2007 and recently Monson 2012: 33–69. On the state of Babylonian demography, see Boiy 2004: 229–34. Gehlken 2005 studies life expectancy in first-millennium Babylonia according to the archival documentation.

factor of nine. This leads him to a (probably too high) estimate of a fivefold increase in population during the time span of 500 to 700 years.[7]

In the light of this state of research, it is hardly surprising that absolute numbers as regards population of the region or even a city are hard to come by. The current estimate for the city of Babylon, still based on a crude estimate of possible inhabitants per hectare (usually fixed at between 150 and 250), reckons with a maximum number of inhabitants of 50,000 during the city's apogee in the Neo-Babylonian period (Boiy 2004: 233).[8]

The Economic Transformation of the 'Long Sixth Century' (626–484)

In 626, Nabopolassar, hailing from a family of high-ranking Assyrian collaborators from the city of Uruk, and who himself likely held the office of a city governor (*šākin ṭēmi*) of the town,[9] defected from Assyrian authority and assumed the title of king. His revolt marks the birth of the Neo-Babylonian (or Chaldean) dynasty, which was to rule over Babylonia for more than eight decades, until the empire was conquered by the Cyrus the Great in 539. However, Achaemenid rule over Babylonia did not at first entail major changes in the institutional framework of the region. It is only with the oppression of two revolts against Xerxes in the latter's second regnal year in 484 that Babylonia's socio-economic fabric started to change profoundly.[10] Not only is the fact that we are dealing with an extended period of relative political stability important here, but above all the fact that the city of Babylon was at the same time at the centre of an empire

---

[7] Adams 1981: 175–252, especially 178; see also Adams 1965: 58–68. Brinkman 1984b is an important caveat as regards the overall representativeness of the survey data (which does not include the most densely settled areas, e.g. the northwestern Euphrates region, including the cities of Sippar, Babylon and Borsippa). While broadly agreeing with Adams' main conclusions, he introduces some regional modifications to the findings for the first quarter or so of the first millennium. Jursa 2010: 36–41 provides a succinct summary of the debate.

[8] This estimate ties in well with Hauser's (1999: 228) reckoning of about 20,000 inhabitants during the Parthian period, when a significantly smaller proportion of the city's surface area was inhabited. In the light of the difficulties encountered (summed up very well by van der Mieroop 1997: 94–7), most scholars avoid committing to absolute population numbers, e.g., Jursa 2010.

[9] His background is discussed in detail in Jursa 2007b and Fuchs 2014.

[10] Briant 2002: 70–6 is still the indispensable starting point; see also Jursa 2007a. For a less optimistic assessment of the impact of the Achaemenid conquest see Pirngruber forthcoming B. Waerzeggers 2014, especially 133–4, also notes significant changes already during the reign of Darius the Great. For the aftermath of the revolts see Waerzeggers 2003/4; Kessler 2004; and Baker 2008; the economic aspects are discussed in Jursa 2014b and Pirngruber forthcoming A.

encompassing large stretches of the Middle East and consequently drew enormous benefits from the associated spoils. In particular, the building projects of the Neo-Babylonian kings need to be mentioned here. They comprised not only prestige buildings – temples and palaces – but also investments in the agricultural infrastructure, to put it anachronistically. Most importantly, the period saw an expansion of the networks of canals. A prime example is the *nār šarri* (the 'royal canal') connecting the Euphrates and the Tigris, which was dug during these years.[11] Even in the Achaemenid period, Babylon remained one of the four capital cities of the empire, although it is clear that especially Susa (already under Darius) and then Persepolis increasingly supplanted Babylon as the empire's focal point, and consequently as the recipient/beneficiary of royal spending.[12]

In addition to an improving climate and demographic growth, this stable political background, combined with significant state expenditure in Babylonia, was another essential component of the economic transformations and growth that characterise 'the long sixth century', to use Jursa's terminology, hence the century and half between 626 and 484. In particular, the traditional model of the Mesopotamian economy as a redistributive temple-centred economy with little need for the institution of a market has increasingly met with criticism over recent years. Scholarship drawing on the rich private and temple archives dating to the long sixth century has brought to light a great deal of information on the structure of the economy of the later period. The new paradigm envisages a process of commercialisation engendering economic growth for the period in question.[13] For the sake of brevity, I shall single out below some of its most characteristic features in the form a list, with no claim to exhaustiveness either in argument or in the references. However, all of the aspects mentioned below are discussed (and most of them exhaustively) at some point in Jursa 2010.

Agricultural Intensification

Cash-crop cultivation became the prevailing economic strategy of the major temple households (Jursa 2004a and 2004b, 2005b). The best documented examples are the Eanna temple in Uruk specialising in sheep husbandry and

---

[11] Jursa 2010: 326–8.

[12] Tolini 2011 is an excellent and detailed discussion of the integration of the province of Babylonia into the Achaemenid Empire. For the construction works at Susa see especially *ibid.*: 275–303; see also Pirngruber forthcoming B.

[13] The indispensible work of reference is Jursa 2010, for a summary see *ibid.*: 754–83. See now also conveniently Jursa 2014b.

the sale of wool in bulk (Kleber 2008: 237–53) and the Ebabbar in Sippar producing dates on a large scale (Jursa 1995). The latter shift is particularly relevant, as date horticulture is not only more labour-intensive compared to extensive cereal agriculture (especially barley in Babylonia), but also yields a much higher output per surface area, allowing the generation of higher surpluses. The period is furthermore characterised by an increasing reliance on rent-farmers and other entrepreneur-type middlemen as mediators between temple/palace and farmers (van Driel 1999), especially from the second half of the reign of Nebuchadnezzar II onwards. Among the factors of production, land was an abundant and thus inexpensive resource compared to equipment such as plough animals and particularly water rights (Stolper 1985:125–34).

Commercialisation

On the one hand, it is clear that temples profited from state expenditure in the form of investments in the agricultural infrastructure such as the digging of the royal canal. On the other, they were pushed into the market mainly by the peculiar nature of taxation in the Neo-Babylonian and Achaemenid periods (Jursa 2011). The state's principal aim was clearly the recruitment of manpower for the army, for building projects, etc., but as the temple households were notoriously understaffed, they were forced to earn silver (by selling their crops or otherwise) in order to be able to hire free – and thus more expensive – workers to perform their duties.[14] *Mutatis mutandis* the same process applies to the other main target of royal taxation, individuals from the ranks of the urban elites.[15] According to Jursa (2010: 681), the demand for labour was so elevated as to create 'something like an urban working class'.[16] The silver thus paid as tax by the temples and well-off individuals was spent locally, especially during the Neo-Babylonian period, thus boosting demand and entailing a positive feedback cycle.

---

[14] See for example Beaulieu 2005. Y. Levavi (Vienna) presented an analysis of the topic from an epistolographic point of view at the Fourth International Congress of the Research Network '"Imperium" et "Officium"' in Vienna in November 2013; publication of the conference proceedings is planned.

[15] On taxation in first-millennium Babylonia see van Driel 2002: 153–328, and Jursa 2009 and 2011/13. The obligations of the priestly upper classes are discussed at length in Waerzeggers 2010: 327–53.

[16] Reliance on labourers external to the temple household is also encountered in the case of minor manufacturing activities such as weaving, which activities were also carried out by women who thus found employment beyond the immediate sphere of the private household (Joannès 2008).

Monetisation

Consequently, a sufficient level of monetisation even of small-scale transactions was a necessary prerequisite for the functioning of the system of taxation, which, again, exerted substantial pressure upon the temples to convert their harvests or other cash-crop commodities such as wool into silver as quickly as possible after the harvest (Jursa 2010: 591–2, 768–72 and *passim*). Even the rations (*kurummatu*) received by temple dependants are best interpreted as 'salaries paid in kind' rather than genuine rations aiming to provide full provisioning of the recipient. Additionally, there was a growing propensity to replace 'rations' with silver payments (Jursa 2008), also in the case of travel rations (*ṣidītu*, see Janković 2008).

Integration

Market integration within Babylonia was favoured by several factors, including regional specialisation and a cash-crop economy, the central role of the capital city Babylon and especially by comparatively low transport costs within Babylonia as a result of the increasingly dense network of navigable canals (Jursa 2010, contribution of Weszeli, 140–52). In general, it can be stated that Babylonia at least from the late seventh century onwards is best described as a fairly well-integrated economic region with a considerable amount of market activity.

Price Quotations in Context

It should be stressed that the ADs are not the only text corpus referring to price equivalents. An important observation in this regard is the fact that thinking in terms of price equivalents is frequently encountered with temple administrators in the Neo-Babylonian period. A particularly interesting corpus is the letters written by various officials of the Neo-Babylonian Eanna temple in Uruk, dating from the long sixth century. Although these documents precede the bulk of the data treated here – there is unfortunately no pertinent material from the Late Achaemenid or Seleucid periods extant – they are contemporary with the earliest diaries and in any case cast light on the historical reality of the price quotations in Babylonia around the middle of the first millennium. Furthermore, they elucidate material conditions and the everyday workings of the temple as an economic household. In these texts, we find several references to quantities of mostly barley and dates, and sometimes other commodities which could be acquired for 1 shekel of silver, or also the rate at which one commodity could be exchanged for another. The value of these instances, which stem from a more immediate context – daily accounting practices – than the abstract notations of the diaries, cannot be emphasised sufficiently. To be sure, it was certainly not the primary purpose of the price quotations of the ADs to facilitate daily transactions or enable the administrators to operate in the most economical manner possible. The passages in the letters, however, betray a firmly rooted awareness of price equivalents and, even more sophisticated, of regional price differences in the ambience of the Babylonian temples, just as they attest to a practice of mutual conversions of commodities on a large scale. In sum, these documents provide examples of the practical implementation of the abstract quotations of the diaries in everyday business transactions of the large, institutional households and shall be discussed in greater detail.

We quote some pertinent passages in full, explaining their respective connection to the data of the price sections of the diaries. A suitable starting point is YOS 3 45, lines 21–5:[17] 'Before barley becomes scarce, my lord shall send 1,000 *kurru* of dates to me so that I can exchange them for barley; I wish to make ready rations for the winter.' Two things are interesting about this passage. First of all, it serves as a reminder that the commodities quoted so regularly in the diaries equally constituted the economic basis of the temples, their regular observation had thus as a corollary at least potentially some practical application.[18] One thousand *kurru* of barley correspond to 180,000 litres, giving an impression of the scale at which the institutional households occasionally operated. Secondly, it nicely illustrates the pattern of seasonality which characterises the price quotations of the ADs. With the barley harvest taking place in spring, the stocks on hand were nearly depleted at the dawn of autumn. As, however, dates were harvested around October, they were at this time of the year readily available to be either directly distributed as rations or, as in this instance, to be exchanged against the more sought-after barley.

[17] *A-di la-i* ŠE.BAR *ta-maṭ-ṭu-ú* 1 LIM GUR ZÚ.LUM.MA EN-*a lu-še-bé-el*-MU *a-na* ŠE.BAR *lud-din u* PAD[HI.A] *a-na ku-ṣu lu-hi-ir*. See Stolper 2003: 281–3, for an edition with translation and commentary. Also Kleber 2012: 227 provides a partial translation of the letter.
[18] This down-to-earth aspect is neglected in Slotsky's (1997a: 23–42) overview of the commodities in the ADs, which collects *inter alia* references about magical and medical qualities of the commodities.

Another most interesting passage is possibly found in YOS 3 81, lines 6–8 and 16–20:[19] '(Concerning) the barley in Babylon, much of it has been expended (…) barley is valued higher here than dates: 240 litres of dates for 180 litres of barley; 40 *kurru* (7,200 litres) of barley (are given) for one *mina* of white silver. 2 *mār bānê* shall bring up dates and exchange them for barley in Sippar; if not they shall make available 10 *minas* of silver and exchange it here for barley before barley gets scarce.' The knowledge of the author of this letter, Innin-ahhē-iddin, of the prevailing economic circumstances is remarkable even by modern standards. Not only is he informed of a difference in value between dates and barley at his current location, but even of the precise range – 1 litre of barley being worth 1.33 litres of dates – and furthermore of the fact that in nearby Sippar, located around 60 kilometres to the north of Babylon, the rate of dates to barley was seemingly more convenient for the purposes of the temple. The letter also clearly indicates that when intending to buy commodities on a larger scale, the temple chose the means of payment, either dates or silver in our instance, according to the prevailing economic circumstances, with the aim of taking as much advantage as possible from the considerable resources at their disposal.

The letter YOS 3 79 (lines 22–7) similarly reports rather substantial regional price differences:[20] 'See, they told us that 1 shekel of silver [buys] 36 litres of dates in Uruk and we did not make purchases. Here they say that 1 shekel of *qalû*-silver (buys) 72 litres of dates or 72 litres of barley, I am searching but cannot find any.' As has been established by Kleber (2012), this letter as well as the two preceding ones, dates from a period of famine at the beginning of the reign of Cambyses. YOS 3 79 shows the temple official Nabû-ahu-iddin striving to acquire commodities to be disbursed as rations to labourers at what he considers a reasonable price during this difficult period. The equivalent at Uruk, merely 36 litres of dates per shekel was judged to be unacceptable. The supply situation in Bīt-Amukānu, situated to the south of Uruk in the Sealand, whence the Eanna regularly

---

[19] ŠE.BAR-a_4 *šá ina* TIN.TIR[KI] ŠE.BAR *ma-at-ta ina lìb-bi a-na te-lit te-lu-ú* (…) ŠE.BAR *a-kan-na ina* UGU ZÚ.LUM.MA *i-ba-áš-šú* 1 GUR 1 (PI) 4 (BAN) ZÚ.LUM.MA *a-na* 1 GUR ŠE.BAR 40 GUR ŠE.BAR *a-na* 1 *ma-na* KÙ.BABBAR *pe-ṣu-ú* 2 [LÚ]DUMU DÙ[MEŠ] ZÚ.LUM. MA *lu-še-lu-ni-im-mu a-na* ŠE.BAR *ina* UD.KIB.NUN[KI] *lid-din-u' ia-a-nu-ú* 10 *ma-na* KÙ.BABBAR *pe-ṣu-ú liš-ku-nu-im-mu a-kan-na a-na* ŠE.BAR *lid-din-u' a-di la-'i* ŠE.BAR *ta-maṭ-ṭu-ú*. Stolper 2003: 283–4 has an edition with translation and commentary; see also Kleber 2012: 225.

[20] *Li-mur šá* 1 PI ZÚ.LUM.MA *a-na* 1 GÍN KÙ.BABBAR *ina* UNUG[KI] *iq-ta-bu-ú-na-a-šú* KI.LAM *ul ni-íp-pu-uš a-kan-na* 2 PI ŠE.BAR *ù* 2 PI ZÚ.LUM.MA *a-na* 1 GÍN KÙ.BABBAR *qa-lu-ú i-qab-bu-ú ù ú-ba-'-e-ma ul am-mar*, mentioned by Jursa 2010: 92[(492)] and 551[(3020)], see now also Kleber 2012: 223–4.

acquired larger quantities of barley in particular, seems to have been hardly any better: although the equivalents were nominally double the amount at Uruk, the commodities do not seem to have been available after all.[21] The practice that the temples seem to have systematically gathered information on the price situation in different towns within Babylonia, at least in periods of exceptionally high prices, is also encountered in the fragmentary letter W 3381z (1; 4–8):[22] 'The equivalent is 48 litres for 1 shekel in Babylon and Borsippa, and sixty litres in Sippar and Opis.' It is telling that the Eanna temple in southern Babylonia was informed of barley equivalents in towns as distant as Sippar and Opis. The passage quoted therefore reinforces in an impressive manner the notion of market integration throughout Babylonia.

As opposed to the letters considered thus far, a more optimistic picture of the economy is drawn in YOS 3 68,[23] conveying the impression of a period of abundant supplies. The generic statement in the letter of the officials Zēru-ukīn and Nabû-ginû (9–10) 'Silver is much (worth) in relation to barley' is specified a few lines later (13–15), '1,000 (*kurru*) of barley, at the rate of 62 (*kurru*) for 1 mina of silver.' This equals an equivalent of 186 litres of barley per shekel of silver, a very favourable rate not encountered in our dataset throughout the fourth century – it was only during the later Seleucid period that the barley equivalent could occasionally rise to such notable amounts. In the same letter (lines 15–17) transport costs at what would seem to be an advantageous rate of 6.7 per cent of the value of the merchandise are also mentioned. As the destination is an unnamed canal, probably the closest, this letter equally illustrates nicely the spatial market integration favoured by the practice of transporting larger bulks of goods by waterways, mentioned above. Additionally, it shows in a similar way to YOS 3 45 that considerable amounts (again 1,000 *kurru*) of basic commodities were acquired by the temple for silver. Again, the awareness of the temple dependants of regional price differences is remarkable.

Another use of price quotations in the first millennium is found in a text category which is – in accordance with the term given to them by A. Leo Oppenheim, their first editor[24] – commonly designated as 'siege documents'.

---

[21]   Kleber 2012. She additionally adduces YOS 3 33 of the same Nabû-ahu-iddin quoting the same barley equivalent of 72 litres per shekel but explicitly referring to the scarce supply situation.

[22]   KI.LAM (…) 1 (p) 2 BÁN ŠE.BAR *ina* TIN.TIR^(KI) *u* BÁR.SIPA *a-na* 1 GÍN *u* 1 (p) 4 BÁN *ina* UD.KIB.NUN^(KI) *u* ^(URU)*ú-pi-ia*, quoted in Jursa 2010: 82^(410); equally adduced by Kleber 2012: 229.

[23]   KÙ.BABBAR *ina muh-hi* ŠE.BAR *ma-a-du* … (13–15) 1 LIM ŠE.BAR *a-na pi-i* 1 + *šu* 2 GUR *a-na* 1 MA.NA … (15–17) ½ DANNA *qaq-qar a-na muh-hi* ÍD *ru-qí-it i-na* 1 GUR 2 BÁN *a-na* UGU ÍD. On various aspects of this document see Jursa 2010: 101, 146 and 489^(2667).

[24]   Oppenheim 1955, see now also Eph'al 2009, especially 114–51.

These texts share the characteristic that they were drawn up during a time of internal warfare when the particular city in which they were written lay under siege. These documents mainly come from Nippur from the period of the war between the Assyrian king Sîn-šar-iškun and Nabopolassar in the 620s. Other examples from Sennacherib's siege of Babylon in 690 in his campaign against Mušēzib-Marduk[25] and from the war between the brothers Assurbanipal and Šamaš-šum-ukīn[26] are also extant. The high prices quoted in these texts are accompanied by other statements, such as, most exhaustively, 'the land was gripped by siege, famine, hunger, want and hard times' (YBC 11377, translation by Brinkman) and serve thus primarily to underline the hardship suffered by the city in this period. Therefore, their historicity is at least questionable.[27] But on the other hand, caution is required because it is exactly one of these *topoi*, namely parents selling their children, which is the transaction at issue in nine of twenty-five tablets in the archive of Ninurta-uballiṭ/Bēl-usāti from besieged Nippur. The sale of children by their parents in a period of famine is also documented in the Astronomical Diaries (AD -273B, U.E.1; and possibly also in AD -373, U.E.1). While the veracity of the prices in these siege documents is thus disputable, they can thus at least help us to establish a minimum range of what was, probably by quite some margin, conceived as famine prices. The variation of the documents at our disposal is, however, minimal, and ranges between 2 litres (YBC 11377) and 2 *sūtu* (i.e. 12 litres) of barley (unpublished document K. 132 in Eph'al 2009: 116[5] and 124) for 1 shekel of silver.[28] The lowest observed equivalent encountered in the data at our disposal stems from the Diadochi Chronicle (ABC 10 = BCHP 3), which quotes – exceptionally for that genre – 6 litres of barley per shekel in the period of extended warfare before Seleucus and Antigonus the One-Eyed. This value can be compared to the lowest equivalent encountered in the dataset of the Astronomical Diaries, which stems from the same period and amounts to 7.5 litres of barley per shekel in 309. These quotations, then, could mean that prices in the siege documents may have a historical reality after all. However, there is also one barley price quotation extant in AD -273B,

---

[25] YBS 11377, published in Brinkman 1973: 93.

[26] San Nicolò 1951, no. 20.

[27] Eph'al 2009: 132–5.

[28] The range of pertinent seventh-century Assyrian documents listed in Eph'al 2009: 125–6 is similar, and the same holds true for attestation from Bronze Age Emar (Eph'al 2009: 141–2). The equivalents that serve to underline the hardship suffered by the country are even lower in the poem 'The Curse of Akkade' (Cooper 1983). During the invasion of the Guteans following the impieties of Narām-Sîn, 1 shekel (of silver?) bought only a quarter of a litre of sesame, a quarter of a litre of grain (barley?) and half a *mina* of silver (lines 176–8).

reporting as mentioned above that 'people sold their children' because of a seemingly grave famine. The price equivalent is, at 1 *pānu* (36 litres) per shekel of silver, considerably higher than those of the letters (and note additionally that the equivalent for dates is not even close to being exceptionally low, as is the case in AD -373, unfortunately without a barley equivalent extant).[29] Hence, the case of AD -273B modifies the quotations in the letters and gives substance to Eph'al's claim (2009) that the equivalents ranging between 1 and 12 litres of barley for a shekel of silver may be literary *topoi*. As to the question from what price equivalent onwards one can speak of famine prices, the guesstimate of Vargyas (1997) of 50 litres of barley and below does not seem too far off the mark in the light of AD -273B.

Continuity and Change in the Late Achaemenid and Seleucid Periods

The archival material used by Jursa in his masterful study came to a sudden end in the aftermath of the rebellions against Xerxes in the king's second regnal year, in 484. The mainly northern Babylonian cities involved in the uprisings – most notably Sippar, Borsippa and Babylon – suffered severe retaliation at the hands of the Achaemenid king, but until recently, the degree of change was hidden behind the near complete end of written documentation. Most importantly, the traditional local power structures were utterly uprooted. In Babylon, the prebendary system, the mainstay of the local elites whence they derived social prestige, political power and material wealth, was abolished. Likewise, the office of *šatammu* (conventionally translated as 'temple administrator' or similar) as the highest representative of local interest vis-à-vis the crown disappears from the record for decades to come.[30] A new elite was created, whose power base was their ties to the crown and its representatives. An illuminating example is Bēlšunu, identical with Belesys, the satrap of Transpotamia, in the writings of Greek historian Xenophon.[31] His clan, the Bābāya, were minor players during the long sixth century, but Bēlšunu himself held during the fifth century first the

---

[29] The famine reported in AD -149A, r4 occurred in Antioch-on-the-Orontes rather than in Babylonia and is thus of no use for our purposes; see van der Spek 1997/8, *contra* Del Monte 1997: 93–4.

[30] These developments are described on the basis of new texts in Hackl 2013, especially 291–5 and 380–93; his results are conveniently summarised in Hackl forthcoming.

[31] His career is discussed in Stolper 1987 and 1995; for an introduction to the archive see Hackl 2013: 413–30.

position of city governor (*pīhātu*) of Babylon and then even rose the office of satrap – a position usually reserved for the Persian nobility – of *ēbir nāri*, i.e. Transpotamia. Moreover, Bēlšunu derived his economic wealth from his dealings with the Achaemenid ruling class, by managing real estate in their possession in Babylonia, which they often held in the form of a royal gift (*nidinti šarri*). Additionally, Bēlsunu himself is also attested as the beneficiary of such crown grants.

This altered institutional framework had of course ramifications for the workings of the economy. For the Late Achaemenid period, a weakening of the market as mode of exchange regarding the factors of production (i.e. land, labour and capital) is clearly in evidence. In particular, the amassing of landed property in the hands of Persian aristocrats (and, to a lesser extent, Babylonian minions of the Great King) and the concomitant power of the new elite to coerce labour services from the Babylonian subjects greatly reduced the scope of land and labour markets.[32] As the discussion of the commodity prices of the Late Achaemenid period will show, a similar case for commodity markets can be made.

Not much is known of Babylon's status during the Late Achaemenid period. In the Murašû archive from Nippur, we find indications that the city was still at least occasionally visited by the Great King, so for example by Darius II in 423 shortly after his accession to the throne and again several years later, in 417.[33] Even some minor royal building activities are attested during the reign of Artaxerxes II (404–359), who added a pavilion, the so-called *Perserbau*, to the south palace.[34] On the local political level, we note with Hackl (forthcoming) the reappearance of the office of *šatammu* in the first year of Darius III, possibly a gesture intended to foster the acceptance of the usurper's claim to the throne. In this context, we should note that Darius III's accession was not unchallenged, as the Uruk King List registers the presence of a rebel king after the death of Artaxerxes IV (Tolini 2011: 577–9).

With Alexander the Great's conquest of Babylon in 331, the city rose to prominence again, and scholars have assumed repeatedly that the Macedonian even intended for Babylon to become the capital city of his new empire.[35] However, Alexander's untimely death in the afternoon of

[32] Jursa 2014a, see also Pirngruber forthcoming A. The impact of the changed institutional framework on the factors of production is discussed in detail in Chapter 3 below.

[33] Discussed extensively by Tolini 2011: 505–24.

[34] Tolini 2011: 539–47.

[35] A recent example is Heckel 2008: 149. On the conquest see Bosworth 1988: 86–7; Kuhrt 1990; and Tolini 2012: 277–87. A political history of Late Achaemenid and Seleucid Babylonia is provided by Boiy 2004: 102–92.

11 June 323 (Depuydt 1997) – famously documented by an Astronomical Diary with the terse phrase LUGAL NAM[MEŠ], 'the king died' – inaugurated a period of lingering warfare for years to come. In particular, the conflict between Seleucus and Antigonus Monophthalmus (the 'One-Eyed') ravaged the province, and it was only with the former's victory and acceptance of the title of king in 305/4 that peace returned to Babylonia.

Babylon subsequently played a key role in early Seleucid royal ideology, as evidenced for example by the fact the Seleucid era begins with Seleucus' reconquest of Babylon in 312.[36] Also on a more concrete level, there can be no doubt about the city's continuing relevance despite the foundation of Seleucia-on-the-Tigris as new provincial capital in its vicinity. It was noted above that the number of chronicle texts displays a clear peak in the period of Antiochus I. These texts show Antiochus in the role of a pious Babylonian king, performing sacrifices to the gods in the different temples and supervising renovation works undertaken at the Esangila temple, Babylon's central sanctuary (BCHP 6, lines 6–7). It is thus hardly coincidental that the last Babylonian royal inscription, the so-called Antiochus cylinder from Borsippa, dates to the reign of the same ruler.[37]

In the later decades of Seleucid reign, Babylon seems to have lost some of its prominence. Even within Babylonia, the eastern region along the Tigris became the focal point of Seleucid colonialisation policy. This trend continued a development that has its roots in the preceding centuries, and which has at its base the increasing (economic) importance of the Tigris river, both as source of irrigation canals and as an artery of trade.[38] Most of the new settlements, urban or village-sized, were actual foundations, rather than expansions of earlier sites, the prime example being Seleucia-on-the-Tigris, the seat of the highest provincial officials, whether satraps or *stratēgoi*, in the third and second centuries.[39] As was the case with the Ptolemaic Empire, the Greek colonisation seems thus to haven taken place mainly in previously economically underexploited areas, namely the Fayyum in Egypt[40] and the Tigris region in Babylonia.

---

[36] According to L. Capdetrey (2007: 35–8), the return to Babylon can thus be said to assume the role of a myth of origin for the dynasty.

[37] On this document see Kuhrt and Sherwin-White 1991; Kosmin 2014a; and Stevens 2014.

[38] Adams 1981: 192 speaks of a 'fundamental shift towards the Tigris as the main axis of trade, settlement, and communications'.

[39] Cohen 2013: 109–77 provides a brief survey of the Seleucid settlements in Babylonia. For a discussion of the underlying policies see Capdetrey 2007: 52–6 and Kosmin 2014a: 183–221, especially 186–90 on the Tigris region.

[40] Manning 2003: 99–125.

At the same time, it is clear that after the battle of Ipsus in 301 and the ensuing territorial gains for Seleucus I in Syria and Asia Minor, the empire's centre of gravity shifted towards the west, with Antioch-on-the-Orontes becoming the empire's primary royal residence and northern Syria the new 'dynastic homeland' (Kosmin 2014a: 110).[41] Also on the political level, the dominant conflict took place on the eastern shores of the Mediterranean. However, the Syrian Wars fought over Coele-Syria with the Ptolemies also had repercussions as far as Babylonia. This is best attested by AD -273B reporting military preparations in the run-up to the First Syrian War, thus attesting to the rather deep integration of the region into the imperial structures.

There is no reason to follow Strabo's assessment of Babylon as a deserted city throughout the Seleucid period.[42] After Antiochus I's residence as vice-king, the city was still on occasions visited by the king. The most notable event was possibly the participation of Antiochus III in the Babylonian New Year's festival in 205 upon return from his *anabasis* into the upper provinces, described in AD -204C. A second visit of the same king to Babylon and further on to Borsippa is attested in early spring 187. Not only the king, but also the high provincial officials from Seleucia regularly visited the city and participated in cultic rites, mainly sacrifices *ana bulṭi ša šarri*, 'for the life of the king' or other dignitaries (e.g. AD -178C).[43]

The continuing importance of the Esangila temple in the Hellenistic period as centre of scribal culture and scientific learning[44] is matched on a political level by the re-emergence of its pre-eminent role in the local social organisation, which in the third and second century is better known than during the Late Achaemenid period.[45] After the reappearance of the office in the reign of Darius III, the *šatammu* is attested as the highest local official well into the Parthian period. Just as during the long sixth century, he represented the local community in their dealings with the crown and its authorities. In the diaries, he is always mentioned together with the *kiništu* of the Esangila, that is, the temple assembly. The composition of the latter must remain elusive, as the prebendary system no longer existed in the city of

---

[41] On the significance of the battle see, e.g., the concise remarks of Anson 2014: 173–4.

[42] Strabo, *Geography* 16 1.5.

[43] These sacrifices are discussed in Pirngruber 2010: 535–42.

[44] Beaulieu 2006: 31 entertains the possibility of Babylon as a role model of sorts for the Mouseion of Alexandria. See Clancier 2009: 106–213 for the impressive amount of tablets and variety of genres produced in the Hellenistic period.

[45] The social structure of Hellenistic Babylon is the subject of several recent contributions, see, e.g., Boiy 2004: 193–225; Clancier 2012b; and Clancier and Monerie 2014.

Babylon,[46] but we are better informed concerning its competences, mainly owing to the information provided by the ADs. It seems that this institution can be compared to the civic assembly (*puhru*) best known from the early Neo-Babylonian period (Barjamović 2004). Besides these local organs, and quite similar to the power structure during the long sixth century, the presence of royal officials is also attested. An example is the *zazakku*, a fiscal administrator installed by the king, presumably to tighten the crown's control over the temple resources.[47] Most intriguingly, however, an assembly of the Greek community, known as the *politai*, is in evidence likely since the reign of Antiochus III, and in line with Babylon's refoundation as *polis*. Just as the Babylonian *kiništu* was headed by the *šatammu*, these *politai* always occur in tandem with the *pāhātu*, maybe in this instance the Babylonian rendering of Greek *epistates*.[48]

In the light of these significant social and political evolutions, one needs to be careful in extrapolating from the findings for the long sixth century for the economy of the ensuing Late Achaemenid and Seleucid periods, a particularly pressing problem in the light of the dearth of archival data. Although there are a few very interesting archives, most famously the Murašû archive from Nippur (Stolper 1985) and the Esangila archive from Babylon (Hackl 2013), there are, for example, hardly any price data extant which could supplement the observations from the ADs. These price notations, identified clearly as market prices (see the discussion in the previous chapter), are thus by themselves the main indicator for the persistence of the markets as an economic mode of integration. Moreover, a few hints can be detected which attest to the same awareness of regional and temporal price differences displayed in the epistolographic sources from the long sixth century also during the Hellenistic period. CT 49 116 (Jursa 2006: 185), for example, alludes to both dimensions, reading: KÙ.BABBAR *ši-mi dan-nu* K[AŠ.SAG (4) *lìb-bu*]-*ú na-dan šá ina* [ITI]KIN MU 49.KAM *ina* E[KI] (5) [*ina-a*]*n-din-nu*, 'the silver price of said vats of prime beer according

---

[46] For the definition of the *kiništu* of the sixth century as a specifically priestly assembly see Waerzeggers 2010: 56.

[47] It is hardly coincidental that this office (discussed by Dandamaev 1994; see also Del Monte 1997: 79 and Boiy 2004: 161 and 210), already attested in the Neo-Babylonian period, seems to have been reintroduced by Antiochus IV. On this king's policies towards Near Eastern sanctuaries, and in particular the temple in Jerusalem see, e.g., Mittag 2006: 225–81 and Honigman 2014: 345–77.

[48] For the possible equation of the two titles see van der Spek 1986: 64–5. The institutions of *pāhātu* and *politai* are discussed in Boiy 2004: 204–9; cf. Kessler 2006: 280, who thinks that the *pāhātu* – being a royal official – acted as an intermediary between the Babylonian community headed by the *šatammu* and the king as well.

to the rate that prevails in Babylon in month VI year 49 (SE = 263/2)'.
Interestingly, the terminology employed to designate the rate (*nadānu*) in
this passage is exactly the one encountered in some of the later price lists
from the Parthian period – S/W texts 9 and 11, both from the last quarter of the second century – as a synonym for the more common KI.LAM
(*mahīru*).[49] A corollary of the document just quoted is that it gives some
insight into the practical use of specifically monthly equivalents, the most
commonly observed entity in the diaries. An important archival document
confirming the reality of price fluctuations as noted in the diaries is CT 49
111 (= Stolper 1993a, text 13), dating to month IX of year 42 SE (December
270). After arranging the repayment (in silver) of a commodity loan similar
to CT 49 116 'according to the rate (*nadānu*) that prevails in Babylonia', an
additional punitive clause specifies that in case of default payment at the
appointed date the repayment shall be according to the lowest prevailing
equivalent, and thus the highest going price, of the current year (*lìb-bu-ú
na-dan ma-ṭu-ú šá* MU 43.KAM).[50] If anything, these two examples just
quoted show that thinking in terms of price equivalents as well as the awareness of price oscillations was as characteristic of Hellenistic Babylonia as it
was for the preceding, much better-documented Neo-Babylonian period.

In general, both the absolute number of prices other than the observations of the ADs and the variety of commodities for which prices are extant
is much smaller in the Late Achaemenid and Seleucid periods, with the
possible exception of prebend sales prices.[51] There are two prices for slave
women from Late Achaemenid Uruk in sale contracts, one dating to 424 and
the other to 418.[52] However, the large difference between the two prices –
38.5 shekels and 75 shekels – is indicative of the general problem with slave
prices, namely the wide range of fluctuation that arises as a result of differences in age, physical constitution, education, etc.[53] Considering the usual
range established by Dandamaev (1984: 204), the 424 price of 75 shekels

---

[49] See Stolper 1993a: 44 on this particular use of the infinitive of the verb *nadānu*, 'to give'. Van
der Spek (personal communication, spring 2015) also considers a reading *nadānu* of the
sumerogram KI.LAM for the attestations in the Astronomical Diaries and the Late Babylonian
commodity price tablets.

[50] Thus, the explanation of this clause by Stolper 1993a: 44.

[51] The following list of prices lays no claim to being exhaustive, but can at least convey an
impression of the data at our disposal and the problems encountered. Several hitherto
unpublished prices from northern Babylonia (not considered here) have now been published
in Hackl 2013 and Hackl and Pirngruber 2015. This data consists mainly of prices of slaves and
house rents and is difficult to contextualise (or even quantify) for the reasons outlined above.

[52] Edited as texts 2 and 3 in Stolper 1993a.

[53] Dandamaev 1984: 204–5. See also *ibid*. 200–2 for the range attested in Neo-Babylonian
documents.

seems to be more characteristic of the Late Achaemenid period. The prices of two *kišubbû*s, empty building lots, are roughly comparable, though they stem from two different cities: the one from Uruk was sold at 10.6 square metres per shekel,[54] the other one (from Borsippa) was sold at 12.25 square metres per shekel.[55] This impression of rather heterogeneous prices for real estate assets is, however, completely reversed by two contracts involving agricultural land 'planted with date gardens and for the cultivation of grain' (ŠE.NUMUN *zaqpi u pî šulpi*) from Uruk, TCL 13 234 and 249 (van der Spek 1986, texts 3 and 2), whose prices per square metre differ considerably.[56] Other contracts involving real estate, both sales and leases, mention plots consisting of different assets that certainly influence the price (an inhabitable *bît qašti* of unspecified dimension and a *bît ritti* in text VDI 1955/4, 3 = van der Spek 1995, text 2) and frequently omit the size of the plot involved. Most other archival documents mentioning occasionally considerable amounts of silver are records of deposit or promissory notes and contain no information on the amount of a commodity that could be purchased with the silver. To my knowledge, they are no straightforward sales of barley, dates or other staple (food) commodities attested throughout the Hellenistic period. This fact highlights the importance of the price quotations of the Astronomical Diaries, which are our only source on the costs of daily necessities.

In part, the scarcity of the documentation at hand can be explained by Seleucid bureaucratic practice. The disappearance of certain types of transactions from the cuneiform record was a consequence of administrative reforms undertaken by Antiochus I during the period of the First Syrian War in the late 270s. The introduction of new taxes on the sale of slaves (*andrapodōn*) and, more important for our purposes, on sales of arable land (*epōnion*) as well as the requirement to register these transactions with the *chreophylax*, a royal financial official, also entailed a change of the language and material medium employed for the documentation of these transactions. Henceforth, the pertinent documents were drafted in Greek and on

---

[54] TCL 13 239, published in van der Spek 1986 as text 7: 5 shekels of silver a paid as compensation for a plot of ~53 m².

[55] CT 49 137, published as text 1 in van der Spek 1995. The price mentioned in the contract amounted to 12 shekels of silver for a *kišubbû* of roughly 147 m².

[56] In TCL 13 249, dating to 316 BCE, 2 minas are paid for a quarter share in a plot of about 3,000 square metres (which are 6.25 m²/shekel); in TCL 13 234, dating only four years later, 9 minas and 15 shekels are paid for a quarter share in a parcel of 21.5 hectares – the price equals thus 96.85 m²/shekel. Note that both contracts date to the period of repeated armed conflict between Alexander the Great's death and the establishment of the Seleucid dynasty. For the impact of warfare on land prices see the assessment in van der Spek 2000a: 303–5 (also discussing both TCL 13 234 and 249).

(perishable) papyrus, which of course means that they are not preserved for posterity.[57]

Although we are thus informed about the introduction of certain cash taxes, the system of taxation of Seleucid Babylonia and how far it constituted a continuation of Achaemenid practice to recruit manpower for building projects and similar purposes cannot be answered adequately. It seems, however, that silver payments played a more important role compared to the earlier periods. There is indeed even evidence for the introduction of a general head tax, denoted in cuneiform texts as the 'silver of the heads' (*kaspu ša qaqqadū*).[58] Moreover, in addition to the cuneiform documentation there is evidence on matters of taxation in form of clay bullae from Seleucia-on-the-Tigris, mentioning a salt tax (*halikē*) and exemptions thereof.[59] It is tempting to interpret this salt tax as a poll tax of sorts (and as such perhaps identical to the 'silver of the heads' mentioned in the cuneiform documentation), as was the case in contemporary Egypt, where it was intended to further the monetisation of the countryside.[60] However, for the time being this idea must remain speculation.

These important developments notwithstanding, the conclusion by Aperghis (2004: 179) of 'rapid changeover to a monetary economy' clearly underestimates the continuing importance of rents and taxes collected in kind and especially grain throughout the Seleucid Empire.[61] Rather, von Reden's (2007: 109–10) caveat for the Ptolemaic Empire, that the fact that taxes in cash are better documented in our evidence does not mean that these exceed the income of the state in the form of grain, clearly applies to the Seleucids as well. This is also the stance adopted in the most recent study of the Seleucid system of taxation, where in analogy with contemporary Egypt the harvests of the royal estates are assumed to constitute the state's main source of income.[62]

Still, regarding everyday transactions, it is safe to assume that Babylonia ranked among the more densely monetised regions of the empire. This trend was furthered by a major innovation of the Hellenistic period, namely

---

[57] Doty 1977: 308–35, on the basis of the documentation from Uruk. However, his results seem to apply for northern Babylonia, too; see Hackl 2013: 54–5. For an analogous practice in Ptolemaic Egypt, see Manning 2003: 171–7.

[58] Mentioned explicitly in CTMMA 5 148 (the so-called Lehmann text) and AD -183A.

[59] Unfortunately, these documents are notoriously reticent and not easily interpreted, see Mollo 1996. In her forthcoming doctoral thesis, Jen Hicks (London) will have a fresh look at the bullae.

[60] Von Reden 2007: 65–7 and 2010: 45.

[61] Bringmann 2005; Capdetrey 2007: 395–428; and Monerie 2013: 266–96.

[62] Monson 2015: 189 and the literature quoted there, and note 79.

the introduction of coinage on a larger scale and the opening of mints in Babylonia in the immediate aftermath of Alexander the Great's conquest of the city.[63] Although coins occasionally circulated in Babylonia during the Achaemenid period, they were treated as bullion and thus weighed rather than counted. Evidence for this practice is contained in a coin hoard from Babylon containing clipped silver coins – both Persian *sigloi* and various denominations of Greek origin – together with Hacksilber and jewellery in silver and bronze (Reade 1986, especially plate 1). However, in spite of the absence of minted coins it is beyond doubt that the Babylonian economy was already deeply monetised in the long sixth century.[64] The introduction of coinage may thus have had less of an impact than one might be inclined to assume at first glance. In order to facilitate dealing with the new means of exchange, the *manûtu ša Bābili*, the 'rate of Babylon', guaranteed the equivalence of 2 Babylonian shekels (16.66 grams of silver) to 1 stater, be it the imperial tetradrachm or the local lion stater.[65] Also, the commonness of coin usage seems to have developed only slowly over a time span of several decades. Importantly, payment in coins never became the exclusive, and not even the predominant method, but was employed alongside the traditional means of weighing silver and, of course, commodity monies, mainly barley and dates. It is interesting to note that according to the cuneiform documentation, coins seem to have been employed only for even sums exceeding 2 Babylonian shekels – hence, sums that could be disbursed in the most common current denominations of lion stater and tetradrachms.[66]

As is amply attested for the sixth century, the quality of the silver, and more specifically of the coins used as means of payment in these transactions, was still important and thus specified in the business contracts, reflecting strong attachment on the part of the Babylonian elites to the real, intrinsic value of coins (Monerie 2013: 449). Of particular interest in this regard are the prebend sales contracts from Uruk in southern Babylonia, the bulk of which date to the third century.[67] These contracts habitually

---

[63] Le Rider 2003: 267–334, also Monerie 2013: 134–49.

[64] Jursa 2010: 469–753; see, e.g., 659: 'silver should not be considered exclusively "high-range" money ... Silver money was used ubiquitously ... It seems unlikely (and can be excluded for all the individuals whose archives have been preserved) that any inhabitant of a Babylonian city in the sixth century could have avoided engaging in silver-based transactions on a regular basis.'

[65] Jursa 2002: 120–1, also Stolper 1993a: 23 and Monerie 2013: 182–6.

[66] Monerie 2013: 184 (fig. 24) and 187.

[67] The most recent discussion of Hellenistic prebend sale (and also lease) contracts is Corò 2005, including editions of all known as well as several unpublished texts. The system is also described by Monerie 2013: 391–428. See Pirngruber and Waerzeggers 2011 for a study of the prices of prebends.

stipulate that the payment is to be settled in coins of the reigning king. For example, OECT 9 25, a sale of a temple enterer's (*ērib bīti*) prebend worth 32.5 shekels of silver dating to the year 86 SE (226/5), demands the payment of the purchase price to be in (lines 9–10) *is-ta-tir-ra-nu šá ¹si-lu-ku bab-ba-nu-ú-tú*, 'silver in staters of Seleucus in good condition', hence Seleucus II (246–226).[68] At first glance this specification is enigmatic, as the Seleucid Empire was known for its 'permissive' stance towards foreign denominations.[69] However, according to H. Seyrig, coins minted in the names of the Seleucid king circulated above their intrinsic value. By specifying the means of payment the sellers of prebendary shares thus ensured payment with the most valuable current denomination.[70] This awareness of the different values of the various types of coins in circulation has recently found confirmation in one of the Commodity Price Lists. S/W 6 (lines r12–15) differentiates in year 175 SE (137/6) between a barley equivalent for 1 shekel of silver in staters of Demetrius and for 1 shekel of silver staters of Arsaces, the former amounting to 84 litres but the latter to 72 litres only. The coins of the Seleucid king is thus attributed a greater purchasing power, and, interestingly, this appraisal seems furthermore to correspond to the greater average weight of the tetradrachms from Seleucia-on-the-Tigris of this king.[71]

The above-mentioned prebend sale contracts from Hellenistic Uruk can be used also to cast light on still another aspect of the Late Babylonian economy. Almost eighty prices from 'single profession prebends'[72] could be used in a comparative analysis between Neo-Babylonian and Hellenistic material. Besides showing that the alleged sharp rise in prebend prices between Neo-Babylonian and Hellenistic periods is purely fictitious and based on a misunderstanding of the contract formulary, the study shows that throughout the whole Hellenistic period, there is no clear pattern of rise or decline in the prices for any group of prebends, with the exception of the brewers' prebend.[73] The prices of this latter type of prebend almost double between

---

[68]   According to the Babylonian king list (Sachs and Wiseman 1954), year 87 SE was the first full year of his successor Seleucus III, which in the logic of this list should mean that Seleucus II died at some point during 86 SE, hence the year to which OECT 9 25 dates. However, there is also numismatic evidence pointing to the death of Seleucus II only during 87 SE, see van der Spek 2010: 376.

[69]   See, e.g., the assessment in Le Rider and de Callataÿ 2006: 73–7 and 125–7.

[70]   Le Rider and de Callataÿ 2006: 77 and 116 (interpreting an observation by P. Vargyas). For a succinct summary of Seyrig's view see *ibid*. 111–16.

[71]   Slotsky and Wallenfels 2009: 94[(65)].

[72]   That is, sale contracts involving only one specific type of prebendary activity, such as brewer, butcher, temple enterer, etc. See Corò 2005: 26–32 for the terminology.

[73]   Pirngruber and Waerzeggers 2011: 115 and fig. 1; cf. Monerie 2013: 419–27.

the period 270–250 and 230, and after a gap in the documentation of about fifty years their value seems to have risen again by more than 50 per cent in the attestations between 170 and 150.

Moreover, it seems possible on the basis of this material to make the case for a general congruence of barley prices in the cities of Uruk and Babylon: some of these prebend sales contracts add a (barley?) equivalent of the purchasing prices, which overall aligns nicely with the prices prevailing at the same time in the city of Babylon.[74] In a maximalist reading, this fact can be interpreted as a hint at a certain degree of market integration throughout Babylonia for this later period, as was the case in the long sixth century. A particularly interesting attestation of a certain degree of market integration also in the Late Achaemenid period stems not from cuneiform documents but from the Greek historian Xenophon, who participated at the close of the fifth century as mercenary in the abortive revolt of Cyrus the Younger against his brother, the Great King Artaxerxes II. In his *Anabasis* he describes the economic relations of the villages along the Euphrates that were passed by Cyrus and his allies on their march into Babylonia with the city of Babylon thus (1 1.5) 'the people who dwelt here [i.e. near the village of Pylae on the Euphrates] made a living by quarrying mill-stones along the river banks, then fashioning them, and taking them to Babylon, where they sold [*epōloun*] them and bought grain in exchange [*antagorazontes*]', with *antagorazō* specifically implying a purchase made with money.[75] The passage suits also remarkably well with what is known about Babylonian soil conditions, namely a scarcity of natural resources but a productive agriculture with high yield rates. Xenophon indeed seems to have been quite well informed about Babylonian agriculture. The passage *Anab.* 2 3.14 for example attests to his knowledge that grain and date beer (which he calls palm wine, *oinon ek tēs balanou tēs apo tou phoinikos*) were the most important elements of the diet of the inhabitants of Babylonia.

Finally, there are also occasional attestations of commodity prices in the Greek authors. Xenophon in his *Anabasis* (1 1.6) provides a price for grain that Cyrus' troops could acquire from the Lydian merchants who were accompanying the army on campaign. However, the price given – 4 *sigloi*

---

[74] The pertinent contracts are OECT 9 30, 36 and 61, the latter two being partially broken. Moreover, the commodity at issue is never specified. However, by comparison with the Neo-Babylonian material, barley is the most likely option. See Pirngruber and Waerzeggers 2011: 120 for a discussion.

[75] See the definition of *antagorazō*, 'to buy with money received in payment for something else' in Liddell and Scott 1968[9]. On the passage in Xenophon see Lendle 1995: 46–7; see also the map on 54 for the location of Pylae.

for 1 *kapithē* of grain (corresponding to 30 obols for 2 choenikes, 1 choenix containing about 1.1 litres) – is probably to be interpreted as a topical price, too. The price can be converted into 5 drachms or 2.5 shekels of silver for 2.2 litres of grain, hence about 1 shekel of silver per litre of grain, which is certainly greatly exaggerated: the mean price of the Late Achaemenid period amounts to 3.37 shekels/*kurru*, hence about 55 litres per shekel. An additional argument for such a reading of the price stems from its literary context as it occurs in a passage dedicated to describing the hardship and deprivation suffered by Cyrus' troops on their campaign.

3 | Land, Labour and Capital: The Factors of Production

Introduction

This chapter considers one of the most decisive elements of commodity price formation, namely the distribution of the factors of production, that is, land, labour and capital. It thus follows an approach advocated by economist Douglass North since the 1970s and focuses on the structures (socio-economic, political, cultural, etc.) that underlie a given economy before tackling the question of the economy's performance.[1] Particular attention is paid to the ownership pattern of the factors of production and its potential impact on prices. As the topic is best documented in the Murašû archive, the focus in this chapter is on the Late Achaemenid period.

However, it is not my intention to confine myself to an analysis of the specific data at hand, but rather to tackle the wider question of the representativeness of its pattern for the Late Achaemenid period at large. After all, the Murašû archive precedes the price data of the Astronomical Diaries, and additionally stems from the rural region of Nippur rather than from the provincial capital of Babylon. However, comparative evidence from two archives dating to the fifth and fourth centuries, but unfortunately not yet fully published – the Kasr archive from Babylon and the Tattannu archive from Borsippa – confirms by and large the representativeness of the Nippur data, especially as regards the question of land tenure for wider regions of Babylonia during the Late Achaemenid period.

The highly volatile commodity prices (see Figure 5.1 for barley prices) prevailing in the first half of the fourth century cannot be explained by exogenous shocks. I will show that economic structure and social institutions, rather than external factors, are the main cause of price volatility in post-Xerxes Babylonia.

Before going *in medias res*, a brief introduction to the Murašû archive is appropriate. Without a doubt, this archive of a family of agricultural entrepreneurs from the city of Nippur, dating to the last quarter of the fifth century and consisting of about 800 documents, qualifies as the most informative

---

[1] Exemplarily North 1990.

source for the topic at hand.[2] The business dealings of the Murašûs – the main protagonists are Enlil-šumu-iddin and his nephew Rēmūt-Ninurta – comprised two main activities. In the first place, they provided credit for small-scale land-holders in the land-for-service scheme so that the latter were able to discharge their fiscal obligations (*ilku*) to the crown. The most frequently recurring designation of an individual plot is 'bow land' (*bīt qašti*), which entailed at least etymologically the obligation to serve as archer. Less often occur the designations 'horse land' (*bīt sisê*) and 'chariot land' (*bīt narkabti*); these describe more substantial plots that may comprise entire villages. Although these tenants are consequently occasionally designated as military colonists, they did not have to serve in person but could equally hire substitutes for that purpose.[3] Furthermore, the system of land held on lease against various obligations had a wider reach in the Late Achaemenid period and also extended to crown land (*uzbāra*) managed directly by royal agents and to land at the disposal of government institutions and persons of high standing, royal minions and even to temple land. Several such bow lands were united in a larger administrative unit called a *hadru*, which was managed by low-level clerks, the *šaknus*, who regularly acted on behalf of the actual tenants and thus often were the direct business partners of the Murašûs.[4]

The second main activity the Murašûs engaged in was the sub-letting of agricultural land and date gardens, but the latter seem to have played only a minor role in Nippur compared to northern Babylonia.[5] The Murašûs had either rented the plots in question from the original tenants or owners, or the land had come into their hands as pledged land (*bīt maškāni*), hence, as a consequence of outstanding debts.

Distribution of the Factors of Production: The Problem of Interlinkage

The Murašûs seem to have started out as agricultural entrepreneurs, leasing tracts of arable land. The main strand of their activities consisted then in the

---

[2] The activities of the Murašû family are at the heart of the monographs by Cardascia (1951) and Stolper (1985), and their work has been supplemented by several important contributions by van Driel (1989, 1999 and 2002: 194–273).

[3] See the succinct description in Stolper 1993b.

[4] The best description of the system of land tenure and the institution of the *hadru* is still Stolper 1985: 70–103. See also Joannès 1982: 8–45 on fiefs and land-holding in the Late Babylonian period. For a reading *hadru* rather than *haṭru* see Beaulieu 1988.

[5] Jursa 2010: 405–18.

letting and sub-letting of these plots. The family's archive is highly informative in relation to the pattern of land ownership in the Late Achaemenid
period and also casts light on the overarching institutional framework. The
issue is therefore treated in some detail. The most obvious way to tackle
the question of ownership of land in Late Achaemenid Nippur is to look at
the lessors who rented out land to the Murašû 'firm'. For this purpose, two
types of documents are at our disposal, rental agreements and rent receipts.
We shall focus first on leases to individual members of the Murašû family –
most often Enlil-šumu-iddin or his nephew Rēmūt-Ninurta – or, rarely, one
of their slaves. Some thirty-five texts are at our disposal, some of which are
fragmentary to the point of being of little use. In the light of Stolper's analysis of the subject matter,[6] it hardly comes as a surprise that the clear majority of the texts deal with bow land (*bīt qašti*) rented out to the Murašûs
either by the tenants themselves or by the *šaknu* of the respective *hadru*
(and in one instance, BE 9 72, exceptionally by a *rab umma*).[7] Four more
texts deal with crown land (*uzbāra*), which in EE 1 and TuM 2/3 147 were
rented out by a canal manager (*ša muhhi sūti* [ID]RN). The latter official is also
mentioned in EE 2, in which the actual lessor provides guarantees against
legal action on the part of a *ša muhhi sūti* [ID]RN. Hence, about three-quarters
of the plots leased by the Murašûs originated in the land-for-service sector,
or were directly rented from the crown and its agents, the canal managers.

In EE 10, the lessor is a certain Aqubia, the bailiff (*paqdu*) of a Persian,
Unnatu. In fact, it is striking that in the remaining texts, that is, those that
seemingly refer to land held privately – in the sense that the lessors are
neither managers of crown land nor officials in the land-for-service sector – Persian aristocrats and their estate managers abound. In PBS 2/1 20
real estate of a member of the royal family, the *mār bīti* Neba'mardu, is
rented out by his bailiff. Two such texts (TuM 2/3 148 and BE 9 102) refer
to *ustabaru*s, royal household officials who appear as absentee landlords, in
a vein similar to Persian aristocrats and members of the royal house: their
possessions are rented out by their *paqdu*s, who also take care of the business of collecting the rent.

Only two texts listed in Table 3.1 cannot be easily accommodated within
this pattern. In PBS 2/1 16, the status of the land is in a lacuna. The plot
is rented out by Nanāya-iddin/Hungama, and is located in Bīt Haššamur.
Nanāya-iddin/Hungama also appears in IMT 43 together with his brother

---

[6] Stolper 1985, especially 36–104.

[7] Pertinent texts are IMT 1, 4, 5; EE 3, 6; BE 9 2, 10, 72, 107; BE 10 15, 53, 99; PBS 2/1 30, 35, 96,
115, 116, 159, 175, 182. The *rab umma*, essentially a military title, is discussed by Stolper 2001/
2: 106–7.

Table 3.1. *Overview of leases to the Murašû firm*

Text (date)	Lessor(s)	Summary of transaction
BE 9 2 (Art 10-12-22)	Ahūšunu/ Šamaš-zēr-ibni	Relinquishment of bow land against payment of dues
EE 3 (Art 22-01-20)	Kāṣir/Bēl-nāṣir, *šaknu ša šušānu mārū hisannu*	Lease of four bow lands for ten years, for 50 shekels of silver annually and payment of [*mandattu*]
IMT 1 (Art 23-06-10)	Šulum-Bābili/Bēl-ittīa, *šaknu*	Lease of [bow(?)] land *ana palāh šarri*
EE 2 (Art 24-05-05)	Iadih-Iama/Bana-Iama	Lease of crown land (*uzbāru*) and water rights; waiver of action of the *ša muhhi sūti* ᶦᴰ[...] Bēl-nāṣir/Bēl-ušēzib
EE 10 (Art 24-xx-04)	Aqubia, *paqdu* of Unnatu	Lease of fields *ana errēšūti*
BE 9 10 (Art 28-03-03)	Zabdā/Iddina, his brother Bēlšunu and Lābâši/Ahu-iddin	Lease of bow lands *ana nukaribbūti* and *ana errēšūti*
IMT 2 (Art 31-x-x)	Ištabuzana	Lease of the *uzbāru ša bīt sinništi ša ekallim*, including bow lands
IMT 3 (Art 31-11-08)	Halabi-Esu/Padi-Esu and Halaba-Esu/ Mukēšu	Long-term lease (30 years)
EE 1 (Art 32-xx-25)	Nabû-uballiṭ/Aplāya, brother of the *ša muhhi sūti* ᶦᴰ[...] Tattannu	Lease of crown land (*uzbāru*) and water rights
IMT 4 (Art 35-01-20)	Bēl-iddin/Nidintu, *šaknu ša bīt rab urāte*	Lease of bow lands
BE 9 48 (Art 36-07-02)	Bagamiri/Mithradata	Long-term lease (60 years) of the field of the lessor's uncle
BE 9 72 (Art 40-06-15)	Marduk-šumu-iddin, the *rab umma*	Lease of bow lands of the priests of Larak
IMT 5 (Art 40-06-18)	Lâbâši/Nabû-ittannu	Lease of lessor's bow lands
EE 6 (Art 41-07-12)	Ahāšunu/Ililāya	Lease of lessor's bow land

Table 3.1. (*Continued*)

Text (date)	Lessor(s)	Summary of transaction
BE 9 102 (Art 41-07-16)	Bēl-bullissu/ Da'mamiazda, *ustabaru* and *šaknu*	Lease of 107;1.4[b] arable land, royal gift (*nidinti šarri*)
BE 9 107 (Art 41-07-16)	Bēl-abu-uṣur/Bēl-ēriš, *šaknu ša šušāne ša* [lú]*mašaka*	Lease of seven bow lands and *gizzetu*- land
BE 10 15 (DarII-01-02-08)	Bēl-idišu/Bēl-asu'a, brother of Lābâši, *šaknu ša bīt umasupitru*	Lease *ana palāh šarri* (6 minas of silver) of bow lands from the crown prince's estate (*bit umaspitru*)
PBS 2/1 175 (DarII-01-03-29)	Lābâši/[..] and his brother Bēl-bullissu, to Rībat/Bēl-erība	Lease of a field of the [LÚ]É. LUGAL.AMA.MU, the lessors' bow land
PBS 2/1 182 (DarII-01-05-11)	Enlil-ittannu/ Mušallim-Enlil	Lease of the lessor's bow land
PBS 2/1 16 (DarII-01-07-20)	Nanāya-iddin/ Hungama'	Status of land broken[a]
BE 10 53 (DarII-01-07-21)	Ahmana' and his brother Barīk-Bēl, the Lydians	Lease of bow land
PBS 2/1 20 (DarII-01-08-08)	Madanu-iddin, *paqdu* of the *mār bīti* Neba'mardu	Lease of 8;0 garden and field
PBS 2/1 30 (DarII-01-xx-18)	Aplāya ... *hadru ša šušānu mārū hisannu*	Lease of bow lands and a share of a horse land
PBS 2/1 35 (DarII-01-xx-xx)	Iddin-Marduk	Lease of land of unknown status
EE 4 (DarII-02-xx-30)	Šulum-Bābili/Bēl-ittiā, *paqdu* of Artaumanu	Lease of land (qualified as *makkūru*)
TuM 2/3 146 (DarII-03-05-20)	Bisde/Dalatani, to Rībat/Bēl-erība	Lease of lessor's bow land (*ana errēšūti u šutāpūti*)
TuM 2/3 147 (DarII-04-07-17)	Libluṭ/Iddin-Nabû, *ana muhhi sūti ša nār Sîn*	Lease of water rights and *uzbāru* land

Table 3.1. (*Continued*)

Text (date)	Lessor(s)	Summary of transaction
PBS 2/1 96 (DarII-04-12-12)	Hašdāya (?)	Lease of bow land of the *ustabaru* Bēl-iqīš, under control of his brother Hašdāya
BE 10 99 (DarII-05-02-18)	Hiduri'/Habṣir, slave of Balāṭu/Ṣiha' and *šaknu* of the carpenters	Land in the *hadru* of the carpenters under control of Balāṭu
PBS 2/1 115 (DarII-05-xx-28)	Rībat/Bēl-erība, to his slave [..]	Lease *ana nukaribbūti* of lessor's bow land
PBS 2/1 215 (DarII-06-06-23)	Quda/Ninurta-ibni, to Bēl-ēṭer-Šamaš, slave of Rēmut-Ninurta	Lease *ana nukaribbūti* of *qutanu*-land of potters, held by Rahim/Barikki-ili and his brother Hannani'
PBS 2/1 159 (DarII-07)	Iltammeš-nūrī, to Tirrakama and Mitirriadaṭa, *mār bītis* of Enlil-šumu-iddin	Lease of bow land *ana nukaribbūti* and *ana errešūti*
TuM 2/3 148 (DarII-08-01-13)	Bēl-ahu-ušabši/ Marduk, *paqdu* of Pitibiri, to Murašû/ Enlil-šumu-iddin	Lease of fields given to the *ustabaru* Pitibiri, under control of Bēl-ahu-ušabši

Notes: [a] According to Stolper 1985: 77, an official of the [LÚ]*šušānū ša bīt Zuzā* is mentioned, which is of course a strong indicator that land from this *hadru* is being rented out.
[b] See Jursa 2010: xviii for explanation of Akkadian numerals and measures.

Padi-Esi (whose second name is Bagadata) as recipient of rent for land (the status of which is again in a lacuna) in the towns of Arzuhini and Bīt Haššamur.[8] The latter town is also attested in IMT 46 as place of bow lands for which Rēmūt-Ninurta pays rent to two individuals who are designated as Arumeans, known to have been organised in a *hadru*.[9] Both the location of the fields and the Iranian family background, as evidenced by the onomastic, point thus to a membership of the sons of Hungama in the *hadru* of

[8] In PBS 2/1 15 Nanāya-iddin rents oxen and seed from an agent of the Murašûs; both PBS 2/1 15 and 16 date to the first year of Darius II: see Stolper and Donbaz 1997: 113–14.
[9] Attestations can be found in Stolper 1985: 72 (entry 1).

the Arumeans, especially given that the reference to a *hadru* can be implicit only; note, for example, BE 9 74. In IMT 3, which is a rental agreement with an exceptional contract period of thirty years, the whole rental sum for which is paid in advance by Enlil-šumu-iddin to two individuals. The status of the land is not specified, but the fact that a long-term lease likely to exceed the life expectancy of the lessors was concluded rather than a sale – a type of transaction not attested at all in the Murašû archive – points to land held on condition: 'fiefs could be leased or pledged but could not be alienated' (Stolper 1985: 25).

Sub-lease contracts are less easily amenable to such an investigation, as the status of land is not always specified. Most frequently, the generic catch-all term *bīt ritti* is employed to describe the land that is the subject of the deal.[10] In PBS 2/1 39, the land to be sub-leased is simply called 'for rent at his [Rēmūt-Ninurta's] disposal', *ana sūti ina pānišu*. However, when fuller information on the status of land is given, then the situation is quite similar to that observed for the primary lease contracts; bow land is the most frequent designation for land,[11] followed by quite some margin by royal land.[12] The evidence of the receipts for rent (*sūtu*) and tax (*ilku*) payments confirms the impression given by the rental agreements, as the overwhelming majority of these payments were made within the land-for-service sector.[13] Again, a majority of land holdings without further designation (i.e. which may be interpreted as privately owned land) are held by people with Persian names.[14]

This general pattern of land ownership finds confirmation in contemporary archives, especially the Kasr archive from Babylon, where royal land grants (*nidinti šarris*) feature even more prominently than in the Murašû

---

[10] It is likely that land of varying status was subsumed under this expression: see van Driel 2002: 305–8. Pertinent texts are EE 11, 17, 27; BE 9 26, 30, 34, 35, 45, 86a; IMT 8, 13, 15, 20, in all of which *bīt ritti* (most often in combination with the lessor's PN) designates part or all of the land to be leased out.

[11] EE 6, 13, 20; BE 9 99, 101; PBS 2/1 150, 163, 210. In some instances, land is not explicitly described as bow land, but the reference to a *hadru* leaves little doubt concerning the status of the land in question (EE 11; BE 10 54, 79, 112; PBS 2/1 106, 123; IMT 9).

[12] The standard designation is again *uzbāra* (IMT 27; EE 11, 23, 25; PBS 2/1 123, 150), but in one instance *zēru ša šarri* (JCS 53 6) occurs, and the first contract recorded in BE 9 65 refers to *muṣanû* – land of the king.

[13] Receipts for rent or tax payments referring to bow or horse land, or to *hadru* organisations or their *šaknu*s, are: BE 9 8, 18, 47, 66a, 74, 106; BE 10 5, 50, 63, 66, 71, 83, 86, 92, 100, 111, 113, 122, 128; EE 36–38, 40, 44–46, 49; IMT 44–46; PBS 2/1 13, 51, 66, 72, 77, 88, 94, 116, 119, 122, 138, 139 188, 192, 197, 205, 211, 218; TuM 2/3 186, 191.

[14] Examples include Uheiagam/Parnakka (PBS 2/1 5), Isipatara'u (BE 9 28a), Daruka (EE 47) or Marduniya (PBS 2/1 37).

archive. This archive is not yet published in a satisfactory manner, but it has already been subjected to preliminary analysis.[15] The main protagonist is Bēlšunu/Bēl-uṣuršu (Xenophon's Belesys), governor of the city of Babylon between 422 and 415, and attested as provincial governor of Transpotamia between 407 and 401. Unlike the principals of the Murašû 'firm', Bēlšunu is hardly active himself in the texts, and sub-leases of land rented by his subordinates and agents (particularly active were Uraš-nāṣir/Ibnāya and Šalammarê) are the best-attested text type. Hence, the activities attested are generally to be located on a lower level in the hierarchy of farms than those of the Murašû archive.[16] Consequently, several of the sub-lease contracts known thus far do not specify the status of land but simply refer generically to rented land, either as *bīt sūti* or land *ana sūti ina pān* PN.[17] But in three leases the land to be leased out is specified as *nidinti šarri*, and in two instances (both from the reign of Darius II) the grant was made to Bēlšunu himself.[18] This compares well to an instance in the Murašû archive (BE 9 102) which specifies that the land held by the *ustabaru* Bēl-bullissu was a royal gift (*nidinti šarri*). Such royal grants also feature prominently in receipts for rent (*sūtu*) payments.[19] As was the case in the Murašû archive, the potential instances of private land were usually held by Persians. Pertinent examples are Ispa'udu/Atebāga in Mich. 46 (= Stolper 2007 15) and Artašata in Dar. 476 (mentioned in Stolper 1995, text 16).

In addition to the types of land discussed so far, temple property was also incorporated into the prevailing patterns of land tenure, which constitutes a crucial difference from the practice of the long sixth century. The rent (*sūtu*) for the fields of the god Bēl (*zēr* [d]Bēl) in the contracts of the Murašû archive was received by canal managers (*ana/ša muhhi sūti* [ID]GN) instead of temple officials, meaning that the temple exerted nominal control only.[20]

---

[15] On this archive see Jursa 2005a: 61. Preliminary analyses of the material are found in Stolper 1987 and 1995; important publications of stray texts are Stolper 2004 and 2007. An in-depth investigation of the Kasr archives by Andrew Dix (Chicago) is in preparation.

[16] In the classificatory system of Stolper 1995: 218, mainly tertiary leases (sub-leases of the agents of the principal) in the Kasr archive as against mainly secondary leases (principal to their agents) in the Murašû archive.

[17] Examples are published in Stolper 2004 (BM 95-4-6,2 and Bellino Q) and Stolper 2007 (BM 116622).

[18] Usko tablet and YBC 11586 = Stolper 2004 text 7. The Usko tablet was most recently edited by Stolper 2004: 534–5. The third rental agreement mentioning a *nidinti šarri* is VAT 15610, which is still unpublished but referred to in Stolper 1995 as text 46.

[19] FuB 14 21 (mentioned in Stolper 1995 as text 55), YBC 11562 (Stolper 2007: 6) and VAT 15975 (mentioned in Stolper 1995 as text 55).

[20] Discussed by Stolper 1985: 42–4. Pertinent texts are EE 41, 48; BE 9 14, 59; IMT 40; and PBS 2/1 1.

After the accession year of Darius II, a change in practice seems to have taken place, as the land of Bēl disappears from the record and the *hadru* of the *širkū ša* Bēl (PBS 2/1 94 and 211) is introduced.[21] The evidence from the Kasr archive points towards similar circumstances: in text BM 47343, Šalammarê, a slave of Bēlšunu, disposes of assets (16 *kurru* of barley) specified as *makkūr* Bēl: the scope of the firm hence seems to have extended over temple properties as well. Alas, it is not known whether Bēlšunu obtained the rights to dispose of these funds directly from the temple or from crown officials, like the canal managers administering lands of Bēl in the Murašû archive. Overall, this balance of power between private and institutional households is a peculiarity of the Late Achaemenid period. Not only were the temples no longer the major economic players in the region,[22] their properties were managed directly by crown agents or even incorporated into the land-for-service system.

Summing up, with regard to the wider institutional framework within which the Murašûs and similar entrepreneurs operated, a very tight nexus between political and economic power is clearly in evidence: agricultural land was either incorporated in the royal land-for-service system and managed by a caste of low-level local officials (*šaknu*s), or directly supervised for the royal administration by crown officials, the canal managers. This latter group also were in charge of another even more lucrative asset, namely access to the all-important canal rights. These are occasionally designated with the expression *ṣibitti šarri*, hence they constitute another right that ultimately derives from royal authority.[23] Finally, the most important characteristic of the majority of people holding seemingly privately owned land – in the sense that the plots were managed by neither group of officials but by bailiffs (*paqdu*s) – is the fact that they bore Persian names, or were local minions of the king.

---

[21] The identity of the *hadru* of the *širkū* of Bēl with the land of Bēl was suggested by Cardascia (1951: 77[(+6)]), but refuted by Stolper 1985: 42 on grounds of the differing management, i.e., by *šaknu*s in the case of the former and by a *ša muhhi sūti* [ID]GN in the latter. However, the distinct diachronic pattern allows for Cardascia's position.

[22] The relevance of the large households, i.e., temples and palace, in the Neo-Babylonian period is underlined by e.g., Joannès 2000a, who designates them as 'le veritable moteur de l'économie babylonienne' (112). See Jursa 2010: 768–72 for a succinct description of the economic strategies and structural weaknesses (and strengths) of Babylonian temples in the first millennium on the basis of the abundant evidence from Sippar (Ebabbar) and Uruk (Eanna). According to his estimates (Jursa 2010: 759), the rather small Ebabbar temple produced about as much as *c.* 150 propertied families engaging in intensive horticulture as attested in the region around Borsippa. See also the assessment of Garfinkle 2012: 10 for the Ur III period, according to whom even small temples managed significantly larger resources than even the wealthiest private entrepreneurs.

[23] Van Driel 2002: 191–2. The management of canals is described in Stolper 1985: 37–51.

The second main activity of the Murašûs was acting as capitalists. Having – by unfortunately undocumented mechanisms – converted the staples at their disposal into cash, they provided small-scale tenants firstly with often high-value capital assets, especially oxen and seed, and secondly with consumption credits. We will encounter the unavailability of liquid assets in a rural ambience again in the discussion of storage in Chapter 4. Indeed, the promissory notes (*u'iltu*)[24] issued by the Murašûs to small farmers are exclusively stipulated in kind – dates, in the overwhelming majority. A handful of documents explicitly state that the dates are owed in lieu of silver which the Murašûs advanced to the peasants so that they could discharge the tax (*ilku*) payments incumbent on their holdings, rather than productive credit.[25] The amounts lent by Enlil-šumu-iddin and, to a negligible extent, his subordinates (his slaves Mušēzib and Ribat/Bēl-erība, his *mār bīti* Tirikam and his son Murašû) in the first year of Darius II (423/2) convey a good impression of the enormous scale of the Murašû family's business: more than 17,172 *kurru* of dates – corresponding to 3,594,975 litres – were owed to Enlil-šumu-iddin by different holders of bow land. This bears comparison with the total annual gross income of a medium-sized temple household such as the Ebabbar temple in Sippar, which generated in year 14 of Nabonidus (542/1) an income of 11,800 *kurru* of dates and 6,000 *kurru* of barley.[26] This finding ties in well with what has been stated above concerning the increased powers of private entrepreneurs with respect to institutional households in the Late Achaemenid period.

Importantly, with two exceptions (BE 10 8 and 11), all these debts were secured by plots of land held in fief by the debtors. The fact that this impressive accumulation of promissory notes dating to a single year was found in the archive of the Murašûs is conventionally interpreted as indicative of a mass default by the tenants,[27] an event that may or may not have been connected to the succession crisis after the death of Artaxerxes I.[28] Most relevant for our purposes is the corollary of this mass default: as all debts, irrespective of the quantity of dates/silver borrowed, were secured by pledges of real estate, the Murašûs now found themselves in the position of being

[24] Jursa 2005a: 42–3 provides a succinct description of the formulary of this type of document; more exhaustive is Cardascia 1951: 27–68. See Jursa 2010: 413 for the role of dates as 'commodity money' in this context.
[25] IMT 79, 80, 88 and 89; EE 66, 76 and 82; BE 9 81, 94, 94a, 95 and 96; BE 10 57, 125 and 126; PBS 2/1 40, 179 and 198.
[26] See the balance sheet in Jursa 2010: 572–5.
[27] For example, Stolper 1985: 104–7.
[28] Stolper 1985: 114–24 argues for such a connection, but see van Driel 1989: 223–4 and now Tolini 2011: 554–63.

Table 3.2. *Loans made by the Murašû family*

Text	Amount (commodity)[a]	Creditor
IMT 81	71;0 dates	Enlil-šumu-iddin
BE 10 8	200;0 dates	Enlil-šumu-iddin
BE 10 11	2;2.3 barley	Mušēzib
BE 10 12	50;0 dates	Enlil-šumu-iddin
BE 10 13	140;0 dates 40;0 barley	Enlil-šumu-iddin
BE 10 14	1,200;0 dates	Enlil-šumu-iddin
BE 10 16	277;0 dates	Enlil-šumu-iddin
BE 10 17	664;3.2 dates	Enlil-šumu-iddin
BE 10 18	138;4 dates	Enlil-šumu-iddin
BE 10 19	134;3 dates	Enlil-šumu-iddin
BE 10 20	117;0.5 dates	Enlil-šumu-iddin
BE 10 21	200;0 dates, 60 vats of beer	Enlil-šumu-iddin
BE 10 22	60;0 dates	Enlil-šumu-iddin
BE 10 23	225;2.3 dates	Enlil-šumu-iddin
BE 10 24	200;0 dates	Enlil-šumu-iddin
BE 10 26	564;0 dates	Enlil-šumu-iddin
BE 10 27	500;0 dates	Enlil-šumu-iddin
BE 10 28	560;0 dates	Enlil-šumu-iddin
BE 10 30	100;0 dates	Enlil-šumu-iddin
BE 10 31	116;0 dates	Enlil-šumu-iddin
BE 10 32	287;3.2 dates	Enlil-šumu-iddin
BE 10 33	287;3 dates	Enlil-šumu-iddin
BE 10 34	315;2.1 dates	Enlil-šumu-iddin
BE 10 35	457;0 dates	Enlil-šumu-iddin
BE 10 36	58;0 dates	Enlil-šumu-iddin
BE 10 37	250;0 dates	Enlil-šumu-iddin
BE 10 38	28;0 dates	Enlil-šumu-iddin
BE 10 40	150;0 dates	Enlil-šumu-iddin
BE 10 41	112;0 dates	Enlil-šumu-iddin
BE 10 42	512;0 dates	Enlil-šumu-iddin
BE 10 45	794;0 dates	Enlil-šumu-iddin
BE 10 46 (= PBS 2/1 36)	372;0 dates	Enlil-šumu-iddin
BE 10 47	164;0 dates	Enlil-šumu-iddin
BE 10 48	185;2.3 dates	Enlil-šumu-iddin
BE 10 49	202;0 dates	Enlil-šumu-iddin

Table 3.2. (*Continued*)

Text	Amount (commodity)[a]	Creditor
BE 10 51	300;0 dates	Enlil-šumu-iddin
PBS 2/1 4	25;0 dates	Enlil-šumu-iddin
PBS 2/1 6	53;0 dates	Enlil-šumu-iddin
PBS 2/1 7	200;0 dates	Enlil-šumu-iddin
PBS 2/1 8	200;0 dates	Enlil-šumu-iddin
PBS 2/1 9	250;0 dates	Enlil-šumu-iddin
PBS 2/1 10	150;0 dates	Enlil-šumu-iddin
PBS 2/1 11	20;0 dates	Tirikāma
PBS 2/1 12	43;0 dates	Rībat
PBS 2/1 14	120;0 dates, 18;0 barley	Enlil-šumu-iddin
PBS 2/1 18	200;0 dates	Enlil-šumu-iddin
PBS 2/1 19	1,100;0 dates, 60;0 barley	Enlil-šumu-iddin
PBS 2/1 22	82;4 dates, 15;0 barley	Rēmūt-Ninurta
PBS 2/1 25	117;3.4.3 dates	Enlil-šumu-iddin
PBS 2/1 26	1,500;0 dates	Enlil-šumu-iddin
PBS 2/1 31	103;2.3 dates	Enlil-šumu-iddin
PBS 2/1 33	71;0 dates	Enlil-šumu-iddin
PBS 2/1 40	*x* dates	Enlil-šumu-iddin
PBS 2/1 41	315;2.1 dates	Enlil-šumu-iddin
PBS 2/1 42	70;0 dates	Enlil-šumu-iddin
PBS 2/1 169	50;0 dates	Enlil-šumu-iddin
PBS 2/1 174	200;0 dates	Enlil-šumu-iddin
PBS 2/1 176	56;3.2 dates	Enlil-šumu-iddin
PBS 2/1 177	200;0 dates	Enlil-šumu-iddin
PBS 2/1 178	367;2.3 dates	Enlil-šumu-iddin
PBS 2/1 179	100;0 dates	Enlil-šumu-iddin
PBS 2/1 180	271;2.3 dates	Enlil-šumu-iddin
PBS 2/1 181	72;2.3 dates	Enlil-šumu-iddin
PBS 2/1 183	500;0 dates	Enlil-šumu-iddin
PBS 2/1 184	26;0 dates	Enlil-šumu-iddin
PBS 2/1 185	70;0 dates	Murašû
PBS 2/1 186	200;0 dates	Enlil-šumu-iddin
PBS 2/1 187	100;0 dates	Enlil-šumu-iddin
PBS 2/1 228	250;0 dates	Enlil-šumu-iddin
CTMMA 3 126	90;0 dates	Enlil-šumu-iddin
Anatolica 14 80	*x* dates	Enlil-šumu-iddin
Anatolica 14 81	*x* dates	Enlil-šumu-iddin

Note:[a] See Jursa 2010: xviii for explanation of Akkadian numerals and measures.

not only creditors, but equally landlords as well as providers of indispensable equipment. This situation is certainly not unique to Late Achaemenid Babylonia, as money lending against corollary was already a common means of acquiring access to land in the third millennium,[29] but both the sheer scale and the fact that we are dealing with one single creditor are.

'The ramifications of this situation are important. In terms of development economics, we are dealing here with a scenario of interlinked markets. This situation has its roots in the desire of those in possession of capital assets to have some sort of insurance against default, which means that credit is extended only to people over whom some kind of control can be exerted.[30] However, the results are detrimental to the socio-economic balance of the country, as the logical result of these mechanisms is a scenario of accumulated powers for those acting simultaneously as merchants, money lenders and landlords. As defined by Bharadwaj,[31] '[M]arkets become interlocked through price and non-price links, given that market and social power is vested in the dominant rural classes and that the dominant party often combines multiple functions, thus enjoying a superior position simultaneously in a number of markets.' This exceptional power of entrepreneurs is possibly hinted at in the so-called *pirku* guarantees in which lessors oblige themselves to renounce exaggerated claims and which not only highlight the asymmetric relationship between contract partners but, at the same time, also imply a situation of patronage sought by lessees.[32]

Before considering further the effects of this situation, the third factor of production, labour, needs to be discussed. One side-effect of this scenario of wide-spread rural indebtedness was to provide those to whom the peasants were indebted, namely the large-scale entrepreneurs such as the Murašûs, with cheap availability of labour, too. The most straightforward manifestation of this phenomenon was the proliferation of servile tenants tied to land no longer in their possession and producing for their creditors.[33] A particularly instructive text in this regard is BE 9 34, in which Hiliti'/Inna-Nabû

---

[29] Steinkeller 2002 with references to similar practices in Classical antiquity. See also Abraham 2004: 13 for these activities in the context of the Egibi archive.

[30] For the concept see, e.g., Basu 1997: 281–99; see also van Zanden 2004: 1030. It is applied by, e.g., van Zanden 2004 and Crow and Murshid 1994.

[31] Bharadwaj 1974: 4, quoted after Basu 1997: 298. The importance of the social context of these transactions is emphasised by Crow and Murshid 1994.

[32] These contracts are discussed in Stolper 2000; see also van Driel 2002: 212–14.

[33] Van Driel 2002: 203–22, most explicitly on 205: 'It is their hold on people which provided the Murašûs, and those underlings who acted for them, with the labour required for the undertaking of the leases we find in the archive'; see also Joannès 1982: 29–30 for the term 'feudatoires dépendantes'. Jursa 2014a likewise argues for a growth in compelled labour during the fifth century.

rents back his own *bīt ritti* (É *rit-ti-ia*) as well as two plough oxen and seed for three years from Enlil-šumu-iddin, against payment of 100 *kurru* of mainly barley but also minor crops such as wheat, emmer, millet, legumes and sesame.[34] Of similar interest is IMT 17, in which two persons, Iadi'im and Hagga, declare their intent to work as farmhands (*ikkaru*) on their own *bīt ritti* for Enlil-šumu-iddin, with the obligation of paying assessed rent (*imittu*) to the latter.[35]

In addition, a handful of documents provide deeper insight into the topic of forced labour. A first example is EE 104, dating to year 37 of Artaxerxes. According to this text, Enlil-šumu-iddin/Murašû holds a certain Kalkal-iddin/Ahhē-utēr in debt bondage, literally 'in prison' (*ina* É *kil-lu*), because of outstanding harvest debts. In the words of Dandamaev (1984: 160), such *bīt kīli*s were 'in essence, workhouses where debtors worked off their debt under supervision of their creditors or their creditors' agents'. Evidence from the sixth century from the Ebabbar temple in Sippar reveals that people detained in *bīt kīli*s usually were obliged to carry out servile and demeaning tasks, in particular grinding flour.[36] While there is no explicit proof for such obligations in the texts from the Murašû archive, texts such as THM 2/3 203 shows that these prisoners could be put at the disposal of the family's agents as a workforce by the Murašûs. A second text, IMT 103, explicitly refers to detainment because of outstanding harvest debts: Rēmūt-Ninurta holds three persons in the *bīt kīli* 'instead of the remainder of the harvest of [his uncle] Enlil-šumu-iddin', *ku-um re-eh-tú* EBUR (lines 3–4). The wording of this document is revealing: the debtors are not detained *because* of their debts, but *instead of* the amount owed; it is more than likely that they had to perform compensatory service for their creditor.[37] A final text to be mentioned in connection with this is EE 91, which stipulates the obligation of several persons to break up the soil on land of Rēmūt-Ninurta/Murašû without any compensation. Indeed, the failure to fulfil this task within the given time frame will result in physical punishment (100 blows), the tearing

---

[34] Other texts which see peasants leasing their own land from the Murašûs include EE 12 and IMT 15.

[35] The terminology of this text is intriguing, as *ikkaru*s during the sixth century were usually tied to an institution, hence the translation 'temple farmer' (see Jursa 1995: 7–8). On *imittu*, *ibid.*, 147–50 and 161–5.

[36] Bongenaar 1997: 113–20; also Joannès 2006: 471. See also Kleber and Frahm 2006: 118–19 for the *bīt kīli* of the Eanna. The social aspects of the task of grinding flour are briefly alluded to by van Driel 2002: 218.

[37] Further references to imprisonment but without specifying debts as the underlying cause are IMT 102; BE 9 57; BE 10 10; PBS 2/1 17 and 23. PBS 2/1 21 refers to imprisonment because of 'property', possibly a reference to theft. Several of these texts are briefly discussed by Dandamaev 1984: 161–4.

out of hair of head and beard – tantamount to a reduction to a slave-like status – as well as detainment in the *bīt kīli*.[38] Most probably, the harsh conditions of this work contract have a background in outstanding debts, because otherwise Rēmūt-Ninurta's power of disposal over these workers is hard to explain.

Finally, besides these instances of forced labour as a result of indebtedness, brief reference also needs to be made to two classes of semi-dependent workforces that are peculiar to the Late Achaemenid period. The more abundantly attested group are the *šušānu*s, who make their appearance in great number in the land-for service system in the Nippur countryside in the later fifth century. They are organised in *hadru*s attached both to the estates of private persons, possibly royal minions, and of government institutions, such as the *šušānu*s of the treasury (*bīt nakkandi*).[39] The second group of unfree labourers are the *gardu*s, possibly the Babylonian equivalent of the Elamite expression *kurtaš* amply attested in the Persepolis archives. So far, they are attested on lands of the royal family such as the estate of the crown prince (*bīt mār šarri*), but BE 10 92 shows that like the *šušānu*s, the *gardu*s could be organised in a *hadru* as well.[40] This proliferation of dependent labour on state holdings – both the land-for-service sector and lands of magnates or even the crown prince – constitutes a significant break with the patterns known from the sixth century and is indicative of a contraction of a comparatively free labour market, which is being superseded by the increased use of coerced labour.[41]

Consequences

Two factors have clearly emerged from the discussion above. Under the prevailing circumstances, it would have easily been possible for the Murašûs to act as catalysts for economic growth, however limited, along the lines of the Ebabbar temple during the sixth century, thus for instance promoting

---

[38] For references to *gullubu* (to shave) expressly denoting punishment and demotion in status see CAD G, 129–30, s.v. *gullubu* 1a 1′–3′. Dandamaev 1984: 229–34 discusses different slave marks.

[39] Stolper 1985: 79–82 (cf. also entries 40–9 in his list of *hadru*s on 76–8) and van Driel 2002: 210–11. The term has a peculiar meaning in the Murašû archive not attested in earlier periods. The CAD defines them as a 'class of state dependants', CAD Š/III (1992) 378–9, s.v. *šušānu* 2.

[40] Stolper 1985: 56–9, van Driel 2002: 211–12. On the *kurtaš* see Aperghis 2000.

[41] Also Jursa 2014a, with an emphasis on the changing pattern of land ownership in the aftermath of the abortive revolts in the second year of Xerxes.

agricultural intensification by means of a change to date horticulture on
a larger scale. However, as far as the evidence allows us to see, extensive
cereal agriculture (with barley as main crop) remained the dominant form
in the Nippur region. Rather than encouraging tenants under their control
to engage in the production of cash crops, the Murašûs kept their tenancies
small scale and dispersed. The problem that lies at the heart of this outcome
is the institutional framework, which could be shown to have differed significantly between the relatively prosperous long sixth century, when, in
the words of Jursa, we see the prevalence of a 'framework of legal and social
institutions which are conducive to furthering commercial activities',[42] and
the years following the abortive revolts against Xerxes. The rather insecure
entitlements to property and factors of production, thoroughly dependent on royal favour, discouraged longer-term investments in agriculture
that would have been necessary to trigger some kind of intensification.
Rather, entrepreneurs like the Murašûs chose to focus on generating maximum revenue in the short term. Also, as the system was based on access
to the Achaemenid administration and royal favour, the Murašûs were not
exposed to competition and could act rather freely – until they became
themselves victims of the system that they had helped to establish and pro-
mote. A telling example of this system of tenuous property rights (or at
least rights of disposition over land) largely dependent on royal favour is
provided by the events following the disputed accession to the throne of
Darius II, who immediately set out to expropriate those Persian nobles who
had adhered to enemy factions during his troubled accession to the throne
(Manuštanu/Menostanes), and rewarded those who had fought by his side
(Artahšaru/Artoxares) as well as members of his family, most famously his
wife (Paurušātiš/Parysatis), with large tracts of land in the Nippur region
and elsewhere; suffice it to call to mind the domains of Aršama/Arsames in
Egypt.[43]. A similar case concerns a plot of land that had belonged to a prince
Situnu, but which was redistributed to an *ustabaru* Pitibiri.[44] The precarious
nature of entitlement to land is also reflected in texts from the Kasr archive,
such as the above-mentioned document YBC 11562 (Stolper 2007: text 6),
in which a tract of land that had belonged to a certain Širiadamuš was given
to Issipitamma as royal grant (*nidinti šarri*): loss of royal support clearly
entailed economic repercussions, too.[45]

[42] Jursa 2010: 785.
[43] The evidence is gathered in Tolini 2011: 525–8.
[44] See Stolper 1985: 67.
[45] BM 30224 (mentioned as text 17 in Stolper 1995) refers to land that was for lease before PN₁
      and is now being leased to PN₂; however, the context of this transaction is unclear.

Moreover, rather than mere accumulation of riches, the interlinkage of markets on several levels benefiting a few powerful entrepreneur-type businessmen as exemplified by the members of the Murašû clan constituted a major impediment for markets to work efficiently. As we have seen, the first effect of a situation of interlinked markets is that they foster disparities in incomes and riches, providing those wielding economic power – which in the Late Achaemenid period is tantamount to social/political power – with an ever-increasing share of total economic output. A first situation of interlinkage is constituted by transactions that ensure the supply of cheap labour for capitalists as a consequence of outstanding debts (labour–capital nexus). Better attested is the confiscation of agricultural land because of debts that could not be redeemed (land–capital nexus). Most abundantly documented by our sources is, however, the interlinkage between commodity markets for agricultural produce and capital markets. Although the hypothesis of a direct link between high interest rates and a high level of seasonal price fluctuation of staple foods can no longer be upheld,[46] a case for the interlinkage of capital markets and the market for agricultural goods contributing to rather elevated levels of price volatility in the context of nineteenth-century CE Java has been made by van Zanden (2004). A similar situation can be postulated for Late Achaemenid Babylonia. Such a link is most clearly visible in the loans of silver for the payment of taxes (*ilku*) that were to be repaid in kind, usually dates, after the harvest (see above). These transactions appear innocuous at first glance but are actually worth consideration in detail. A suitable example is text EE 66:

[320 *ku*]*rru* of dates, of Enlil-šumu-iddin [son of Murašû, owed] by Šumu-iddin, son of Anu-uballiṭ and his co-proprietors [*bēlū qašti*] [from the *had*]*ru* of the people from the city of Dēr which is located in the town of Ālu-ša-Maqtūtu [on] the banks of the Harri-piqūdu canal. In the month of *tašrītu* (VII) of year 41 (of Artaxerxes I), they will pay the above-mentioned 320 *kurru* of dates in the large 'measure' (*mašīhu*) of Enlil-šumu-iddin (delivering them) to the drying ground (*haṣāru*). Their plot, their bow land, (comprising) fields planted (with date palms) and in stubble, located in Ālu-ša-Maqtūtu on the banks of the Harri-piqūdu- canal, are as pledge for the above-mentioned 320 *kurru* of dates at the disposal of Enlil-šumu-iddin. No other creditor will be granted usufruct until Enlil-šumu-iddin, as creditor, has been compensated. The dates are the equivalent [lit. 'price'] of the silver that was paid for the *ilku*, flour of the king, *bāra*-tax,[47] and all other deliveries to the royal treasury incumbent on them and their bow. They guarantee for

---

[46] See van Zanden 2004 and Földvári, van Leeuwen and Pirngruber 2011 for modifications of the view of McCloskey and Nash 1984.

[47] On this fee see van Driel 2002: 269–70.

one another for the discharge of the debt, whoever (of them) is available will pay (Witnesses, Scribe, Date).

The first important observation concerning the text is that this transaction is insured by a pledge of the debtors' bow land; we are thus in the second place dealing with a transaction interlinking land and capital. But more importantly, the deal is also interlinked between commodity (dates) and capital (silver). The lessor provides the silver for the tax payment (*ilku*) and is entitled to a sizeable amount of the debtor's harvest, expressed in dates. However, as dates are rather to be considered as commodity money in the context of the Murašû archive in a region where extensive cereal agriculture was the predominant form of farming,[48] the interlinkage concerns in all likelihood various commodities at once. The effects of this way of phrasing a record of transaction are not trivial. The key problem here is that transactions like this one obfuscate information on the actual supply and demand situation of the individual commodities, which is a primary function of a price notation. Thus, it fosters uncertainty and price instability. In the present case (and comparable ones), the situation is aggravated by the fact that the date equivalent of the silver paid for the *ilku* includes two surcharges for the debtors, who had to come up with transport costs – they had to deliver the commodities from the fields into the city (of Nippur) to the drying place (*haṣāru*)[49] – and furthermore were also subject to the payment of interest: at least this is how we interpret the 'large measure' of Enlil-šumu-iddin. Such an understanding of the *mašīhu rabû* seems to be indicated by PBS 2/1 127, which reads (lines 6–7) *ina* GIŠ*ma-si-hu tar-ṣi ša* 1 PI *ša* ¹*Re-mut-*dMAŠ, 'in the "right measure" of one PI of Rēmūt-Ninurta': a measure of 36 litres was also customary in sixth-century Sippar, where the 'large measure' contained 45 litres.[50] The additional 9 litres per *mašīhu* would thus amount to an interest rate of 25 per cent. Moreover, the coexistence of several such personalised 'measures' – the measures of Enlil-šumu-iddin and Rēmūt-Ninurta, the big measure (*mašīhu rabû*), the measure of the obligation (*mašīhu ša ušištu*), the right measure (*mašīhu tarṣu*), as well as measures specifying the interest such as the *mašīhu* of 38 litres (1 PI 2 *qa*) attested in IMT 108 – will hardly have improved this situation.[51] And finally, such 'price-fixing loans'

---

[48] Jursa 2010: 408–14.

[49] These places are located in cities; attested are, e.g., the *haṣāru*s of the towns of Abastanu (IMT 73), Galia (EE 73) and Bīt-barena' (EE 77). If unspecified, we assume that Nippur is meant, whence the Murašûs originated.

[50] See Jursa 1995: 151–2.

[51] See Johnstone 2011: 35–61 on the difference between abstract, standardised measures (*kurru*) and notional, practical measures (*mašīhu*) in the Greek world (*medimnos* and *phormos*).

establishing a fixed relationship between produce and capital (and various other factors, as we have seen) can be safely assumed to have reduced the income of peasant households by fixing the repayment at below-market prices.[52]

The accumulation of different types of capital assets in the hands of a few also means that those at the other end of the social ladder face worsening conditions, and thus raises the probability of default. One expected consequence is rising interest rates, which is indeed what we find for the Late Achaemenid period: whereas during the sixth century interest rates around 20 per cent were the norm, values of *c.* 40 per cent were closer to the norm in the fifth and fourth centuries.[53] But the wide-spread indebtedness also meant that these peasants had to deliver their produce immediately after harvest, thereby granting substantial market power in the commerce of dates to the Murašûs. Especially in rather isolated markets such as the Nippur region, such entrepreneurs came to exert both a monopoly – they are the only providers of capital, both credit and capital assets, as well as land – as well as a monopsony – they are the only large-scale buyer of agricultural produce. The commercialisation of produce following the harvest by such near-monopolists may in the short term have depressed prices substantially, much to the detriment of those small-scale farmers who had to sell their own produce in order to be able to come up with *ilku* of their plots. Consumption loans on the other hand were usually taken on in the pre-harvest period when commodities were scarce and expensive – a vicious circle that is not easily broken.

The scenario just described is not only conducive to seasonal fluctuation, but comparatively minor exogenous shocks can also be expected to have comparatively large repercussions under the prevailing circumstances. In that sense, the recently advanced claim by Tolini according to which the events of the first year of Darius II were triggered by a simple harvest failure should not be dismissed too lightly.[54] Another expected effect of the interlinkages described above concerns market efficiency: the fact that an increasing number of small-scale tenants were tied to their land implies less scope for a market as mode of allocation of basic commodities, as peasants will strive towards self-sufficiency for lack of funds. Additionally, the

[52] According to the calculations of Crow and Murshid 1994: 1021–4, Bangladeshi farmers who took on such loans in the 1980s CE had to repay their debts in produce at a price of between 25 per cent and 45 per cent below market price level.
[53] Jursa 2010: 490–9; Földvári, van Leeuwen and Pirngruber 2011: 187–9.
[54] Tolini 2011: 554–63.

factor of dependent labourers drawing rations on state-assigned holdings will have aggravated this situation.

In the end, although the pattern of volatile prices in Late Achaemenid Babylonia exhibited by the price quotations of the Astronomical Diaries cannot be explained in a straightforward manner, an investigation of their socio-economic background based on the Murašû and related archives shows that the organisation of agriculture in the post-Xerxes period was not at all conducive to economic stability. The reliance of the later Achaemenid kings on a few large-scale entrepreneurs brought about an accumulation of a wide range of assets in the hands of a few. This situation clearly had wider economic repercussions than the mere enrichment of an élite utterly dependent upon royal favour. Most visibly, it entailed an impoverishment of a larger section of the rural population and a comparative instability of prices for basic goods.

Outlook: The Seleucid Period

Considering the relevance of the distribution of the factors of production for the functioning of the market, it is even more unfortunate that we possess hardly any information for the Seleucid period. As what little evidence there is has received ample treatment recently, I shall confine myself to a few observations.[55]

In addressing the question of continuities and changes from the Achaemenid to the Hellenistic period, it has become commonplace to compare the scant Babylonian material with data from other parts of the empire. Asia Minor, with its wealth of epigraphic material, is an obvious point of reference here. Analyses of the various types of land attested, its administration and the king's powers of disposition in this region feature prominently in recent research. While a basic dichotomy between (Greek) *polis* and *chōra* is still often maintained, the focus has shifted to the broad variety of statuses of land that the latter term comprises. Concomitantly, the concepts of royal sovereignty and the king's powers of disposition have come to occupy a prominent position, replacing the rigid legalistic framework of debates such as whether the king should be regarded as the actual owner of all land.[56] Other scholars go a step further and argue for a much

---

[55] Van der Spek 2014b: 209–21 gives a succinct discussion of land tenure in Seleucid Babylonia; see also the in-depth treatments in van der Spek 1986: 45–129 and now Monerie 2013: 205–64.

[56] See Mileta 2008 (especially 20–61) and Capdetrey 2007: 135–66, especially 139: 'l'expression de terre royale renvoyait en fait à cette capacité du roi d'exercer sans mediation sa souveraineté

less rigid division between *polis* and *chōra*, with van der Spek concluding on the basis of Babylonian material that 'Greek and non-Greek cities were not treated differently as a matter of principle.'[57]

In the following paragraphs, we will discuss the only recently fully published Lehmann text (CTMMA V, texts 148A and B) and its implications for the topic at hand. The text is a protocol recording a meeting of the *kiništu* of Babylon in 236 concerning plots of arable land and related incomes, and can roughly be divided into three different sections. It starts with the account of the *šatammu* remembering a grant of land located along the Euphrates river and concomitant income rights granted by Antiochus II to his wife Laodice and her sons. The latter subsequently donated the land to the Babylonians, Cuthaeans and Borsippaeans and decreed that the tithes due on these plots should be given for maintenance of these cities' main temples. The *šatammu* then goes on to record a variety of exemptions from taxes incumbent on these fields, which were confirmed by the reigning king, Seleucus II, as well as additional donations of fields and incomes to named individuals. In the last section, besides the decision to erect a commemorative stele attesting to the benefactions rendered by Antiochus II and his family, legal stipulations are written down. Most importantly, the *kiništu* decrees the perpetuity of the land grants – both arable fields and date orchards are mentioned – to the individual citizens. Additionally, the obligation to register these holdings on wooden writing boards (in a sort of central inventory?) is proclaimed.

The first point to make is that the original grant by Antiochus II to Laodice concerns land taken from the king's own estates (*bīt ramānišu*, 'his own house') on the Euphrates in the vicinity of Babylon. The passage is thus clear evidence of genuine crown property, that is, land that was managed directly by the royal administration in Babylonia. There are a few more references to such royal domains in Babylonia,[58] but their precise extent must

---

sur une partie du territoire … cette expression recouvrait des statuts fonciers, divers et multiples'. Mileta attempts a sub-classification of the *chōra* as consisting of *ethnē* (tribal territories), *dēmoi* (rural villages and colonies, as well as indigenous cites) and territory under direct royal administration, on which the domains of the king and his family were located. For the incomparably richer documentation on land tenure and the state's claim over land in the contemporary Ptolemaic Empire see Manning 2003.

[57] Van der Spek 1993b: 64, and similarly Schuler 2004: 515–19, who emphasises the different statuses of *poleis*, according to the prevailing political constellations. Capdetrey 2007: 209–24 provides a classification of the various modes of integration within the empire for cities newly annexed or conquered, but insists on a basic difference between Greek and indigenous cities (criticised by van der Spek 2012).

[58] Another text from the Hellenistic period referring very likely to royal estates is Stolper 1993a: 73–7, text A2-3.

remain unclear. The vast estates of members of the Achaemenid royal house attested in the Murašû archive[59] find no parallel in the very scanty documentation from the Hellenistic period.

Secondly, it seems to be the case that the grip of the crown on arable land was less tight compared to the Late Achaemenid period. Legal guarantees assuring ownership rights against arbitrary confiscations play a prominent role in the Lehmann text. The fact that the original recipients of the grant gave the land in question to the inhabitants of Babylon, Borsippa and Cutha is of course reminiscent of similar stipulations in analogous documents from Asia Minor, where the land received by the beneficiary is to be attached to a city. The dossiers documenting the donation (or sale) of land by the king to Aristidokides and, again, Laodice constitute the closest parallels.[60] This clause is usually explained as a safeguard for the recipient, as the fact that the land now belonged to *chōra politikē* rather than to royal land is assumed to have strengthened his proprietary rights.[61] The peculiarity of the Lehmann text is that it points to an outright 'privatisation' (van der Spek 2014b: 214) of formerly royal land in these instances.[62] The expression *šalaṭu nadānu* (CTMMA 5 text 148A:11), 'to give authority or right of disposal', is unequivocal in this regard; moreover, the text also refers to the possibility of alienation of the plots. Only income rights – the tithe (*ešru*) is mentioned explicitly – seem to accrue to the original beneficiaries of the grant, but Laodice and her sons decided to put (part of?) these proceeds at the disposal of the Babylonian temples.

Summing up, the Lehmann text not only corroborates to some extent van der Spek's assumption of a fundamental parity of Greek and non-Greek cities, it also allows us to postulate a greater relevance of private property in Seleucid compared to Late Achaemenid times. The case of Asia Minor shows that this may have been a slow, gradual process,[63] but overall, the

---

[59]   Stolper 1985: 52–69.

[60]   For a recent edition of this material, see Aperghis 2004: 312–18 (appendix 2, texts 2 and 3). The first scholar to point out the similarity of the dispositions was Sarkisian 1969 (1953).

[61]   Capdetrey 2007: 151–3; similar is Mileta 2008. Bresson 2016: 110–17, especially 112, adds to this aspect of ownership the additional advantage of a lower tax rate. Aperghis 2004: 107 assumes a different economic rationale, namely the extension of the tax base by increasing the cities' agricultural production.

[62]   Similar is Monerie 2013: 226–9; he speaks of 'une prise de possession effective' (226). Briant's interpretation of the Laodice dossier (1973a: 104 = 1982: 106), to which Monerie refers, implies an assumption of precariousness of the grants for the beneficiaries, which may hold true for the income drawn by the original beneficiaries, but is unlikely to extend to the plots of land themselves, now part of the *chōra politikē*.

[63]   Thoneman 2009 shows that during the reign of Alexander the Great, Achaemenid practices of land tenure still prevailed in that region.

sources at our disposal, often fragmentary, confirm a basic protection of the property rights of individuals and institutions over their land. Instructive is the early example (dating to 308/7) of a verdict reversing the encroachment of a royal official Iltalimatu' on land belonging to the Ebabbar temple (of Larsa?), confirming 'des précautions avec lesquelles avaient été traitées les institutions locals en Babylonie'.[64]

Finally, a crucial but elusive question in any discussion of land tenure in central Babylonia in the Hellenistic period is that regarding the fate of the extensive *hadru* system. A functional equivalence of the Hellenistic *klēroi* with the earlier types of military fiefs (*bīt qašti*, etc.) and, on the administrative scale, of the rather elusive *(h)ekas* with the earlier *hadru* is often cautiously assumed.[65] Whether these lands reverted to the new overlords and were henceforth treated as royal land of sorts or whether they were given the status of *klēroi* and saw a drive towards privatisation similar to the development in Egypt[66] cannot not be answered at present. In any case, contrary to what we saw in the discussion of the Murašû archive, temple lands were no longer integrated into a state-sponsored superstructure such as the *hadru* system. In the verdict concerning the lands of the Ebabbar temple mentioned above, the fields are designated as *makkūr* Šamaš, 'property of Šamaš' (the temple's main deity), rather than referring to a *hadru* of Šamaš. This does not seem to be a coincidence, as the same expression '*makkūr* (of a god)' occurs several times in texts concerning both arable land and urban real estate in Seleucid Uruk.[67] This may also indicate a weakening of the crown's direct control of land.

It was pointed out in Chapter 2 that the centre of gravity of the ongoing demographic expansion, and hence also the area where new settlements consisting to a certain extent of Greek colonists, was located along the Tigris. The Euphrates region, the traditional Babylonian heartland comprising besides the capital city of Babylon also places such as Sippar and Borsippa, with which this study is mainly concerned, may have experienced little impact from this secular trend. This means essentially that the new dynasty had no need to resort to major requisitions of arable land in

---

[64] Joannès 2006: 113–15 (quotation at 115). The text in question is Porter Travels II (1822), pl. 77g, edited with commentary as text 5 in van der Spek 1986: 202–11. See also van der Spek 1993b: 65–6.

[65] Cohen 1978: 47–50 and van der Spek 2014b: 215; but cf. Monerie 2013: 216.

[66] Manning 2003: 178–81. Bresson 2016: 114–17 emphasises the stability of the rights of *klērouchoi*.

[67] For example, YOS 20 18 and 19 and TCL 13 234 (arable land and date gardens), and YOS 20 16, 38, 48, 67, 68, 80 and 83 (urban property).

the latter region in order to settle their followers, as was already seen by G. Cohen (1978: 21) in his study of Seleucid settlements. In that sense, the Tigris and Euphrates regions may be compared to the Fayyum and Upper Egypt in the Ptolemaic Empire, respectively – the former hitherto under-exploited region becoming the focal point of Greek colonisation, and the latter mainly indirectly affected by the land policies of the new overlords.[68]

---

[68] Manning 2003: 6–8 and then, in detail, chs. 3 and 4.

4 | Price Volatility and Storage

Introduction

In the discussions of the commodity price series of the Astronomical Diaries in this chapter, price volatility, which is most commonly measured by the coefficient of variation (or, a cruder yardstick, by the standard deviation), will play a central role. The underlying cause of price volatility are frequently supply and demand shocks, the most prominent factors being exogenous shocks and seasonal fluctuations. According to K.-G. Persson, a high level of price volatility is indicative of weak market integration.[1] Indeed, spatial market integration, hence trade between different regions, will level out price differences between those regions that are integrated into the trading network because of the 'law of one price' and thereby reduce volatility within the individual regions. On the basis of archival documents it is indubitable that within Babylonia a certain extent of market integration had been achieved by the sixth century,[2] and it is likely that the situation was not all that different in the Late Achaemenid and Hellenistic periods. However, trade – and other modes of long-distance exchange such as payments of tribute – with regions beyond Babylonia seems to have been confined to luxury goods (ivory, lapis lazuli, etc.) and material not available in Babylonia, such as timber. The main obstacle for inter-regional trade with staple goods such as barley or other grains was, as was the case for much of the pre-industrial world, of course the prohibitively high transport costs.[3]

---

[1] A quintessential statement is Persson 1999, especially 91–113.

[2] The most detailed treatment of the question is Jursa 2010: 61–99; see his assessment of the city of Babylon 'as the central node within a network of exchange covering all of Babylonia' (140) in the sixth century. See there also ch. 2 on regional integration in Babylonia. On the comparatively low transport costs within Babylonia thanks to the existence of regional waterways see the contribution of Weszeli in Jursa 2010: 140–52.

[3] On various aspects of long-distance exchange in first-millennium Babylonia, Graslin-Thomé 2009, in particular 271–3 on the absence of long-distance trade for staple goods because of high transport costs. She also provides an extensive discussion of the objects of long-distance exchange, most prominently textile products, metals and woods (187–283). The only commodity of those recorded in the ADs for which trade was possible and even likely is wool; see the following chapter.

Among alternative risk-aversion strategies with the aim to stabilise prices, Földvári and van Leeuwen 2011 list diversification of the consumption structure and inter-temporal risk-reduction techniques such as storage. The former clearly played an important role in the economy of Babylonia in the first millennium, which can be qualified as a 'dual-crop economy' based on the production of barley on the one hand and of dates on the other. That the two commodities are complementary has been shown for the first time by P. Vargyas, who noted that the date harvest had an alleviating effect on barley prices.[4] Hence, the peculiar structure of Babylonian agriculture contributed to price stability by reducing seasonal variation to a considerable extent. Additionally, the fact that the commodities were negatively correlated to one another, with the harvest periods of these two commodities being about half a year apart – barley in spring, dates in autumn – was certainly no disadvantage in that regard.

The final strategy that needs to be considered is inter-annual storage, or carry-over. To put it simply, the availability of sufficient stocks of foodstuffs in case of crop failure will attenuate the concomitant price increases and thus contribute to a lower level of price volatility. In spite of these stabilising effects of carry-over, its level is usually assessed at fairly low rates in pre-modern societies. Particularly influential was an article by McCloskey and Nash arguing that one major impediment to inter-annual storage in medieval England was the high interest rate: the net profits from storage (accruing from ever-increasing prices in the months after the harvest) need to be at least equal to the opportunity cost of interest forgone.[5] Hellenistic Babylonia was similarly a society with high interest rates. Direct evidence is sparse but telling. Although the very high interest rates – usually 40 per cent in the case of silver loans, and even higher in cases of loans in commodities (barley) – found in the business archive of Mūrānu and his son Ea-tabtanâ-bulliṭ, which make up the bulk of attestations for Seleucid Babylonia, are to be interpreted rather as penalties for delayed payment,[6] the few extant

---

[4] Vargyas 1997, in particular 339–40. Földvári, van Leeuwen and Pirngruber 2011 provide a precise estimate on the impact of the dual-crop structure on the seasonal variation of both commodities. See also Figure 5.22, especially the bars for the period 225–140.

[5] McCloskey and Nash 1984. See also Persson 1999: 55–62 and 67–72 for the same conclusion (based on different price series and a different argumentation) that carry-over in pre-modern societies was negligible.

[6] Jursa 2006 provides an edition of this archive and a discussion of the *modus operandi* of Mūrānu and his son, see particularly 161–2 for interest rates. Table 6 in Földvári, van Leeuwen and Pirngruber 2011 (187–9) charts all interest rates from Late Achaemenid and Hellenistic Babylon published to date; the data contained therein is also included in table 57 in Jursa 2010: 497–9, which centres on the material from the sixth century.

genuine rates of interest from Late Achaemenid in Hellenistic Babylonia attest to an annual interest rate range of between 20 per cent (Jursa 1998, text 16) and 40 per cent (Stolper 1993a: A2-10). In sum, it is safe to conclude that in the Hellenistic period, the interest rate on silver loans was close to the standard Neo-Babylonian rate of 20 per cent per annum and probably higher. Additionally, one has to consider that interest on loans in barley or dates was even higher. One possible explanation of this phenomenon was given by Flynn and Gíraldez (2002): because of the comparatively small extent of monetisation, silver was a more sought-after commodity. Repayments in kind were hence charged a disproportionately high interest to make repayment in cash more attractive. Such a line of argument is also congruent with a notion of (comparatively) high interest rates as a result of a (comparatively) low level of monetisation and low availability of silver.[7] These silver loans usually stem from an urban context, and the people involved in these transactions were high temple officials or urban entrepreneurs (or both) with comparatively easy access to cash. As regards small-scale farmers in a rural setting, however, the evidence points quite unambiguously to a lack of access to capital markets. The promissory notes from the Murašû archive from late fifth-century Nippur (as well as those from several other smaller archives) show that in a rural context credit was in most cases extended by specialised entrepreneurs to tenants of fiefs (i.e. land on which service was incumbent in a general way) so that the latter could pay their tax obligations – but not for productive purposes.[8] This claim is justified in so far as repayment in this substantial text corpus is invariably (a) stipulated in kind and (b) due in the harvest month. The importance of loans to fulfil tax obligations is shown by other archival evidence which in general shows also an increasing tax burden for the later part of the Achaemenid reign over Babylonia, starting with Darius I (523–486).[9] Credit for productive purposes on the other hand, for example in the form of so-called *harrānu* (trading) partnerships, is again confined to the higher strata of (urban) society.[10] Thus, although the opportunity costs (the

---

[7] This approach also provides a partial explanation of why interest rates on silver loans tended to be lower – in general close to the iconic 20 per cent value – in the long sixth century: this period was characterised by an extension of the monetary economy, silver was thus comparatively readily available; see Jursa 2010: 490–9.

[8] The system was first described by Stolper 1985; on credit see particularly 104–7.

[9] Jursa 2009. In addition, Jursa 2010 emphasises the dependence of small-scale farmers 'on outside funds in order to be able to fulfil their tax obligations' (252) which he considered 'potentially disruptive to the economy' (60)

[10] Jursa 2010: 206–8. On the distinction between rural consumption loans and urban credit for business activities see also the succinct summary remarks in Wunsch 2002a: 249–50. In

interest forgone) of these peasants was at least in theory low because they simply did not have access to liquid assets, they cannot be expected to have engaged in storage on any significant level because of tax obligations and/ or the requirement to repay consumption loans.

Besides the high level of interest rates, another important factor militating against carry-over on a larger scale in first-millennium Babylonia for the major producers such as the temples was the underlying political structure: in order to meet tax requirements, Neo-Babylonian temples were forced to sell the lion's share of their cash crops immediately after harvest. To quote Jursa (2010: 597), who detected a seasonal pattern in sales of the Neo-Babylonian Ebabbar temple's date harvest with a distinct peak immediately after the harvest, 'by and large the temple did not hoard dates with the intention of making them available to outsiders after the intensive phase of selling following the harvest', which he interprets as 'a reflection of the temple's pressing need for money: the evidence suggests that Ebabbar had to attempt to sell a maximum amount of its major cash crop in as short a time as possible'.

The Price Data from the Astronomical Diaries and Their Relevance for Storage

A promising way of additionally testing the hypothesis that carry-over was small also in the Hellenistic period is an investigation of the attestations of old (*labīru*) and new (*eššu*) barley and dates occasionally mentioned in the ADs and Commodity Price Lists of the Hellenistic period. Such an investigation is all the more interesting as it offers one of the few possibilities to ascertain economic structures of the Late Achaemenid and Hellenistic periods independently, without recourse to the sixth century. The reasoning behind this analysis is that *eššu* should refer to freshly harvested produce and *labīru* to produce already in the storehouse for an extended period. As may be expected in a society in which storage played a marginal role, there are only very few references to 'old' barley or dates, and, indeed, the whole dataset contains only two instances that can be interpreted as referring to carry-over, one for dates and one for *kasû*.[11]

---

addition, van de Mieroop 1997: 197–214 deals exclusively with credit for productive purposes in an urban context.

[11] Such an approach focussing on 'old' and 'new' grain was also suggested by McCloskey and Nash 1984 in their analysis of storage in medieval England; see 174–5 for the paucity of attestation of 'old grain' in the manorial account at their disposal. It may be true that the

Tables 4.1 and 4.2 chart all attestations of 'new' barley and 'new' dates in the ADs and the price lists. In the column headed 'Time period', the precise points in time of the price observations within the month are given, and the attestations of barley (dates) and new barley (new dates) are placed in the respective separate sub-cells. New barley, as one might think, indeed generally appears during the harvest period, hence the Babylonian months *nisannu* (I) and *ayyaru* (II), *mutatis mutandis*, new dates only appear in autumn. Barley designated as *eššu* either replaces barley without additional attribute (as in AD -308) or runs parallel to it (S/W texts 9 and 12) for a short period. The column headed 'Difference in equivalent' shows the increases in the equivalent (i.e. price decreases) which occur with the change from barley to 'new' barley; note that there is not a single instance of 'new' barley being more expensive (and the same holds true for dates and 'new' dates). This effect can first and foremost be explained as a consequence of the alleviation of the supply situation with the arrival of the new harvest rather than as a difference in quality or otherwise. Taking the two findings together, it seems clear that the designation 'new' refers less to a specific quality of a commodity but rather points simply to the fact that a new harvest has arrived on the market. The fact that 'new' barley most often simply takes the place of the commodity without further designation can be interpreted as pointing to the absence of larger stocks of that commodity, especially when considering the (almost complete) absence of attestations of 'old' barley.

The fact that the price difference between 'regular' and 'new' produce is notably larger with dates than with barley as well as the fact that new dates when parallel in time to regular ones are usually cheaper can be tentatively explained by the particularities of storage: in order to store dates, the fruit has to be dried, resulting in a much higher caloric value per litre (as well as per kilo). A similar reasoning could equally apply to the same phenomenon in the barley data, where, too, new produce is cheaper than the 'regular' one in instances where attestations run parallel. One can tentatively argue that this cereal is stored without its hulls. Note that according to Charles (1984: 29), the hulls are usually removed prior to consumption.

The same phenomenon is also visible, although to a much lesser extent, with the price data of *kasû* and cress. Also the documentation is more meagre for these commodities. For cress, there are only two telling instances

---

difference in source material – manorial accounts in medieval England and observational texts in the Late Babylonian period – potentially yields too low a number of instances for carry-over in the latter period. However, the results of this investigation are not affected by this hypothetical shortcoming. References to 'old grain' are also attested in Greek sources, see Bresson 2016: 431[(+59)].

Table 4.1. *Attestations of new barley*

Attestation	Date	Commodity	Time period[a]	Difference in equivalent
AD -308	April/May 309	Barley New barley	b e	+6
S/W text 12	?? month II	Barley New barley	m m	+18
S/W text 9	April/May 126	Barley New barley	11–e 15; 16–17; 18; 19– 22; 26–e	+15; +24; +15; +12; +19
AD -119B[1]	April/May 120	Barley New barley	–e m–e	+2.5
AD -118C[1]	April/May 119	[Barley] New barley	18 [...], [...], 26–27, 28, 29, 30	+14; +16; +11; +17; +20; +38?
AD -105C	May/June 106	Barley New barley	7 7–13	+??
AD -94	May/June 95	Barley New barley	[...] 22–e	+5 or +41
AD -85A	May/June 86	Barley New barley	[1?]7 19–[...]	??
AD -73	June/July 74	New barley	w	??

Note:[a] b = beginning of the month; m = middle of the month; e = end of the month; w = whole month.

(AD -105C and AD -77A). The cress equivalent in month III of year -105 is effectively the same as it is for new cress harvested at the end of month II in the same year. The new cress harvested in the last days of month III in -77 is slightly cheaper than cress without additional designation at the beginning of the same month.

For *kasû*, the situation is much the same. Most telling is the instance in AD -124, giving an equivalent for new *kasû* that is 36(+) litres higher than the one for regular *kasû* in the same month. The large difference between ADs -182 and -181 can be explained by the fact that the price of -181 is the price for new *kasû* during the ongoing harvest (month IV, hence June/July) and thus a period a high supplies, whereas the earlier

Table 4.2. *Attestations of new dates*

Attestation	Date	Commodity	Difference in time period	Difference in equivalent
AD -328	September/October	Dates	m	
	329	New dates	m	+27
AD -251	September/October	New dates	w	??
	252			
AD -218	September/October	New dates	w	??
	219			
S/W text 5	October/November	New dates	VIII	??
	170			
AD -144	October/November	Dates	w	
	170	New dates	w	+18
AD -140B	November/	Dates	e	
	December 141	New dates	e	+72
AD -132	October/November	Dates	[…]	
	133	New dates	m	+60
S/W text 9	September/October	Dates	b	
	126	New dates	m	+36(+)
S/W text 9	October/November	Dates	12–20	
	125	New dates	23–26	+18
AD -123B	August/September	Dates	−e	
	124	New dates	−e	+42
AD -118A	October/November	Old dates	m	
	119	New dates	w	+26 (new)
AD -99	October/November	Dates	w	
	100	New dates	w	+18
AD -86B	October/November	Dates	[…]	
	87	New dates	1–3	+??
S/W text 17	?? month VII	Dates	w	
		New dates	w	+24(+)

reference dates from month XI, hence the period right in between of two harvests.

Commodities can equally be designated as 'old'. The price for *kasû* designated as old in month X of year -186 (this instance is the only one of old *kasû*) is lower than the price for regular *kasû* in the immediately following month. It is unlikely that this passage refers to the harvest, as both

Table 4.3. *Attestations of old dates*

Attestation	Date	Commodity	Difference in time period	Difference in equivalent
AD -203	November/ December 204	Old dates	b–m–e	??
AD -193B	September/ October 194	Old dates	w	??
AD -156B	November/ December 157	Old dates	w	??
S/W text 6	May/June 137	Dates–Old dates	b–w	−6(+)
S/W text 6	June/July 137	Dates–Old dates	w = w	+18(+)

attestations of new *kasû* arriving at the market date to month IV. Although the possibility of a second harvest cannot be entirely discarded,[12] we might be dealing with an attestation of carry-over here. In this interpretation, *kasû* without an additional attribute would refer to the commodity of the harvest of ~July 187, the old variety thus at least from the year 188. Being obviously less appreciated, the price of old *kasû* was notably cheaper.

In addition to one fruitless reference to old barley in S/W text 17, there are a few occurrences of old dates. The equivalent in AD -336 is unfortunately broken, and the evidence from S/W text 6 is ambiguous as regards the equivalent. In month IV, old dates are clearly cheaper than regular dates, but in month III old dates are slightly more expensive than regular dates at the beginning of the month. If, however, the date price (for regular dates, specifically) increased during that month, which is a quite probable scenario considering the effects of seasonality, we would have the same pattern of old dates being cheaper than their regular equivalent. The only explicit attestation of both old and new dates together in one passage is AD -118A. In this diary, old dates are more expensive than new ones. The fact that old dates were thus not necessarily perceived as being of inferior quality becomes explicable when one notes that dates have to be dried in order to be storable, and the caloric content per litre (as capacity measure) is thus higher as they contain less water. The most interesting point of S/W text 6

---

[12] See Stol 1994: 175 for the uncertainty regarding the harvest of *kasû*.

is, however, that it is the only instance referring to either old or new dates not during the harvest season. One possible interpretation of this passage is to explain it – like the instance of old *kasû* in AD -186B – as referring to inter-annual storage: if the regular dates stem from the preceding harvest of autumn 138, then the dates designated as old must be from an earlier harvest, possibly autumn 139.[13] As date palms bear fruit only once every year, the possibility of a second harvest can definitely be excluded in this case.[14] S/W 6 is thus the only reasonably certain attestation for inter-annual storage in the corpus of the ADs for a staple good.

Archival Evidence and Storage Facilities

Evidence for 'old' produce, i.e. produce that was stored for longer than one harvest year is thus very meagre in these abstract price notations discussed so far. This is consistent with the notion of carry-over having played a very minor role only in the Late Babylonian economy. The evidence from the administrative documents from the temple households, which equally sometimes distinguish 'new' and 'old' produce, points in the same direction. As there are only very few pertinent documents from Hellenistic Babylonia, we will also consider the Neo-Babylonian evidence. The letter corpus of that period adds some interesting passages with reference to specifically 'old' dates. The letter CT 22 84, dated by Ebeling (1949: 51) on prosopographical grounds to the late seventh century, reads (lines 16–22) *ul-tu a-gan-na* ZÚ.LUM *eš-šu-tu ù* ZÚ.LUM.MA *la-bi-ru-tu šá ana sat'-tuk-ku ṭa-a-bi ana* AB-*iá ú-še-bi-la*, 'From here I have sent up old and new dates, fit for the regular offerings, to my father.' There is no indication as to the precise date of the letter within the year. However, after what has been said about commodities specified as 'new' in the discussion of the Commodity Price Lists and Astronomical Diaries, a date in autumn shortly after the date harvest seems to be the only possible option. This precious instance of a coexistence of new and old dates is another one of the few attestations of carry-over from Babylonia. An additional observation is that, if the reading *sat-tuk-ku* is correct, no difference seems to have existed between old or new dates as

---

[13] There is an analogous nomenclature for wine produced in Vienna: white wine (mostly from Veltliner grapes) is called 'Heuriger' (i.e., 'this year's') only until the following grape harvest, after which it is (normatively) sold as 'Alter (Wein)'.

[14] See, e.g., Cocquerillat 1968: 30–5 for the fruit cycle of the date palm: pollenisation in Mesopotamia usually takes place in the month of *nisannu*. After a ripening period of *c.* 180 days, the fruits are harvested in the month of *tašrītu* (October/November).

to cultic purposes.[15] CT 22 104 and 203 mention quite impressive amounts of old dates. In the former, 20 *kurru* (3,600 litres) of old dates are to be sold in the city of Babylon,[16] while the latter concerns a delivery of 5,400 litres of old dates (30 GUR ŠE.BAR SUMUN-*ti*).[17] Finally, one should mention BM 75787, a text which documents the sale of old dates from the *šutum šarri*, a storage facility in, according to Jursa (2010: 582–3), 'an attempt to clear out the storehouse in the expectation of the new harvest'. This instance and its interpretation are telling: although carry-over was thus theoretically possible in Mesopotamia, it seems not to have been among the economic strategies usually adopted by the larger institutions.

From the Late Achaemenid and Hellenistic periods, the evidence is as usual more meagre. CT 49 102, is a promissory note dating to 24(?) SE which mentions [15 GUR] ŠE.BAR *pe-ṣe-tu₄ eš-še-tu₄*, fifteen *kurru* of new white barley (completion Stolper 1993: 51). This transaction, the date of which is severely damaged, seems thus to have taken place at harvest time. Important documents for our purposes stem from the so-called 'Brewers' archive' from Borsippa.[18] CT 49 4 is part of this dossier. It is a letter order issued by the two paymasters (*bēl minde*) Tattannu and Nabû-uṣuršu dating from month VI of year 5 of Artaxerxes III (354/3). The text records the payment of 180 litres of barley of the previous year: 1 GUR ŠE.BAR TA ŠE.BAR *šá* ᴸᵁLÙNGAᴹᴱˢ *šá* MU 4.KAM, '1 *kurru* of barley from the barley of the brewers of year 4'. At first sight, this letter order could be interpreted as recording an attempt of the temple authorities to clear the stores for the incoming harvest (as we have seen before with BM 75787). If this were case, text CT 49 4 would be one of the few documents directly attesting to the possibility of carry-over in Hellenistic Babylonia, since according to this interpretation the Ezida temple still had a considerable quantity of dates left at the time of the new harvest. There is, however, another, more convincing interpretation of this text, namely, that it points to occasional arrears in payments. The temple has not been able in year 4 of Artaxerxes III (355/4) to meet its obligations vis-à-vis the persons entitled to income and was

---

[15] This interpretation suggested by Ebeling 1949: 51 is, however, far from being certain. The copy in CT 22 actually reads *šá-ti-ki*.

[16] Note the semi-syllabical writing SUMUN-*ru-tu*. Alternatively, one may consider a reading *be-ru-tu*, which generally is attested with various commodities, cf. CAD B (1965), s.v. *bēru* A, 'choice, select.'

[17] This instance does not allude to the possibility of using old dates as seed, SUMUN NUMUN, as read by Ebeling. The reading suggested here, SUMUN-*ti* was confirmed by photo collation by J. Hackl (Vienna).

[18] See Oelsner 1971: 165–6 for a short description of this archive. A full treatment is now provided by Hackl 2013: 476–522.

dependent on the arrival of the new date harvest to settle this liability. This latter interpretation is clearly to be preferred in the light of the usual phrasing of the letter orders of the Brewers' archive.

These texts register the disbursal of a commodity, usually barley or dates, to the brewers (or other professional groups) of the temple, upon order of the *bēl minde*. The designation of a commodity as 'of year x' is not infrequent in these letter orders from Borsippa and usually refers to annual 'ration' of a given commodity (attested are barley, dates and wool) to which a professional group was entitled. To give two examples, tablet CT 49 18, dating from year 6 of Alexander IV, orders the issue of '6 minas of wool, from the wool of the master-builders of year 6' to an individual. The key support for the interpretation given here is, however, those instances where the commodity is explicitly stated to be (part of) the ration (PAD[HI.A], *kurummatu*) of the current year, to which the professional group as such is entitled. Examples include CT 49 2 and 3, the latter of which reads (lines 4–6): 2 GUR ŠE.BAR TA ŠE.BAR PAD[HI.A] *šá* [LÚ]LÚNGA[MEŠ] *šá* MU 4.KAM, '360 litres of barley from the rations of the brewers, of year 4 (Artaxerxes III)'.[19] With the exception of CT 49 4, the year in which the transaction was recorded and the year which is referred to are the same. Attestations from CT 49 include texts numbers 16, 17, 18 and 49 for wool, as well as numbers 22, 36, 38, 40, 42 and 56 (dates). Hence, rather than referring to carry-over, we get the impression of occasional scarcities, better reconcilable with a lack of carry-over as economic strategy.

As regards storage facilities, the written evidence for our period is even scantier, although it should go without saying that no society can make do without intra-annual storage, which is necessary to ensure consumption throughout the year of commodities harvested at one point in time.[20] Several designations for 'storehouse' were in use in the Hellenistic period.[21] The diaries mention the 'property' (NÍG.GA, *makkūru*) of the goddesses Zababa and Ninlil (AD -254, 13) in connection with a theft, and of the Esangila (AD -330A+B, r5; AD -168A r6), with one instance (-168A r6) referring to gold dedicated to the temple stored therein. Other facilities attested in our period are a *bīt qatē* in the Esangila complex, where the guardians of the statues had a room (AD -200, r13–15), and the treasury,

---

[19] Other instances (CT 49 118, 123//122//182 and 124) which explicitly refer to rations of a given year can be found in the Mūrānu-archive, see Jursa 2006: 191–3.

[20] Johnstone 2011: 74–7 discusses this often neglected topic of intra-annual storage in Classical Greece.

[21] See additionally the table in Jursa 1995: 92 for an overview of the different storage facilities of the Sipparean Ebabbar temple.

bīt bušê (AD -187A, r11, r12; AD -168A, r19, r20), which was located in the juniper garden, and rebuilt in the early 160s. According to AD -187A, it served *inter alia* as the storage room of some cultic paraphernalia. The evidence from the Hellenistic chronicle series is similar to the picture drawn in the diaries: the so-called 'Judicial chronicle' (BCHP 17, first published in Joannès 2000a) describes the proceedings after a theft in the *bīt bušê*, again precious metals (gold and silver) are mentioned and a connection to property of the gods is made (lines 3–4). All these instances thus seem to refer to storehouses of various valuables rather than of basic commodities. Recourse to Neo-Babylonian material, however, shows that hirelings were employed during the date harvest for the *dul-lu šá* ZÚ.LUM.MA in a *bīt makkūri* (É NÍG.GA).[22] Traces of such a practice are equally attested in Hellenistic Babylonia. Several records of deposit and related texts published in Stolper 1993a specify the commodity deposited as NÍG.GA of a god (mostly Bēl and/or Nabû). There is good reason to assume that these properties of the god(s) were also stored in the *bīt makkūri*. Firstly, there is the obvious correspondence of NÍG.GA and É NÍG.GA, which is strengthened by text A2-7 which mentions explicitly a disbursal from the É NÍG.GA rather than designating the commodity given out as 'NÍG.GA DN' as is customary in these texts. Furthermore, the items given as deposit were mostly silver, as one would expect according to the attestations in the ADs.[23] There is, however, at least one instance (Stolper 1993a, text A2-4) in which dates specified as NÍG.GA ^{d}AG are given as deposit. Meagre as the direct evidence may be, the term 'general purpose storehouse' coined by Jursa (2004a: 160) seems thus appropriate for our period as well.

Another important matter as regards carry-over is storage loss, which together with the prevailing rate of interest was one of the most important cost factors involved. Storage loss has been estimated to amount to at least 10 per cent for both medieval England (McCloskey and Nash) and Ancient Egypt (Adamson), the latter tentatively envisaging a somewhat higher rate for Mesopotamia on account of climatic conditions more conducive to fungal attacks.[24] This latter phenomenon is indeed well attested in Babylonian written sources, most explicitly on tablet 12 of the omen collection *šumma ālu*. A few pertinent lines read:[25]

[22] CT 56 582 and 588; see Jursa 2010: 537.

[23] Stolper 1993a, texts 2, 3, 16, 18, A2-7, A2-10.

[24] McCloskey and Nash 1984 and Adamson 1985. Adamson explicitly refers to the 10 per cent spoilage rate as 'conservative estimate' (7). See also van der Mieroop 1997: 152–4 for problematic aspects of storage.

[25] We follow the edition of Freedman 1998 (191–205 for tablet 12).

(15) DIŠ KA.TAR <BABBAR> *ina* É *iš-pi-ki* GAR É BI *i-har-*[*ru-ub*],

If there is white fungus in a storehouse, that house will be devas[tated]

(37) DIŠ *ka-tar-ru na* Ì.DUB:Ì.KUN₄ IGI Ì.DUBᴹᴱˢ DIRᴹᴱˢ SUDᴹᴱˢ

If fungus is seen in a storage-bin/on a threshold, full storage-bins will become empty[26]

(75) DIŠ KA.TAR SIG₇ *ina* Ì.DUB GAR ŠE *ina* É LÚ NU GAL-*ši*

If there is green fungus in a storage-bin, there will be no grain in the man's house.

(81) DIŠ KA.TAR SIG₇ *ina* ŠÀ Ì.DUBᴹᴱˢ GAR Ì.DUBᴹᴱˢ DIRᴹᴱˢ SUDᴹᴱˢ

If there is green fungus inside storage-bins, full storage-bins will become empty.

There is thus little doubt about the consequence of a fungal attack: all apodoses refer essentially to the same outcome, namely loss of the infested crop. The places where such fungal decay occurred are either the storehouse in general (as in line 15) or directly the storage jars. Another interesting place for a (in that instance white) fungus to occur is the lower millstone (*um-mat* ᴺᴬ⁴HAR.HAR). In addition to these occurrences of fungal attacks, tablet 13 of *šumma ālu* deals with lichen infections in various storage facilities: distinct storehouses for grain, sesame, oil and dates are mentioned (lines 47–50). The prominence of both fungi and lichen in the omen series – to each of them is dedicated a whole tablet of the series – points to these infections being a widespread problem in Mesopotamia, the risk of high storage loss being therefore considerable.

Summing up, the evidence from both administrative documents and Astronomical Diaries points to only a very minor role for inter-annual storage (or carry-over). The scarcity of attestations of 'old' produce both in the ADs and archival documents and the fact the 'new' produce usually replaces the variety without further designation at the harvest unequivocally point in that direction, as do the texts from the early Hellenistic period pointing to arrears incurred by the temples. Additionally, the high interest rates in combination with rather small seasonal price increases[27] and the tax structure (at least as it is known from the Achaemenid period) were certainly not conducive to storage. It is not surprising that the commodity for which there are at least a few indications of storage is dates, not barley, as dates can be dried and hence increase in value as the caloric value per litre thereby increases.

---

[26] The same apodosis is given in the case of the appearance of a red *miqtu*-fungus on the roof a man's house (line 64).

[27] See Földvári, van Leeuwen and Pirngruber 2011 for a more detailed elaboration of this point.

Overview: Old (*lābiru*) and New (*eššu*) Commodities

AD -366 iv, 17: Month VI, 38 Art. II (16 September–15 October 367)

Commodity	Designation	Period	Price equivalent (litres/shekel)
Dates	Old	w	36(–71)

Note: In the preceding months IV and V, the date equivalent fluctuates between 60 and 66 litres per shekel

AD -328, 24: Month VI, 8 Alexander III (14 September–13 October 329)

Commodity	Designation	Period	Price equivalent (litres/shekel)
Dates	–	m	51
	New	m	78
	–	e	54
	New	e	[…]

AD -308, 17: Month VI, 8 Alexander IV (10 April–9 May 309)

Commodity	Designation	Period	Price equivalent (litres/shekel)
Barley	–	b	7.5
	New	e	13.5

AD -251, 7: Month VI, 60 SE (4 September–3 October 252)

Commodity	Designation	Period	Price equivalent (litres/shekel)
Dates	New	w	108

AD -218, 3: Month VII, 93 SE (30 September–28 October 219)

Commodity	Designation	Period	Price equivalent (litres/shekel)
Dates	New	w	102

AD -203, 9: Month VIII 108 SE (12 November–10 December 204)

Commodity	Designation	Period	Price equivalent (litres/shekel)
Dates	Old	b	240
	Old(?)	m	210
	Old(?)	e	198

AD -193B, 12: Month VII 118 SE (23 September–22 October 194)

Commodity	Designation	Period	Price equivalent (litres/shekel)
Dates	Old	w	96

AD -186B, r11: Month X 125 SE (2–31 January 186)

Commodity	Designation	Period	Price equivalent (litres/shekel)
Mustard	Old	w	450

AD -181, r3: Month IV 130 SE (14 July–12 August 182)

Commodity	Designation	Period	Price equivalent (litres/shekel)
Mustard	New	w	405

S/W text 5: Month VIII 142 SE (28 October–26 November 170)

Commodity	Designation	Period	Price equivalent (litres/shekel)
Dates	New	b	450(+)

AD -156B, 16: Month VIII 155 SE (2 November–1 December 157)

Commodity	Designation	Period	Price equivalent (litres/shekel)
Dates	Old	w	[…]

AD -144, r15: Month VIII 167 SE (21 October–18 November 145)

Commodity	Designation	Period	Price equivalent (litres/shekel)
Dates	–	w	300
	New	w	318

AD -140B, r6: Month VII 171 SE (6 October–4 November 141)

Commodity	Designation	Period	Price equivalent (litres/shekel)
Dates	–	e	432
	New	e	504

S/W text 6: Month III 175 SE (27 May–25 June 137)

Commodity	Designation	Period	Price equivalent (litres/shekel)
Dates	–	b	216(+)
		m	[…]
	Old	w	210

S/W text 6: Month IV 175 SE (26 June–25 July 137)

Commodity	Designation	Period	Price equivalent (litres/shekel)
Dates	–	w	162
	Old	w	180(+)

AD -132B, r15: Month VII 179 SE (8 October–6 November 133)

Commodity	Designation	Period	Price equivalent (litres/shekel)
Dates	–	[…]	240
	New	m	300
	New(?)	[…]	[180]+144
	New(?)	e	288(–323)

S/W text 9: Month II 186 SE (27 April–25 May 126)

Commodity	Designation	Period	Price equivalent (litres/shekel)
Barley	–	1	18(–35)
		until 7	20
		8–10	18
		11–e	21
	New	15	36
		16–17	45
		18	36
		19–22	33
		26–e	40

S/W text 9: Month VII 186 SE (21 September–20 October 126)

Commodity	Designation	Period	Price equivalent (litres/shekel)
Dates	–	b	72
	New	m	108(–125)

AD -124, r3: Month IV 187 SE (13 July–10 August 125)

Commodity	Designation	Period	Price equivalent (litres/shekel)
Mustard	–	w	216
	New	w	252(–288)

AD -123B, 13: Month VI 188 SE (30 August–27 September 124)

Commodity	Designation	Period	Price equivalent (litres/shekel)
Dates	–	–	41.5
		-e	60
	New	-e	102

S/W text 9: Month VII 187 SE (10 October–8 November 125)

Commodity	Designation	Period	Price equivalent (litres/shekel)
Dates	–	12–20	114
	New	b	[…]
		23–26	132
		-e	114

AD -119B[1], 7: Month I 192 SE (20 April–19 May 120)

Commodity	Designation	Period	Price equivalent (litres/shekel)
Barley	–	b	32
		-e	33.5
	New	m–e	36[a]

Note:[a] Variant AD -119A$_2$: 33.5 litres/shekel for new barley in an unspecified period (w?).

AD -118A, 16: Month I 193 SE (9 April–8 May 119)

Commodity	Designation	Period	Price equivalent (litres/shekel)
Barley	–	1–3	30
		4–9	27
		10	25,5
		11–12	24
		13	27

Commodity	Designation	Period	Price equivalent (litres/shekel)
	New[a]	14–17	30
		18	28
		19	[...]
		[...]	42
		[...]	44
		26–27	39
		28	45
		29	48
		30	[66?]

Note:[a] All the equivalents after day 19 should refer to new barley.

AD -118A, r16: Month VII 193 SE (4 October–2 November 119)

Commodity	Designation	Period	Price equivalent (litres/shekel)
Dates	Old	-m	61
		-e	60
	New	w	87

AD -105C, 27: Month II 206 SE (16 May–13 June 106)

Commodity	Designation	Period	Price equivalent (litres/shekel)
Barley	–	-6	60
		7	72
		8–e	75
	New	7–13	72(–107)
Cress	New	-m	24
		-e	30

AD -99: Month VII 212 SE (4 October–2 November 100)

Commodity	Designation	Period	Price equivalent (litres/shekel)
Dates	–	w	72
	New	w	90

AD -94, 16: Month II 217 SE (14 May–12 June 95)

Commodity	Designation	Period	Price equivalent (litres/shekel)
Barley	–	[...]	[36/72]+31
	New	22–e	108

AD -86B, 5: Month VII 225 SE (10 October–7 November 87)

Commodity	Designation	Period	Price equivalent (litres/shekel)
Dates	–	[...]	[...]+ ½
	New	1–3	30
		4	[...]

AD -85A, 11: Month II 226 SE (5 May–3 June 86)

Commodity	Designation	Period	Price equivalent (litres/shekel)
Barley	–	[1?]7–19	48
	New	[...]	[...]

AD -77A, r4: Month III 234 SE (5 June–3 July 78)

Commodity	Designation	Period	Price equivalent (litres/shekel)
Cress	–	B	6
	New	3–e	9

AD -73, 14: Month III 238 SE (20 June–19 July 74)

Commodity	Designation	Period	Price equivalent
Barley	New	w	45 (81!)

S/W text 12: Month II, undated (possibly 171 SE = 141/0)

Commodity	Designation	Period	Price equivalent (litres/shekel)
Barley	–	b	204
		m	174
	New	[...]	162
		m	192
		e	[...]

S/W text 17: Month IV, undated

Commodity	Designation	Period	Price equivalent (litres/shekel)
Barley	Old	w	105(+)

S/W text 17: Month VII, undated

Commodity	Designation	Period	Price equivalent (litres/shekel)
Dates	–	w	[180?]+120
	New	w	324(–359)

PART III

Performance

5 | A Price History of Babylonia, *c.* 400–*c.* 140

Introduction

The aim of the present chapter is to discuss the characteristics of the price data provided by the Astronomical Diaries, with the addition of a considerable number of prices stemming from the Commodity Price Lists edited by Slotsky and Wallenfels 2009. In particular, we will focus on the statistics of the sample, such as the mean price and deviations thereof – the level of price volatility – as well as on the general trends discernible over time. The earliest period for which Astronomical Diaries are extant, the sixth and fifth centuries, are very scarcely documented, with only one and three surviving diaries respectively (ADs -567, -463, -453 and -418). Only from the early fourth century onwards (December 385, to be precise), we do have a sufficient number of prices at our disposal, amenable to closer analysis. The chronological frame for this investigation is thus the period from the reappearance of price data in the Late Achaemenid era during the reign of Artaxerxes II until the Parthian conquest of Babylonia in 141. From the point of view of the historian it is hardly justified to consider this long stretch in time – about 260 years – as a uniform period. Therefore, we will subdivide this period into several smaller units of time each characterised by a reasonably stable socio-political background. A first break suggests itself at the Macedonian conquest of Babylonia, not only a moment of major political disruption but an event which also had profound repercussions in the price data. The cessation of the long-term warfare between the Successors constitutes a second caesura, and as an emblematic point in time we chose the acceptance of the royal title by Seleucus I in 305/4. Finally, we also distinguish between an earlier and a later Seleucid reign in Babylonia – we shall see below that there are indeed good reasons to do so in terms of price movements – and the lacuna in the price documentation early in the reign of Antiochus III during the 210s provides a fitting watershed.

Another point of interest is the relationship between the prices under discussion to both the data from the 'long sixth century' analysed by M. Jursa in his fundamental *Aspects of the Economic History of Babylonia in the First Millennium BC* (2010) and the few scattered price quotations from

Table 5.1. *Barley prices in the sixth and fifth centuries*

Period	Mean barley price (shekels per *kurru*)	Standard deviation
Long sixth century	2.56	2.54
575–530	1.04	0.44
Fifth century	7.85	1.98

the diaries of the fifth century.[1] Owing to the survival of substantial private and institutional archives throughout Babylonia,[2] the sixth century is exceptionally well documented. This holds true for price data of a wide range of commodities, comprising foodstuffs such as barley and dates, as well as sheep, slaves and date gardens.[3] The years between 575 and 535 in particular are densely covered, the period of the later Neo-Babylonian Empire from the final years of Nebuchadnezzar II onwards until the first years of the reign of the Achaemenid Cyrus II over Babylonia. These years were also characterised by very low barley prices, variable but usually below 1 shekel per *kurru*. However, around 540 prices started to increase dramatically as a result of inflationary pressures stemming from an increased amount of silver in circulation no longer matched by economic expansion (Jursa 2010: 745–53), and around the last decade of the sixth century, this inflationary movement reached its apex, when barley prices frequently amounted to 10 shekels per *kurru*. The main underlying cause of this phenomenon in his interpretation was an expansion of the monetary supply (rather than a rise in demand or, alternatively, a drain on commodity supply). However, towards the end the reign of Darius I, the prices seem to drop again to the level of the 520s, a trend which Jursa tentatively brought in connection with the dislocation of the centre of the empire and a concomitant diversion of the monetary flow. Prices fell again to a level between 3 and four 4 shekels per *kurru*, before the documentation virtually ceases

---

[1] These are collected in table 6.9 in Hackl and Pirngruber 2015: 119.

[2] For a concise overview see Jursa 2005a. The most important institutional archives are the Eanna archive from Uruk (e.g., Kleber 2008) and the archive of the Ebabbar temple in Sippar (e.g., Jursa 1995; Bongenaar 1997). Among the private archives, the archive of the Egibi family, which stems mainly from the city of Babylon, stands out in size (see Wunsch 1993 and 2000). The private archives from the city of Borsippa, which are particularly informative about the social fabric of a Babylonian city, are the focus of Waerzeggers 2010.

[3] Jursa 2010, see especially 443–68, 576–94, 595–623 (contribution of Kleber) and 745–53 for the price analyses of different commodities (*inter alia* barley, dates and wool).

in the second year of Xerxes. The mean barley price for the whole period 626–484 was calculated at 2.56 shekels/*kurru*.[4]

In contrast to the sixth century, data on commodity prices for the fifth century is rather scanty. As far as the evidence allows us to see, this period was characterised by high price levels. Our principal source of information is AD -419. In this year (420/19), the barley price fluctuated in line with the usual seasonal pattern of decreasing prices in the period after the harvest (which usually takes places in month II, *ayyāru*, of the Babylonian calendar, hence roughly April)[5] between 5 and 10 shekels per *kurru*, the mode being 7.5 shekels. During the pre-harvest season of 452, the barley price was even higher, oscillating between 10 and 12 shekels per *kurru*. The general impression is thus one of high prices prevailing throughout the fifth century; the mean price amounted to 7.85 shekels/*kurru*. The postulated 'reversal' after the year 500 of the inflationary process taking place in the second half of the sixth century – that is, the lower prices of 3 to 4 shekels per *kurru* in the first decade or so of the fifth century; see the last entries in table 49 in Jursa 2010: 447 – seems to have been a temporary consolidation only. However, neither can it be excluded that our extant prices are among the highest of the fifth century. The evidence at our disposal is simply not adequate to sustain any certain conclusions. Unfortunately, for this period there is hardly any data from private or institutional archives on commodity prices.[6]

The Late Achaemenid Period: The Issue of Price Volatility

From a Babylonian point of view, the final decades of the Achaemenid dynasty pose considerable problems to the historian, mainly owing to the scarcity of source material. Archival documents, important as they are for elucidating crucial aspects of socio-economic fabric, generally provide little information about political history.[7] The few extant historical

---

[4] Jursa 2010: 447–8. We chose shekels (8.4 grams) of silver per *kurru* (180 litres) as unit of measurement in order to provide easy comparison with his data.

[5] This year should be added to the list of unanimous instances of seasonal fluctuation in van der Spek and Mandemakers 2003: 526–8.

[6] The documentation of northern Babylonia is edited in Hackl 2013; for the price data contained see Hackl and Pirngruber 2015.

[7] But note for example the relevance in this respect of date formulas, which are indispensable in establishing the precise duration of the reign of kings. See on this aspect Oelsner 1971 and Boiy 2007a. The later Achaemenid Empire in general is dealt with in several chapters in Briant 1996 (with updates in Briant 1997 and 2001).

sections of ADs as well as chronicle ABC 9 dating to the reign of Artaxerxes III give us rare insights into the activities of the king. The chronicle gives an account of the capture of the Phoenician city of Sidon, AD -381 possibly relates to the subjugation of the Cypriot king Evagoras,[8] and AD -362 (edited by Hunger and van der Spek 2006) refers to otherwise undocumented armed strife in Babylonia involving the royal family. The most formative sources on Late Achaemenid history, however, are the works of various Greek historians, in particular Ctesias and Xenophon. Not only do their accounts outnumber all other source material at our disposal, they furthermore quite decisively created an impression of a decadent empire in continuous decline: weak kings are being manipulated by women and eunuchs while squandering the heritage of the more positively assessed earlier kings Cyrus II and Darius I (both of whom were awarded the epithet 'the Great').[9] This Greek view of the Achaemenids strongly influenced modern scholarship, and it is only since the 1980s CE, in particular with H. Sancisi-Weerdenburg's provocatively entitled 1987 essay 'Decadence in the Empire or Decadence in the Sources', that this orientalising stereotype has been abandoned. This more balanced approach to the Achaemenids, culminating in Briant's masterly *Histoire de l'émpire perse* (1996, English edition 2001), entailed a re-assessment of various events mainly or even exclusively known through Greek historians.[10] For example, the so-called 'Great Satraps' Revolt' of the 360s, described by Diodorus Siculus (especially 15 90) as a concerted attempt to overthrow Artaxerxes II was shown to have been a series of loosely related local upheavals hardly reaching beyond the main scene of friction in Asia Minor.[11] The furthest that this rebellion might have expanded was Upper Mesopotamia. According to van der Spek 1998a, lines 2–5 of AD -366A deal with the Great Satraps' Revolt, more precisely with the rebellious satrap of Cappadocia, Datames. We know from Polyaenus (7 21.3) that this Datames, a high imperial dignitary and one of the officials in charge of the forces deployed against Egypt in the abortive campaign of 373 (Ruzicka 2012: 123–5), crossed the Euphrates and fought against the royal troops. Datames was considered a rebel as early as 368, and so actually precedes the bulk of events that make up the Great Satraps' Revolt in Asia Minor between 366 and 360. He operated mainly in southwestern Anatolia, in his own satrapy Cappadocia and in

---

[8] See van der Spek 1998a for this interpretation (also Briant 1996: 1010–11).

[9] Wiesehöfer 2007: 12–18 provides a concise overview of the Greek vision of an empire in decline.

[10] But see now also Harrison 2011 for a critical review of recent scholarship on the Achaemenids.

[11] Weiskopf 1989, whose view was accepted and expanded by Briant 1996: 675–94.

Cilicia.[12] Temporally and locally it is thus not too difficult to link him to the present diary, which speaks in line two of a clash between royal troops and troops of an unknown leader, whose name is broken off. Datames' crossing of the Euphrates has commonly been interpreted as an attempt to defend the eastern portion of his satrapy against an army led by subordinates of the king.[13] He was subsequently engaged in bellicose episodes with Autophradates, satrap of Lydia, and Mithridates, the son of the former rebel satrap Ariobarzanes, both commissioned by the Great King with the abatement of the rebellion. His death at the hands of Mithridates is usually dated to 361.[14] However, doubt has been cast on this interpretation of AD - 366,[15] and, indeed, there is no external evidence to support van der Spek's thesis. But unless we want to assume an event unknown to the Classical sources, it is difficult to see who else among the insurgent satraps could be understood in connection to this diary, considering the point in time and the region.

More important for our purpose than the identification of the rebel of this diary is the general picture this diary reveals of political circumstances during the late Achaemenid Empire. Localised warfare and attempts at sedition were a rather common phenomenon throughout the fourth century, in particular in the western parts of the Achaemenid realm. In addition to rebellious satraps, we know mainly thanks to the account of Diodorus of frequent incursions of Spartan kings – most prominently Agesilaus – affecting the coastal cities of Asia Minor in the aftermath of the revolt of Cyrus the Younger.[16] We furthermore have evidence of conflicts on Cyprus, in Phoenicia and in Egypt, the latter culminating in a short-lived reconquest in 342 after several abortive attempts.[17] Moreover, in Babylonia, and thus at the very core of the empire, there was occasional conflict, as attested by AD -362 quoted above. However, the magnitude of these events should not be overestimated. The mere fact that the Great King could repeatedly campaign against a province as far away as Egypt, which was notoriously difficult to access, betrays the considerable resources at his disposition, financially as

---

[12] Datames and his highly interesting (and much-debated) coinage from Tarsos in Cilicia issued under the name of Tarkumuwa were discussed most recently in Wiesehöfer 2003. On his rebellion see also Ruzicka 2012: 125–32.

[13] Weiskopf 1989: 58–9.

[14] Weiskopf 1989: 61, endorsed by Wiesehöfer 2003.

[15] Briant 2001 93-4, especially as regards methodological aspects.

[16] Lewis 1977.

[17] The conflict between the Achaemenid central power and Egypt is analysed in depth by Ruzicka 2012.

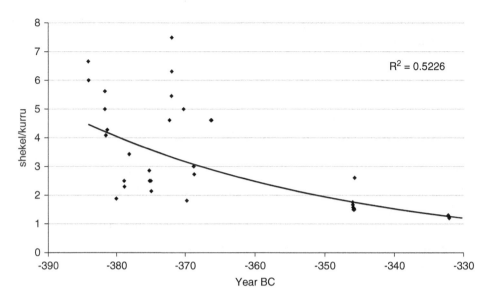

Figure 5.1 Barley prices in the Late Achaemenid period

well as in terms of manpower.[18] The same holds true for the interventions
on Cyprus and for the deportations into Babylonia of captives taken after
the Phoenician city of Sidon was 'pacified'. The revolts and skirmishes in
Asia Minor even took place without any kind of royal involvement; it was
left to loyal satraps to deal with those colleagues perceived as rebels and
with pugnacious Spartan kings. None of the events cited here is likely to
have influenced prices in Babylonia. More likely is an economic repercussion of the events in 363/2 (described in AD -362), some kind of rebellion
and fighting within Babylonia involving a son of the king. Unfortunately,
not only is the historical interpretation of this episode rather elusive, but
there is equally no price data extant for almost two decades after this event
(see Figure 5.1 for barley prices).

Thus, just as is the case for historical information, the price data for
the period between 400 and 330 is rather meagre. In general, the Late
Achaemenid barley price data aligns remarkably well with the prices found
in the late sixth and early fifth century, for which the mean price ranges
between 3 and 4 shekels per *kurru*.[19] The mean of the Late Achaemenid

18 See Briant 1996: 803–9 and 815–20 (and see also 799–800) for an analysis of the heavily biased
    accounts of various Greek historiographers of the Late Achaemenid army, which were 'très
    généralement paraphrasés par les historiens d'aujourd'hui' (804); see 820–32 on the economy.
19 See the last entries in table 49 in Jursa 2010: 443–47. For the whole sixth century, the mean was
    lower and amounted to 2.56 shekels per *kurru* (Jursa 2010: 448).

Table 5.2. *Commodity prices in the Late Achaemenid period*

Commodity	Mean price (shekels per *kurru*)[a]	Standard deviation
Barley	3.37	1.79
Dates	2.02	0.82
Kasû	0.75	1.01
Cress	7.05	7.07
Sesame	9.67	5.56
Wool	1.54	0.75

Note:[a] Wool price in shekels per 5 *minas*.

sample amounts to 3.37 shekels per *kurru* – corresponding to an equivalent of 70 litres per shekel – with a standard deviation of 1.79. As is the general rule with foodstuffs, the value of the median (2.79) is lower than the mean of the sample because of demand inelasticity.[20] These values are much lower than the high prices seemingly prevailing during the fifth century (with a mean and median price of 7.85 and 7.5 shekels/*kurru* respectively), which, it must be kept in mind, rely on only a few known prices. Price volatility is quite high, especially in the period between 385 and 366, when the price oscillated between 1.82 shekels/*kurru* in March/April 370 and 7.5 shekels/ *kurru* in January 372.

This feature is peculiar to the Late Achaemenid period, since, contrary to Vargyas' (2001: 130) assertion that 'the price of barley fluctuated strongly within the economic year', the intra-annual price variation in Babylonia in the second half of the first millennium is in fact in general rather low compared to, for example, medieval England, mainly because of the dual crop structure of barley and dates in Babylonian agriculture.[21] Vargyas' conclusion of 50 per cent fluctuation within a harvest year and up to 100 per cent fluctuation around harvest time based on the price data of the ADs gives a very inflated impression of the magnitude of intra-annual price movements.[22] By accounting also for the negative growth rate of the barley price

[20] On that point see also van der Spek and Mandemakers 2003: 523–4.
[21] For a comparison of the level of inter-annual price fluctuation between Hellenistic Babylonia and medieval England see Földvári, van Leeuwen and Pirngruber 2011. The interdependency of barley and dates was also postulated by Vargyas 1997: 339 and 2001: 177–83.
[22] Also, he confuses changes in the barley *equivalent* with changes in the barley *price*; see van der Spek and Mandemakers 2003 for the frequent confusions of this kind in both Slotsky 1997a and Vargyas 2001.

in autumn, which was caused by the demand-alleviating effect of the date harvest, an average intra-annual growth rate of 15.3 per cent for barley (and a similar value for dates) gives a more realistic idea of the magnitude of seasonal fluctuation.[23]

Figure 5.1 also seems to show that volatility was much lower in the final years of the Achaemenid Empire. This impression is, however, in need of much qualification: one reason for the reduced volatility in the period between *c.* 350 and 330 is certainly the fact that the data comes from two years only, ADs -346 and -332. Because of the scarcity of data, further corroboration of these results for the Late Achaemenid period is difficult, and achievable only by means of crude methodology. One solution is simply to compare the standard deviation from the mean of the periods from -386 until -366 and from -346 until -332 to the mean of the intra-annual standard deviations for the whole period. The results thus obtained confirm our expectations: the standard deviation from the mean of the barley price (in shekels per *kurru*) for the earlier period amounts to 1.65, but in the later period, which is based on two diaries only, it decreases to 0.37.[24] The mean of intra-annual fluctuation as measured by the standard deviation is even lower, only 0.31.[25] These results find confirmation in other periods. For example, for the whole of the reign of Antiochus I (281–261), the standard deviation was 1.14, but the mean annual value (based on ADs -278B, -277, -273B, -270B and on S/W 3) only 0.15. The intuitive assumption of van der Spek (2000a: 297) that considerable price jumps do not occur frequently within one year can thus be corroborated. Finally, it has to be emphasised again that intra-annual fluctuations in general conform to the expected pattern of seasonality: prices were lowest in the period shortly after the harvest

---

[23] See Földvári, van Leeuwen and Pirngruber 2011: 180 and tables 4a, 4b, 5a and 5b (183–6).

[24] A similar pattern is obtained when looking at the coefficient of variation (CV), which decreases from 0.41 in the period between -389 and -366 to a mere 0.23 in the years -346 to -332. Although the CV is generally a more reliable means of comparison, because of the scarcity of data especially as regards the intra-annual oscillations, the cruder standard deviation is more appropriate for the period under investigation.

[25] This value is the mean of the standard deviations of the price data of ADs -384, -381A and B, -380B, -379, -378, -375A and B, -372, -369, -366, -246, -332. AD -370 was not considered because only one price is extant in this diary. Note, however, that three of the included diaries (-380B, -378 and -366) have only two identical prices for one month. Their deviation of zero was included in order to avoid a disproportionate impact of exceptional prices such as the high price of March 346, an outlier in all probability caused by an invasion of locusts (discussed in Pirngruber 2014). However, even if those three diaries with zero deviation were omitted, the value would still amount to only 0.42 and hence be substantially below the value of the earlier of the two periods analysed.

Table 5.3. *r² of the trend-lines of the Late Achaemenid period*

Commodity	Value of r^2
Barley	0.52
Dates	0.62
Cuscuta	0.70
Cress	0.74
Sesame	0.38
Wool	0.87

and rose thereafter.[26] This fact also has to be taken account of in order to reach a more realistic impression of price volatility.

Another conspicuous feature of the Late Achaemenid data is the fact that the prices of all commodities – the five foodstuffs as well as wool – decrease considerably in this period. The explanatory power (r^2) of the (exponential) regressions is quite high for all commodities, usually between 0.5 and 0.7 or more. In spite of the paucity of price data, this overall trend seem beyond doubt. This evidence can be interpreted as another argument against the over-simplifying portrayal of an empire in simple decline.

Like barley, all the other commodities in the diaries do not only exhibit a price decrease during the fourth century (exemplified in Figure 5.2 showing sesame prices) but equally a substantially lower mean than in the fifth century. For dates, the mean diminishes from 4.42 to 2.02 shekels per *kurru*,[27] for sesame even from 30.64 to 9.27.

It must be noted that the first value of the Late Achaemenid sesame series of the ADs (7.5 litres per shekel in May 382, corresponding to 24 shekels per *kurru*) is still close to the values of the fifth century, which oscillate around 5 to 6 litres per shekel. However, already shortly afterwards the equivalent trebles. We cannot tell whether this price was exceptionally high or whether it was in line with the regular equivalent for sesame in the early fourth century. As can be seen in Jursa 2010 (452–4, table 50, listing sesame prices of the sixth century), during the reign of Darius high prices of around 30 shekels per *kurru* of sesame start to appear with a certain regularity. It seems thus plausible that during (most of) the fifth century and also the first decades of the fourth century a

---

[26] See most exhaustively Vargyas 2001: 89–130, and in particular 86–9, for the fluctuation of the barley price within a harvest year; see also van der Spek and Mandemakers 2003.

[27] Not considering the dubious reading of 17 litres per shekel of AD -418, month II, which would raise the mean of the earlier cluster to 5.45.

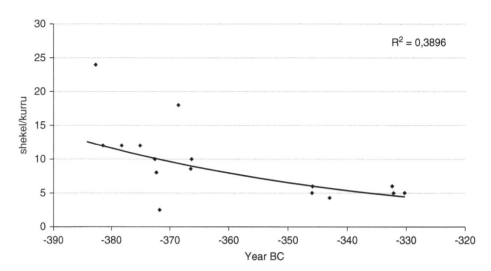

Figure 5.2 Sesame prices in the Late Achaemenid period

high sesame price prevailed. The mean of 9.27 shekels per *kurru* for the period between *c.* 390 and 330 is then again closer to and even below the sixth-century value of 13.37.[28] For dates, the mean of the Late Achaemenid period (2.02) lies above the mean of the long sixth century of 1.24 shekels per *kurru* but slightly below the values for late sixth and early fifth century.[29]

That a downward trend for all commodities for the Late Achaemenid period is beyond doubt was shown by Slotsky's work; however, by confusing equivalences and prices she overstated the magnitude of this trend.[30] The reasons for this downward trend are not clear. Taking again the barley price as point of departure, it is immediately clear that the cause of the low prices cannot be sought in the seasons recorded in the diaries; quite the contrary. The low prices of AD -346 are even pre-harvest prices and consequently *ceteris paribus* among the higher prices of the year in question. The fact that all commodities are affected militates in any case strongly against explanations in terms of harvest variation of the single commodities. It is remarkable that even the price of wool, which is clearly the most stable of all commodity prices of the diaries, declines significantly during these decades.

The prices during the first half of the fourth century oscillate between 1.67 and 2.5 shekels per 5 minas and are thus, as is the case with the other

[28] For this value and a graph of sixth-century sesame prices see Jursa 2010: 454–5.
[29] Jursa 2010: 586 and 592–4, see in particular the latest values from Darius I, year 17 (505/4) onwards.
[30] Slotsky 1997a: 57, speaks of a two- to sevenfold price decrease. Taking the mean price as base point, the decrease is rather two- or at most threefold.

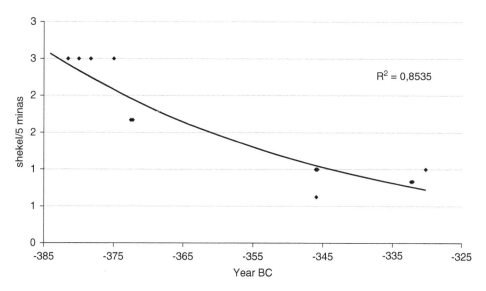

Figure 5.3 Wool prices in the Late Achaemenid period

commodities above the sixth century mean, calculated at 1.4 shekels per 5 minas by Jursa 2010: 618–19. In the 330s and 340s, however, the price fluctuates between 0.83 and 1 shekel per 5 minas only. This unevenness in the price level is also reflected in the coefficient of variation of the Late Achaemenid period, which is, at 0.49, remarkably high for wool, a commodity not prone to seasonal fluctuation and with a higher demand elasticity compared to the basic foodstuffs barley and dates. For comparison, throughout the whole third century that value amounts to only 0.30.[31] It is equally notable that the magnitude of this downward trend in prices amounts to about 50 per cent for all six commodities.

By and large, there are three different explanatory approaches to a universal price decrease. The first possibility to consider is a decrease in demand. This would imply a decline in the population level, which is a very unlikely suggestion. Although the demographic pattern can vary locally, a general rise in the population level in Mesopotamia can be ascertained, starting about the middle of the first millennium and extending well into the Sassanid period.[32] The short time period in particular militates against this hypothesis – unless we want to assume mass deportations or a plague carrying off a large proportion of the population, for which there are no

[31] This difference is all the more remarkable as according to Földvári and van Leeuwen 2011, the CV tends to be higher the longer the period analysed.
[32] Adams 1965 and 1981. See Kessler 2005 for a caveat on local variations, using the example of the city of Uruk.

indications whatsoever – as the two documented periods (380s–360s and 340s–330s) are separated by about two decades only, and do not exhibit any downward trend within themselves. Additionally, the decline in prices is rather steep. The second option, an increase in the level of supply is *eo ipso* improbable as this would presuppose a more or less uniform rise in the productivity level of the most variegated commodities. The third possibility, in a similar vein to Jursa's (2010: 746–53) suggestion for the 'inflation', or rather monetisation, in sixth-century Babylonia, is to assume a change in the monetary base. In our case this would mean a contraction of the monetary supply, and an increase in the value of silver with respect to the commodities. But again, there is no plausible scenario in which there might have been a siphoning off of silver resources from Babylonia in these years. We do read for example that Demosthenes received large sums of money from the Great King in order to organise resistance against the Macedonians in 335/4, but whether those alleged 300 talents of gold constituted a major drain of precious metal for the Persians is extremely doubtful.[33] The abortive campaign launched by Artaxerxes II against Egypt in spring 373 or the interventions on Cyprus against Evagoras in the 380s were certainly more costly enterprises for the royal treasury, but Babylonian commodity prices were not visibly affected. Furthermore, the bribing of the Athenian orator was no singular affair, as we see various Great Kings meddling in Greek affairs – a prominent example is the King's Peace of 386[34] – which certainly involved financial outlays. The case of the Late Achaemenid period nicely reflects the difficulties involved in analysing the data of the Astronomical Diaries: complementary sources are usually scarce, and often a definite explanation cannot be given for apparent trends or even singular phenomena.

Summing up our findings for the Late Achaemenid data, we firstly note that the mean prices are in general higher than the low mid-sixth-century prices, but substantially lower than the high prices caused by the monetisation shock in the last quarter of the sixth century. Any direct comparison between the two datasets is, however, rendered problematic by the scarcity of price data throughout the fifth century, leaving all attempts at a solution on shaky ground. The general impression is of a fairly high price level in this period. There is no convincing mono-causal explanation for the ongoing price decrease in the fourth century. Most striking is the rather high level of price volatility, as epitomised in the wide range of prices in the

---

[33] Diod. 17 4.7–9; see Heckel and Yardley 1997: 87.
[34] On this episode (described by Diod. 14 110.1–4) see Briant 1996: 668.

period between *c.* 385 and 369, pointing to some kind of market imperfection. Analysed from the point of view of performance, the combination in the Late Achaemenid period of both a comparatively high price level as well as a considerable volatility can most satisfactorily be explained by an interplay of several smaller factors. The prices of the earlier cluster saw much bellicose imperial activity in various parts of the empire and beyond (Cyprus, Egypt) involving the Great King himself. Some of the campaigns might have had their starting point in Babylonia, for example that against the land of Razaunda described in AD -369, thereby causing a drain on the province's resources. Ominous references repeatedly point to various difficulties in Babylonia in this period, among which disease (AD -382) and famine (AD -373A), and also the lack of success of several military enterprises (Egypt, Cadusians) might have played their part. Finally, the outcome of the harvest, the dark horse of Babylonian price history, may also have favoured the later years in question here, thereby decreasing price and volatility of one or another commodity. The stable political climate of the 340s seems to have favoured rather low prices, and the only outlier can be explained by the occurrence of a natural disaster, a locust invasion (see Pirngruber 2014). The even lower prices in September–November 333 put in perspective the impact of military actions in regions far from Babylonia: the crushing defeat at Issus of the Persian imperial army with a subsequent looting of the Persian camp at Damascus (Just. 11 9.9–11) left no obvious trace in Babylonian commodity prices.[35] The occurrence of disease, famine and high prices in the first half of the fourth century may still have been encouraged by the continuous campaigning of the king in that period; it is, however, misleading to assume an automatic causal relationship between military campaigns and high prices. Unfortunately, the sources do not permit us to investigate the history of these decades in more depth. However, the Murašû archive from Nippur and the Kasr archive from Babylon allow for a complementary analysis of the economic structure of the Late Achaemenid period, something no longer possible in the Hellenistic era owing to the lack of pertinent sources. It was shown in Chapter 3 that the institutional framework is very likely to have contributed to market instability and high price volatility during the latter part of Achaemenid rule over Babylonia.

A final point remains to be made. It was suggested above that the level of inter-annual price volatility in the Late Achaemenid period – in particular within the period between the 380s and the 360s – is quite high.

---

[35] On this battle, see the detailed treatment in Heckel 2008: 57–65.

The barley price, for example, was shown to range between 1.82 and 7.5 shekels per *kurru*. This pattern of comparatively high volatility applies also to the other commodities not represented in this chapter's figures, although often to a lesser extent. This is not a surprising finding, considering that as the main staple crop barley is particularly prone to larger fluctuations and especially that arable farming is a much less fruitful type of agriculture in terms of output per surface area when compared to date gardening.[36]

It is then an odd finding that the coefficient of variation of barley (0.53) was at a lower level than during the sixth century, when this value amounted to 0.99 (Jursa 2010: 448). This impression is in need of qualification, as this high value is determined by the very high prices (exceeding 10 shekels per *kurru*) prevailing at the end of this century. However, there is also an obvious discrepancy in the coefficient of variation for the densely documented period between the years 573 and 539, which amounted to 0.42 at the very narrow range of a maximum and minimum price of 2.3 and 0.4 shekels per *kurru*, respectively.[37]

This shows once again that statistical values taken by themselves are not necessarily reliable and need to be contextualised. The main difference in the datasets is that in the Neo-Babylonian period the data clusters narrowly around the mean value whereas this is not the case with the widely divergent Late Achaemenid data. However, the scatter band has no influence on the value of the mean, which is both the denominator in the formula to calculate the coefficient of variation as well as an integral part of the formula for the standard deviation, which itself is the numerator in the formula of the CV (coefficient of variation).[38] To concretise by means of a simple example, the mean value of a dataset consisting of two values would be the same if the values were 4 and 4 or 7 and 1. This case is thus a good reminder of the limits of the informative value of conventional gauges and the need to always review in detail the data to be analysed. In the present case, it is less the CV but rather the very wide range of commodity prices that is indicative of imperfect working of the market in the two decades or so between -385 and -366.

[36] In northern Babylonia, the yield of a date garden of 1 hectare amounted on average to 5,328 litres, the yield of a barley field of the same size only to 1,728 litres; at roughly equal caloric value, it has to be noted. See Jursa 2010: 48–53 for a full discussion.
[37] Jursa 2010: 448. The huge difference in the ranges of the years 573–539 and 381–369 is immediately visible when comparing his fig. 8 (448) to our Figure 5.1.
[38] See Feinstein and Thomas 2002: 47–51 for the respective formulas.

The Early Hellenistic Period from the Conquests of Alexander the Great to the Consolidation of the Seleucid Kingdom: The Issue of Monetisation

This period has been repeatedly at the centre of interest of modern research, with the person of Alexander the Great eliciting an abundance of literature since antiquity. The documentation for the decades following Alexander's death until the consolidation of the Seleucid Empire in the huge territory 'from Samarkhand to Sardis', to quote the influential account of Sherwin-White and Kuhrt (1993), is less impressive and varies considerably in quality and quantity. From among Greco-Roman accounts, books 17 to 19 of Diodorus stand out for the wealth of information provided. For Babylonia, important chunks of source material, both archival and historiographical have been analysed and made available in a 2006 congress volume entitled *La transition entre l'empire achéménide et les royaumes hellénistiques* (Briant and Joannès 2006).[39]

Whereas cuneiform documents play an important role in the reconstruction of the controversial chronology of the period,[40] they provide us with little historical information. The most notable exception to this rule is AD -330A+B, giving an account of the battle of Gaugamela as well as some details of Alexander's entry into the city of Babylon. Another interesting scrap of information is a short note inserted into the astronomical section of 11 June 323 reading LUGAL NAM^{MEŠ} – a reference to Alexander's death. This passage is also often referred to in order to point out the sober and emotionless style of the diaries.[41] From the decade between 320 and 311, there is no extant diary at all, leaving us with an unfortunate gap also in the price data. The most important cuneiform source of the period is the so-called Diadochi Chronicle (ABC 10 = BCHP 3). This text originally covered the period between *c.* 320 and 308, but information is preserved only for the years 320–316 and 311–308, and still with gaps. It describes the continuous fighting between the Successors of Alexander the Great for the satrapy of

---

[39] Important contributions to this volume are Joannès 2006, Jursa 2006 and van der Spek 2006a. Note that also the archives referred to in the preceding section on the Late Achaemenid period do not suddenly break off with the Greek conquest but continue for quite some decades into the Hellenistic period.

[40] The chronology followed here is the one suggested by Boiy 2007a, the most complete and convincing attempt thus far. See also the contributions of Anson, Boiy and Wheatley in Heckel, Tritle and Wheatley 2007 as well as Boiy 2000, 2001 and 2002.

[41] For example, in Del Monte 1997: 11. The passage is also discussed by Boiy 2004: 115–17 and Depuydt 1997.

Babylonia from which ultimately Seleucus emerged victoriously.[42] The text gives a very bleak picture of the prevailing circumstances, listing a sequence of battles, slaughter, destruction and requisitions of silver throughout the country. Uniquely for a chronicle of the Hellenistic period, it also mentions a barley equivalent as a means to substantiate the level of dearth in Babylonia: in year eight of King Alexander IV (309/8), 1 shekel of silver only bought 6 litres of barley. This enormously high price finds confirmation in the diaries of the same period, which give 7.5 litres of barley per shekel for April 309. These are the highest equivalent of the whole period covered by the ADs, and it is only during the later Parthian period that such equivalents would reoccur (AD -82).

It has been repeatedly argued that the continuous warfare which in the decades after the death of Alexander the Great took place in Babylonia had major repercussions on Babylonian prices.[43] A brief glimpse at Figure 5.4 shows us that there was indeed a massive price increase during that period. However, there seem to have been economic problems already during Alexander's lifetime, as not only are prices higher already during the 320s compared to the last decades of the Late Achaemenid period – they are back to the rather elevated level of the period 380–360 – but there even occurred a market failure in spring 325 shortly before that year's harvest, when no barley could be found in the city (AD -324B).[44] It was only with the death of Alexander, however, that the situation turns into a veritable crisis without precedence, as can be seen at one glance from the graph plotting the barley price of the last thirty years of the fourth century.[45] The first decade of the third century has been included to show just how large the difference in price was between the stable period after the consolidation of the Seleucid empire and these crisis years.

---

[42] Among the histories of the Hellenistic period, see, e.g., the detailed account of Will 1979[2] and 1982[2] and the relevant sections in vol. VII.i of the *Cambridge Ancient History* (Walbank, Astin, Frederiksen and Ogilvie 1984). More recent (but less exhaustive) works include Shipley 2000 and Anson 2014 (for the years until 281). Boiy 2004: 104–37 provides a history of Babylonia in this period.

[43] Most prominently by van der Spek 2000a: 299–305 and Grainger 1999: 317–18.

[44] See van der Spek and Mandemakers 2003: 528–30 on the interpretation of this and similar passages, against Slotsky 1997a: 22 and *passim*.

[45] Unlike the graphs in the preceding section on the Late Achaemenid period, Figures 5.4 and 5.5 are not on an exponential scale but a third-degree polynomial. The reason for this is very simple: an exponential scale would result in a trend-line moving downwards from a higher point at around 330 to the low prices in the 290s in a one-directional movement at a very low R^2. This form would not account in an adequate manner for the high prices recorded between 323 and 308.

A direct connection between the political history and the movement of the prices seems thus unavoidable. As just mentioned, prices were already rather high in the years 325 and 323, at about the level of the earlier cluster of the Late Achaemenid period and thus oscillating between 3 and 5 shekels per *kurru*. In January and February 322, after a gap of half a year in the documentation, prices were at an unprecedentedly high level of 13–15 shekels per *kurru*. An explanation can be found in the historical circumstances in Babylon after Alexander's death. There was no heir to the throne, and the succession was much disputed. In the end, both Alexander's mentally impaired brother Philipp Arrhidaeus and his yet unborn son with the Sogdian princess Roxana, Alexander (IV), were formally accepted as kings, whereas actual authority was distributed among Alexander's generals.[46] This compromise was, however, contested by the Macedonian infantry under Meleager. As a consequence, the higher ranks, and notably the cavalry under Perdiccas, left the city, cut it off from its hinterland and put it under siege in order to enforce their settlement of the succession. These measures brought success – the rebellion was quelled and Meleager executed – but caused *inopia primum deinde fames* in the city, as according to Quintus Curtius (10 8.12–13) the army cut off grain destined for Babylonia.

A correlation of domestic warfare and high prices in the diaries is also strongly suggested by the events between 310 and 308. The data yields even higher prices of up to 30 shekels for 1 *kurru* of barley (the equivalent of the 6 litres per shekel mentioned the Diadochi Chronicle BCHP 3 = ABC 9, lines r29 and r33), which are to be interpreted against the background of the tenacious military operations by Antigonus the One-Eyed and his son Demetrius, who tried to wrest the satrapy of Babylonia from Seleucus and his general-in-command Nicanor. Some of the military actions and their consequences are described in the chronicle, which for those years specifically refers to repeated plundering of both city and countryside, SAR-*ut* URU *u* EDIN (BCHP 3 = ABC 9, r25 and r38), and to illegal requisitions of an unknown commodity (BCHP 3 = ABC 9, r30). This latter notice responds well to AD -309, which relates requisitions of foodstuffs, dates and possibly also barley. Babylonia was in a desolate state throughout these years: *bikītu u sipdu*, wailing and mourning, are said characterise the country's emotional state.

---

[46] See Will 1979[2]: 19–26 and Boiy 2007a:148. The leading roles were played by a 'triumvirat théorique' (Will) consisting of Craterus, Antipatros and Perdiccas. Note also that documentary sources from both Egypt and Babylonia only mention Philipp in their date formula until his death in 317: van der Spek 2010: 371.

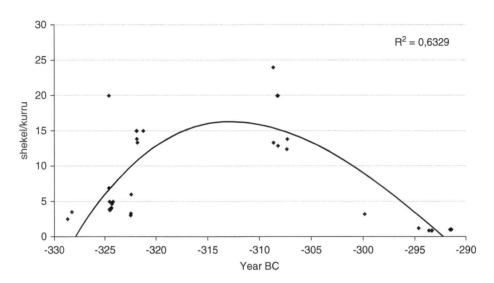

Figure 5.4 Barley prices during the early Hellenistic period, *c.* 330–300

It is unfortunate that the decade between these two price peaks is not covered by any price data at all. There are, however, a few glimpses which allow us to infer that prices were above average throughout the whole early Hellenistic period, though maybe on a more moderate level than during the climaxes of 322 and 310–308. A handful of references attest to military activity in the period between the final acceptance of the outcome of the Babylon conference and the recapture of Babylon by Seleucus and the ensuing conflict against the faction of Antigonus in spring 311. Most of these incidents seem to have been minor in scale or took place mainly outside of the city of Babylon. After the conference at Triparadisus, when Seleucus was installed as satrap of Babylonia, he likely had to remove his predecessor Docimus by military means.[47] A few years later, on his flight from Antigonus, Eumenes spent the winter of 318/17 with a small army in the so-called Carian villages in Babylonia.[48] However, since Seleucus did not grant him any support, he was forced to leave the region early in 317 and turned eastwards towards the Susiane. Spring 317 saw the arrival of Antigonus with his army in Babylonia, but the battles against Eumenes were fought beyond the Zagros mountain range in Paraetacene and Gabiene. In spring 316, Seleucus was forced to leave Babylonia and Antigonus himself took over the office of satrap, but no military encounters between the two

---

[47]　Boiy 2004: 119, with the relevant Classical sources.
[48]　On the presence of Carians in Babylonia according to cuneiform sources, see Waerzeggers 2006.

of them are reported. The political history of the period of Antigonus' rule over Babylon is virtually undocumented, and it is only with the return of Seleucus from his Egyptian exile that the documentation resumes.

Cuneiform sources add interesting details to this period characterised by an uneasy ceasefire interrupted by several flare-ups. According to BCHP 3 (= ABC 10) 33–35, in October 317 the palace in Babylon was captured from someone during some kind of skirmish involving the troops of the kings. These lines are normally interpreted as an episode in the conflict between Eumenes and Seleucus,[49] but it has to be noted that there is no definitive proof that Eumenes ever reached the city or had supporters there. Be that as it may, the passage shows that the silence of the sources may be misleading and that we have to reckon with occasional unrest in the city of Babylon. Finally, the economic circumstances remained precarious throughout the 310s. The Diadochi Chronicle reports a forceful levy of silver in 318 on the orders of Seleucus.[50] Text A2-7 in Stolper 1993a gives proof that the Greek administrators did not hesitate to interfere in the temple economy: in October 314, a disbursal of the substantial amount of 3 minas of silver is made upon the command of a certain Kallinikos to another Greek.[51] The peak of the trend-line at about 314 is thus an artificial outcome of the mathematics rather than historical reality: far from being a period of peaceful stability, the 310s saw occasional outbreaks of bellicose enterprises in Babylonia, most prominently during the campaigns of Eumenes. Consequently, we have to reckon with a price level close to but maybe lower than those of 322 and between 310 and 308, the decisive phase of the warfare between Antigonus and Seleucus for supremacy in the East. The final decades represented in Figure 5.4 show that the economy recovered quickly from this troubled period of the wars of the Successors. Already by 300, the barley price returned to the level between Macedonian conquest and Alexander's death, and in the first decade of the third century, the crisis was definitely overcome: the final consolidation of the Seleucid Empire was reflected in a hitherto unmatched low price level.

Comparison by numbers with the preceding Late Achaemenid period pinpoints the markedly higher price level and volatility of the Early Hellenistic period. Whereas in the former the mean value amounted to 3.37 shekels per *kurru* of barley (70 litres per shekel) with a standard deviation of 1.79, the mean during the Hellenistic period (not including the very low

---

[49] Boiy 2004: 120–1 and 2010.
[50] BCHP 3 (ABC 10), 29–30.
[51] Stolper 1993a: 82–6; see also van der Spek 2000a: 302–3.

Table 5.4. *Commodity prices in the Early Hellenistic period*

Commodity	Mean price (shekels per *kurru*)[a]	Standard deviation
Barley	10.38	7.08
Dates	7.06	3.22
Kasû	0.8	0.4
Cress	13.09	4.56
Sesame	29.55	12.43[b]
Wool	4.11	1.41

Notes: [a] Wool price in shekels per 5 minas.
[b] This value is inflated by the still regular price for sesame in 331. If we were to omit this instance, standard deviation drops to 8.09, with a concomitant rise in the mean to 33.06 shekels per *kurru*.

prices from the beginning of the Seleucid period shown in the figure) was almost three times that value, 10.38 shekels per *kurru*, with a standard deviation of 7.08.[52] Table 5.4 shows that barley constituted no exception to a general pattern of massively inflated and volatile prices.

The differences are impressive: the date price more than trebled from 2.02 to 7.06, and similarly also the price of sesame almost trebled from 9.67 to 29.55 shekels per *kurru*. The cress price almost doubled from 7.06 to 13.06 shekels per *kurru*, and the wool price rose from 1.54 to 4.11 shekels per 5 minas. The only commodity not to show a significant increase in its price (from 0.75 to 0.80 shekels per *kurru*) was *kasû*, a phenomenon which is partly owed to the very high prices of this commodity in 383/2.

The extended warfare of the last quarter or so of the fourth century might, however, not constitute the only reason for the inflationary price movement of that period. P. Temin hypothesised a substantial increase in the monetary supply mainly as a result of the minting of the treasures of the Great Kings looted in the course of Alexander's campaigns as the major factor behind the massive price increase visible in all commodities. It is indeed remarkable that non-vital commodities for which a rather elastic demand can be posited, such as cress (see Figure 5.5), also show a price increase similar in extent to that seen for barley and dates. In his explanatory approach, the treasures captured by Alexander's army – a total of 180,000 talents of silver, according to Strabo (15 3.9) – were minted and put into circulation

---

[52] The CV is also substantially higher than it was in the Late Achaemenid period; 0.7 is a very high result considering the very short period of only thirty years under investigation.

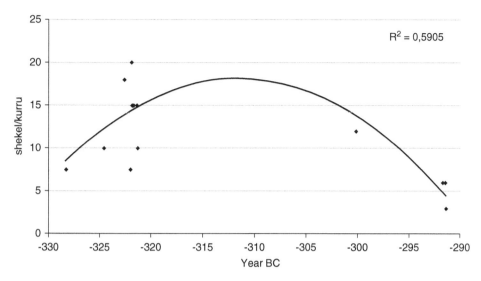

Figure 5.5 Cress prices during the early Hellenistic period, *c.* 330–300

mainly by the Successors, after Alexander's death.[53] The question that arises is thus how much of the price increase was actually due to military activities proper, and how much is better explained by other factors such as an increase in the supply of money.

Gauging the different magnitudes of price increases during comparable episodes of domestic warfare or sedition show the necessity for complementary explanations more clearly. In order to arrive at a plausible conclusion, a variety of factors such as the overall price level of the period investigated, the per cent and absolute change in prices, the duration of the period of high prices and the war campaign, the size of the army (which in addition to the scale of warfare also impacted the demand side as the presence of an army raises demand for food) and so on need to be considered. During the period of the warfare among the Successors, thus between *c.* 323 and 308, the barley price oscillated between 12 and 24 (or even 30, if one were to consider the equivalent given in the Diadochi Chronicle) shekels per *kurru*, with the mean price amounting to 14.35 shekels/*kurru*. This is still higher than the mean price of 10.38 shekels/*kurru* given in Table 5.4, which is significantly deflated by the lower prices prevailing during the 320s. As already noted, the difference from the Late Achaemenid period is considerable. In spite of the extended warfare that troubled the region for almost two decades, prices recovered fast once

[53] Temin 2002: 56. On the monetisation of the Achaemenid treasures see de Callataÿ 1989.

peace was made. In 300, after a gap in the documentation of about eight years, the barley price was back at 3 shekels per *kurru* in the pre-harvest period. This downward trend continued through the early Seleucid period, and the next attestations in the late 290s saw the barley price at below 1 shekel per *kurru*.

The difficulty in assessing this pattern, as so often, is finding source material appropriate for comparison. The reports at our disposal of domestic warfare comparable to the period of the successors in terms of army size and/ or duration, and thus comparable also with regard to potential economic impact, are often not accompanied by adequate price data. This for example is the case with the campaign of Ptolemy III into Syria and Babylonia, which started the Third Syrian War (246–241).[54] However, there are also several cases of correlations between insurrections or warfare in Babylon and rising prices. A prime example is the decade or so between *c.* 240 and 230 (discussed in greater detail in the following section), when the Astronomical Diaries provide us with reports of repeated internal strife involving parts of the army and high officials. Additionally, natural disasters seem to have contributed to the high prices in this period. What is striking is the comparatively small absolute increase in prices: the maximum price during this decade amounted to 6.67 shekels/*kurru* (January 232), compared to a mean price of the Seleucid period of 2.09 shekels/*kurru*. Figure 5.6 shows that throughout the whole period between *c.* 300 and 225, the barley price never exceeded 8 shekels/*kurru*, with outliers usually ranging between 4 and 6 shekels/*kurru*. In the early Hellenistic period, on the other hand, the barley price regularly arrived at a level of 12 or 13 shekels/*kurru* and occasionally could even rise to a level exceeding 20 shekels/*kurru*. In other words, outliers of both the Seleucid and Late Achaemenid periods only ever ranked below the mean price of the quarter century or so between *c.* 325 and 300.

It is not a convincing approach to try to explain these differences exclusively with reference to the duration of the war of the Successors, since during the 230s Babylonia also faced quite an extended crisis period. Nor can it be attributed only to the superior size of the army, as the numbers given by Plutarch in his Life of Demetrius are rather modest, in spite of the fact that generally Greek authors had a tendency to overstate their guesses.[55] Demetrius was sent out in autumn 311 by Antigonus to recapture Babylonia from Seleucus with 15,000 infantry and 4,000 cavalry. Having

[54] On which see most recently Grainger 2010: 153–70. In his discussion, there is no reference to BCHP 11 giving an account of Ptolemy's invasion of Babylonia. The chronicle is published online as Ptolemy III Chronicle (BCHP 11) at www.livius.org/babylonia.html (accessed 21 October 2016).
[55] Plut. *Dem.* 7.2–3; see also Diod. 19 100.3–7.

captured one of the city's citadels, he immediately returns west, leaving Archelaos as commander over only 5,000 infantry and 1,000 cavalry for the siege of the second citadel. Similarly, the reconquest of Babylon by Seleucus was allegedly achieved with 800 infantry and 200 cavalry only.[56] There are no reports with quantifications of the size of the army of Antigonus for his campaigns in Babylonia of 310 and 309. Considering that the resources of what was Alexander's empire were now divided among several competing fractions (Ptolemy, Lysimachus, Seleucus, Cassander and Antigonus), and that Antigonus as *stratēgos* of Asia had a substantial territory to guard, it cannot possibly have been much greater in number than the army at Demetrius' disposal in 311. This was certainly a considerable number of troops but far below the (often inflated) numbers given by various authors for Hellenistic royal armies.[57] According to App. *Syr.* 6.36, 50,000 (of a total of 70,000) of Antiochus III's soldiers were killed in the battle at Magnesia under Sipylos against the Roman army in 190. The total of the royal armies clashing at Raphia (218) amounted to almost 150,000 persons, according to Polybius 5 65, 79 and 82. Regarding the troops of Alexander, Justin 11 12.5 gives the size of the Persian army at Gaugamela with 400,000 foot-soldiers and 100,000 horsemen – a modest number compared to the 800,000 infantry and 200,000 cavalry in Diodorus 17 53.3.

The fact that the price increases during periods of warfare after the early Hellenistic era are much less pronounced, especially in absolute terms, can thus be taken as an indicator that factors other than warfare contributed to the exceptionally high prices in the last quarter of the fourth century. Temin's hypothesis that a steady increase in the monetary supply added to the extent of the inflation presents itself thus as a tempting explanation. However, there are several problems attached to this approach that need to be addressed before further investigation, the first being that it is not clear over what period the silver stocks of the treasury were minted and put into circulation. The estimates of de Callataÿ (1989) give a period of roughly forty years and thus the whole of the period of warfare between the Successors, which would square nicely with the duration of high prices, to which this increased minting activity will have contributed.[58] On the other hand, Grainger (1999: 318) attributes little importance to the silver influx from the Achaemenid treasuries in his explanation of the high prices of the last quarter of the fourth century. In the most recent contribution to

---

[56] Diod. 19 90–91.
[57] The Seleucid army is the subject of an extended study by Bar-Kochva 1976.
[58] Similarly Temin 2002: 56.

this topic, a similar stance was taken by Aperghis, according to whom the coining of the Achaemenid silver left no traces in the Babylonian price data at all, and who argued for a rapid drain of silver from the heartland of the former Achaemenid Empire towards the Mediterranean.[59]

Considering that the main source of expenditure was the armed forces, and that Alexander campaigned with his army in the east for years to come and did not return to Babylonia before early 323, one would *a priori* expect that a major influx of silver should not have taken place before that date, or only slightly earlier with the arrival of advance parties.[60] Le Rider additionally points to substantial financial needs of Alexander beyond military expenses during these years on campaign (city building, court expenses, and more). Of particular interest in his discussion are several passages found in Curtius Rufus and Plutarch which record that mules and camels accompanying the army trek carried substantial amounts of precious metals.[61] On the other hand, one has to consider that soon after the capture of Babylon – the exact point in time is elusive – the city was made the centre of the financial administration of the empire, and that additionally a prolific mint, the first major one operating in the east of the empire, was opened there.[62] Especially during the tenure of office of the notorious squanderer Harpalus between *c.* 327 and 325, one might expect that more silver than was beneficial for the market for basic commodities was put into circulation.

A quantification of the output of the Babylon mint indeed confirms this train of thoughts: according to Le Rider (2003: 318–19), only 1,750 talents of silver were struck during Alexander's lifetime, mainly as tetradrachms, by far the most common denomination of that period. However,

---

[59] Aperghis 2004: 29–30 and 214, especially 30: 'no general increase in prices of an inflationary nature is observed, such as could have been caused by a large influx of gold and silver'. The possibility of inflation is also neglected by Le Rider and de Callataÿ 2006: 233. They envisage structural problems, rather than single events, at the basis of the high prices in the last twenty-five years of the fourth century, but only refer to a potential increase in demand due to continuous army presence.

[60] This presupposition that the Persian treasures were mainly used to pay for army wages is virtually undisputed in modern scholarship, see e.g., Temin 2002: 56; Le Rider 2003: 312; and Bresson 2005: 48. That the army was by far the largest post in the expenditures of the Seleucid kings has also been postulated by Aperghis 2004: 189–205, see also 236–45 for his concept of 'wartime' coinages. See also the interesting assessment of modern European states by de Callataÿ 2000: 337–41. This article is generally a powerful case for warfare as major cost factor throughout history, concluding that 'l'essentiel des monnaies a servi à payer l'armée' (355).

[61] Le Rider 2003: 310–16, in particular 311–12 for the accounts of Curtius and Plutarch.

[62] Bosworth 1988: 245; Le Rider 2003: 270–3; Boiy 2004: 44–5 and 107–10; and Le Rider and de Callataÿ 2006: 30–1. The known financial officers were Asklepiodorus, son of Philon, Antimenes of Rhodes and Harpalus. For increased minting activity in Babylon around 320 see now also van der Spek, Földvári and van Leeuwen 2015.

as he takes into account only extant obverse dies[63] his estimate is certainly too low under the assumption of a per-die productivity of 20,000 coins. Nevertheless, a more sophisticated approach gives an only marginally higher coin output. Based on the treasure of Demanhur (630 tetradrachms using 172 different obverse dies from Babylon), we expect a total number of about 203 obverse dies used in the mint of Babylon in the period between *c.* 324 and 318 according to the Carter method.[64] At an output per die of about 20,000 coins as suggested by de Callataÿ,[65] we arrive at 2,706 talents of silver minted at Babylon, corresponding to about 4 million tetradrachms in these years. At first glance, this is a low amount compared to the alleged total of 180,000 talents (Strabo 15 3.9), but when converted into the metric system, the conclusion that the minting activity of these years is at least part of the explanation for the increased prices seems inevitable. Within six years only, roughly 70 metric tonnes of silver were put into circulation in the form of tetradrachms only. The focus on the increased activity of the mint also provides a good explanation as to why prices started to increase Babylon already in the 320s, during Alexander's lifetime. This approach, it has to be emphasised, is still underestimating actual inflationary tendencies, as it does not even consider smaller denominations and especially uncoined silver in circulation.

The next question is then for how long money was minted in Babylonia at such an elevated level that this might be responsible for increased prices. One certainly has to account for the fact that the Achaemenid treasure was spent in large part in forms other than coinage – one only has to remember Diodorus' description of the sumptuous chariot which was to transport Alexander's body back to Macedonia (18 26.3–28.1) as an instructive example of the many ways in which the looted silver and gold were used. However, there is good evidence that during the reign of Seleucus I (including also the years before his acceptance of the royal title in 305/4) the mints in the eastern part of the empire near or in Babylonia were more productive than

---

[63] He also considers extant dies of dekadrachms and gold staters, which he converts into tetradrachm equivalents; see Le Rider 2003: 318–19.

[64] See the concise description of this method in Esty 1986: 203–4. This method was also employed e.g., in de Callataÿ 1989: 265–6 (with a table of Newell's analysis of the tetradrachms of the Demanhur treasure). Aperghis 2004: 240 (table 11.3) made used of a still more complex method suggested by Esty 1986: 204–27 (also briefly described by Aperghis 2004: 17[(+29)]). In the light of the coins/dies ratio in the Demanhur treasure, the results are essentially the same for both approaches, cf. Esty 1986: 204. As for the date of the issues of the Alexander-type tetradrachms, we follow Le Rider 2003: 297–9.

[65] De Callataÿ 2011: 23. In his earlier papers, De Callataÿ 1989: 271–2 and 2005: 77–8, he suggested a higher ratio of 30,000 coins per obverse die. In that case, the numbers would amount to 4,060 talents, or about 6 million tetradrachms.

under subsequent rulers. As can be seen in Table 5.5, there is quite a discrepancy in the number of annual coin issues particularly from the mints at Babylon, Seleucia-on-the-Tigris, Susa and Ecbatana between Seleucus I and his successors.[66] This can partly be interpreted as resulting from reserves of precious metal still at the disposition of the first ruler of the dynasty, who consequently could mint coinage with a frequency no longer possible for the later kings. The numerous military campaigns of Seleucus I – first the struggle for Babylonia against Antigonus and his son Demetrius, then the campaign into India resulting in a treaty with Chandragupta Maurya and finally his western campaigns culminating in the final defeats of Antigonus at Ipsus 301 and later Lysimachus at Corupedium 281 – also contributed to this pattern. A comparison with the minting activities during the reign of Antiochus III, who similarly spent many years of his reign on campaign, shows that the annual output of the eastern mints was significantly higher during the reign of Seleucus I.

The surprisingly high difference in issues between Seleucus I and Antiochus III thus needs explanation. Firstly, under the later king, the minting system seems to have been less centralised. To the issues in Table 5.5 one has to add notable tetradrachm outputs in Sardis (fourteen issues), Soli (fourteen issues), Tarsus (seventeen issues), the 'Rose' mint, perhaps from Edessa (fourteen issues), the so-called ΔI-mint in southern or eastern Syria (fourteen issues) and especially the 'Uncertain mint 68, in Mesopotamia' (thirty-six issues).[67] Another difference is that Antiochus III inherited from his predecessors a well-established monetary system, whereas at the moment of Seleucus' takeover in 311, coinage based on the Greek standard had just been introduced with the arrival of Alexander's army. Hence, the substantially higher level of coinage issues during the reign of Seleucus I should in part be attributed to an inadequate base supply of money, a factor which gains additional importance when considering the above-average demand of the royal administration for money in order to satisfy its military expenses during the reign of this king.[68] Especially the

---

[66] A methodological caveat is in order here: coin issues are a very imperfect yardstick only and in particular cannot be used to calculate total coin output, for which a full die study would be required. However, such a study is at present not available for Seleucia-on-the-Tigris. We have thus to make do with such an approximation, which follows the model provided by the numismatic study of Houghton 2004 (see especially 74, table 1, listing issues according to geographical region for the Seleucid kings between 246 and 165 (Seleucus II to Antiochus IV)). A similar approach was followed by Aperghis 2004: 216–18 and de Callatay and Le Rider 2006: 219–21.

[67] Houghton and Lorber 2002 II: 152–6.

[68] Aperghis 2004: 245–6 goes as far as hypothesising that in peacetime, coins were struck in such quantity only as to replace money lost by wear and tear by Seleucid kings. Le Rider and de

Table 5.5. *Minting activities of Seleucid kings*

Ruler	Reign	Mint	Number of tetradrachm issues[a]	Issues/year[b]
Seleucus I	311–281	Babylon	46	2.7
		Seleucia-Tigris	128	9.85
		Susa	48	1.6
		Ecbatana	55	1.83
		Antioch-Orontes	6	0.3
		Laodicea-Sea	8	0.4
Seleucus II	246–226	Seleucia-Tigris	7	0.35
		Susa	7	0.35
		Ecbatana	7	0.35
		Antioch-Orontes	14	0.7
Antiochus III	222–187	Seleucia-Tigris	24	0.69
		Susa	18	0.51
		Ecbatana	12	0.48
		Antioch-Orontes	44	1.26
		Laodicea-Sea (?)	21	0.6

Notes: [a] The table was compiled on the basis of the overview in Houghton and Lorber (2002 II: 133–56). In the case of a mint producing different types of tetradrachms, e.g. with Zeus Aetophorus or Zeus Nikephorus on the reverse, the different issues were simply added up. An issue is defined by Houghton and Lorber as coinage 'with unique types, inscriptions, controls and/or control positions' (133). Only issues that were definitely attributed to the respective mints were considered. On the coinage of Seleucus I see also Golenko 1993.
[b] The mint at Babylon closed *c.* 294 (Houghton and Lorber 2002 I: 40), one thus has to reckon with a period of seventeen years (311–294) during which coins were struck at this mint. Afterwards, the atelier moved to Seleucia-on-the-Tigris, to which an active period of thirteen years is assigned for the reign of Seleucus I. The ateliers at both Antioch-on-the-Orontes and Laodicea-on-the-Sea came into the possession of Seleucus I only after the victorious battle at Ipsus in 301.

tetradrachm type depicting Zeus on the obverse and an elephant chariot on the reverse, which with eighty-two issues is by far the most numerous series

Callataÿ 2006: 217–21 warn against such an all-too-schematic assessment of minting practices and emphasise the irregular rhythms of coin issues. However, their own approach, according to which 'on peut présumer que, en temps ordinaire, ils émettaient des espèces seulement quand le besoin s'en faisait sentir' (226) does not *de facto* differ too much from the concept of war- and peacetime issues. They also accept the army as important factor for coin production, but importantly allow for greater flexibility in the analysis of individual issues.

from Seleucia-on-the-Tigris, seems mainly to have served the purpose of monetisation of the new capital city and its environs.[69]

These results support the notion that a period of intense minting activity in the province of Babylonia, which began, according to the chronology of Le Rider, around 324 and continued well into the reign of Seleucus I. This interpretation is congruent with the evidence from the Meydancıkkale treasure, which shows that during the decade 300–290 the larger-scale production of Alexander-type tetradrachms came to an end in correlation with the cessation of warfare among the Successors. It is furthermore striking that the mint at Babylon was one of the most productive mints of tetradrachms according to this treasure.[70] What we do not know, however, are the exact years during which coinage was struck, not to speak of the respective quantities. In the light of the increased minting activity during period of warfare in order to pay for armed troops,[71] important outputs of the Babylonian mint should be dated to the years between 323 and autumn 320 (the arrival of Seleucus, to whom the satrapy was awarded at the conference of Triparadeisus), to 318/17 when Babylonia was invaded by Eumenes and his troops,[72] and to the years of the final battle for Babylon between Seleucus and Antigonus and Demetrius between 311 and 308. Higher minting activity can also be reasonably postulated for 316, when Antigonus returned victoriously with his army from Gabiene to Babylon with 20,000 talents of silver seized in Susa (Diod. 19 55). The sizeable issues of lion staters during the tenure of office of the satrap Mazaeus (330–328),[73] on the

---

[69] According to Houghton and Lorber 2002 I: 52, this type of coinage mainly circulated in Babylonia. An alternative methodology, namely a comparison of extant and estimated obverse dies from Seleucia-on-the-Tigris from the reigns of Seleucus I and Antiochus III would possibly yield a more accurate result in relation to total output. However, as the numbers found in the secondary literature vary to a considerable extent such an exercise should ideally start with an exact assessment of both extant obverse dies and extant coins, which clearly lies beyond the scope of the present work. In general, the information found in recent secondary literature does not point to fundamental changes to the results here obtained. For the reign of Antiochus III, Aperghis (2004: 239–40 and table 11.3) refers to a figure of forty-nine extant obverse dies from Seleucia-on-the-Tigris, based on a 1993 count by Le Rider; Houghton 2004: 77 has sixty-nine obverse dies (see also 53[(17)]) for that mint under the same ruler. For the reign of Seleucus I, the only count available to me was Newell 1938, which gives seventy-three extant obverse dies. In the light of the very low ratios of obverse dies to reverse dies and obverse dies to specimens, and accounting for discoveries made since his study, this number is most likely to have increased considerably.

[70] Le Rider and de Callataÿ 2006: 89–92.

[71] Houghton 2004: 52–4 and Aperghis 2004: 236–42; similarly de Callataÿ 2000.

[72] BCHP 3, 29–30 speaks indeed of a forceful levy of silver in September/October 318. Van der Spek in his completion of the line at livius.org hypothesises that it was destined for army payments.

[73] On his coinage see Le Rider 2003: 274–6.

other hand, are less problematic to date, as is the period of intense minting in the city of Babylon shortly before and shortly after Alexander the Great's death (*c.* 324–318).

The closing date of the Babylon mint in or around 294 is telling as it corresponds to the shift of the imperial centre of gravity towards the Mediterranean and the tetrapolis around Antioch-on-the-Orontes. This event is, however, unlikely to have caused a negative monetary shock as the city was from that moment on provided with coinage from Seleucia-on-the-Tigris. A coin hoard from the city of Uruk shows that the mint at Seleucia quite likely provided the whole of the satrapy of Babylonia with all kinds of denominations, including bronze coinage.[74] Such a major mint in a provincial centre is by no means unusual in the Seleucid Empire.[75]

This intense minting activity very likely exerted inflationary pressures on prices in Babylon, thus contributing to the period of high prices. There are, however, also problems with this approach, the major one being the suddenness of the increase. The prices of all the different commodities shoot up immediately after Alexander's death in June 323 to an unprecedented level. This is of course not what one would expect in a scenario of a steadily increasing money supply. The barley price doubled in the immediate aftermath of Alexander's death (June/July 323) from 3.33 to 6 shekels per *kurru* of barley – both certainly high values but in the general range of prices in the mid-320s – and skyrocketed soon afterwards (January 322) to values of 13 and more shekels/*kurru*. This pattern holds equally true for other commodities, though as so often on a less impressive scale: wool doubles from 1 to 2 shekels per 5 minas between June 325 and December 323. The price of cress oscillated around 15 shekels in the first year after Alexander's death (with one low outlier of 7.5 shekels/*kurru* in winter 323, rising back to 15 shekels by February 322), which likewise means a doubling of the Late Achaemenid mean of 7.05 shekels/*kurru*. Dates show a more peculiar pattern and seem to have risen in two distinct stages. They first about doubled from a price between 2 and 4.5 shekels per *kurru* in the early to mid-320s to values between 7 and 9 shekels in the late 320s, and rose even further to levels of 11 to 12 shekels/*kurru* in 309. Again, the scarcity of data often prevents us from seeing more clearly. Sesame was sold at about 5 shekels/*kurru* in the

---

[74] Leisten 1986, especially his conclusion (336) of a 'fast vollständigen Abhängigkeit Orchois von der Münzstätte in Seleukeia'. For the reading Orcha instead of the more common Orchoi see van der Spek 1987: 73[(+29)].

[75] Aperghis 2004: 214–16; Le Rider and de Callataÿ 2006: 64–5.

late 330s; after an unfortunate gap the price in winter 323/2 had risen sixfold to 30 shekels/*kurru*.

The most plausible scenario for the years between *c.* 330 and 300 sees a combined impact of all three relevant factors, supply, demand and monetisation level. In addition to being ravaged by armed conflict on various scales at an almost yearly rate, Babylonia saw a massive increase in demand once Alexander's army returned from its eastern campaign, and it stayed at an elevated level for much of the following two decades as various generals fought for supremacy, as well as a concomitant influx of silver on a large scale. Against this background, it is easily understandable that the unstable political situation after the death of Alexander the Great and especially the repeated flaring up of hostilities between various fractions exerted particularly strong pressure on the market. The result was that prices soared to unprecedented heights, which in the decades and centuries to come were hardly ever reached again. In the following sections, I expand further on the topic of price increases in periods of warfare and attempt a rough estimate of the magnitude of the impact of the factor peculiar to this period, namely monetisation on a larger scale, once the average increase of prices during episodes of warfare in period documented by our dataset has been established.

The Early Seleucid Period, Seleucus I to Seleucus III, *c.* 305/4–223: The Issue of Outliers

The history of the first eighty years of the Seleucid Empire is not easily reconstructed.[76] The vast territory included culturally very diverse regions, stretching from the Hellenised coastal regions of Asia Minor to Babylonia with its time-honoured local culture, and further still, deep into the steppes of central Asia. We do not have adequate source documentation for all of these regions at our disposal. The works of Greco-Roman writers, such as Justin's epitome of the work of Pompeius Trogus, Appian's *Syriakē* and the very fragmentary later books (Book 20 onwards) of Diodorus Siculus, are important in that they provide us with a rough framework of Seleucid history. But in general, their focus is on the western regions of the empire only and in particular on the (more often than not hostile) interactions

---

[76] For accounts of the political history see, e.g., the relevant sections in Will 1979² and 1982² and Shipley 2000: 271–312. For early Seleucid Babylonia see Boiy 2004: 137–54, see also van der Spek 2010. For more conceptual approaches see Bikerman 1938, Sherwin-White and Kuhrt 1993 and Capdetrey 2007.

with the Ptolemies, the smaller dynasties in Asia Minor and with Rome. With the failure of Antigonus the One-Eyed to wrest control over Babylon and the provinces further to the east from Seleucus and his consequent return to the west in 308, Babylonia disappears from the focus of Greek and Roman historiographers. For many events, nothing is known beyond the mere fact that they happened. To give just one example, even such a well-known episode as the foundation of the new capital city Seleucia-on-the-Tigris cannot be dated with desirable precision.[77]

For Babylonia, this scarcity of information is to a certain extent compensated by the Hellenistic chronicle series (BCHP).[78] These documents shed light for example on the activities of Antiochus I in the city of Babylon during his reign as crown prince and vice-regent in the east (294–281). We see him repeatedly participating in cultic activities in Babylonian temples, organising the clearance of the rubble of the Esangila by means of elephants or giving orders to resettle the Greek population of Babylon in the newly founded city of Seleucia-on-the-Tigris. Another recently discovered tablet, BCHP 11, narrates with considerable detail the war campaign of Ptolemy III into Babylonia, previously known only by means of very brief accounts and boastful inscriptions of Ptolemy himself.[79] Equally valuable is some of the historical information gleaned from the Astronomical Diaries. The best-known document is AD -273B, which provides us in its historical section with an account of the preparations for the First Syrian War fought against the Ptolemies.[80]

This tablet is not only of great importance because the Classical sources are almost completely silent on this conflict. What is more, it also narrates measures undertaken in the course of the war preparations that were bound to have an impact on Babylonian prices: lines r30/1 specify the requisition of 'much silver, clothing, valuables and equipment' from the cities of Seleucia-on-the-Tigris and Babylonia alongside the sending of twenty elephants from Bactria for the royal army in Syria. These measures were accompanied by – or possibly even caused – a scarcity of precious metal (silver) resulting in purchases being carried out in Greek bronze coins, or

---

[77] There is a generic agreement on the last decade of the fourth century, cf. Boiy 2004: 135. For example, van der Spek 2010: 374 gives 'around 305' as approximate foundation date.

[78] This corpus is edited online as BCHP by I. Finkel and R. van der Spek on www.livius.org/babylonia.html (accessed 21 October 2016). See also van der Spek 2006a for a commented edition of BCHPs 5, 6 and 8.

[79] None of the accounts (e.g., App. *Syr.* 65), including Ptolemy's own inscriptions (such as the Adoulis inscription OGIS 54), give any detail as regards the precise course of events.

[80] On the perpetual conflicts between the Seleucids and the Ptolemies see Grainger 2010, on the First Syrian War see especially 81–6.

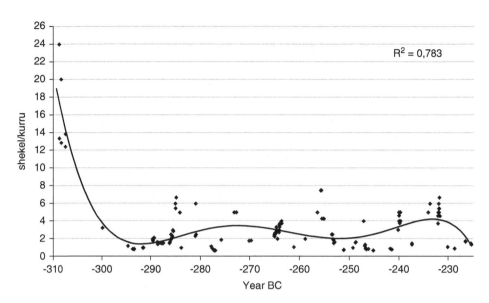

Figure 5.6 Barley prices in the earlier Seleucid period, *c.* 300–225

'copper coins of Ionia' (r33) in the words of the Babylonian author of the diary. AD -273B furthermore yields price data which indeed shows a strong increase in the prices for barley and cress, but not for the other commodities. Barley stood at 5 shekels/*kurru* in both November 274 and April 273, hence at about two and a half times the price prevailing during the 270s, which usually ranged below 2 shekels/*kurru* (see Figure 5.6). Similarly cress ranged far above its average price during the same time. Indeed, the most notable outliers of the whole dataset for this commodity date to winter 274/3, when the price stood at 22.5 shekels/*kurru* (as with barley, the peaks date to the months of November 274 and April 273), compared to a mean price of 6.19 shekels/*kurru*. [81]

The precise cause of this peculiar pattern is disputed in the scholarly literature. Whereas Del Monte attributes the pattern in the barley price to a bad harvest and allows only for a minimal role of the war fought in Syria, van der Spek explains the non-occurrence of the expected deflationary effect of silver requisition by the contemporaneous confiscation of land (and the harvest of this land) alluded to in lines r34–8. [82] This latter explanatory approach – a deflationary effect of withdrawal of silver from

---

[81] The extended period of time under discussion and the elevated number of outliers and oscillating price levels in the dataset justify fifth- and sixth-degree polynomial trend lines in the following sections.

[82] Del Monte 1997: 28–31 and van der Spek 2000b: 305–7.

circulation being offset by a decrease in supply – is certainly tempting but also problematic. Above all, we have no indication as to the surface area of the land to be confiscated. It is more likely that we are dealing with a case similar to the dispute discussed earlier between the royal administration and the Šamaš temple (of Sippar or Larsa) in 308/7 concerning temple land. Such an affair can hardly be expected to have had any kind of impact on prices.

In the light of the uncertainties of the previous interpretations focussing on the supply situation of barley, we suggest setting the focus on demand. There is one factor that has hitherto not received due consideration and this is that fact that the imperial army – including contingents from regions as far away as Bactria – was mustered in the city of Babylon (AD -273B, r32). This military conscription is likely to have caused a boost in the demand of not necessarily all commodities, but especially cereals (thus barley), providing us with a simple explanation of the partial price increase. The passage describing the requisitions (AD -273B, r30–2) is thus best interpreted as referring to an appropriation by the royal administration of bullion from Babylonian citizens and more importantly temples, the silver being used to cover army expenses. The soldiery supplied itself partly while still in Babylonia; barley and also cress were, to judge from the price increase, acquired by the troops as travel provisions for the journey into Syria.[83]

This approach has much to commend to it. The non-occurrence of a price increase in commodities other than barley and cress can be explained by preference, different supply situations and even dietary habits (hence a comparatively small increase in demand for dates and *kasû*). An additional advantage of this demand-centred approach is that we no longer need to postulate a large-scale siphoning off of silver and other precious metals away from Babylonia and into Syria, which in theory should have diminished prices of all commodities in more or less (depending on different demand elasticities and similar factors) equal measure – a phenomenon which failed to occur.[84] The hypothesis of a decrease in the silver supply in Babylonia is also difficult to reconcile with the fact that throughout the reign of Antiochus I, Seleucia-on-the-Tigris seemed to remain an exceptionally productive mint of the empire. This mint alone put into circulation eighteen issues of the tetradrachm type showing the ruler's portrait on the obverse and Apollo seated on the *omphalos*

[83] Incidentally, these are the commodities disbursed as travel rations (*şidītu*) by Babylonian temple households in the sixth century (Janković 2008).

[84] Van der Spek 2000a: 306–7 argues for such a scarcity of silver mainly on the basis of AD -273B, r33 mentioning 'copper coins of Ionia', but see below.

on the reverse, and an additional five issues of drachms of the same type.[85] This higher minting rate at Seleucia is exactly the scenario one would expect as a consequence of the presence of the army in 274/3. Such a correlation has been shown by A. Houghton[86] for the campaigns of Antiochus III, when both the suppression of the revolt of Molon and the passing of the army through Babylonia during Antiochus III's *anabasis* into the Upper Satrapies triggered minting activity at Seleucia. All this evidence thus suggests strongly that there was no general scarcity of silver in Babylonia during the gathering of the army and other preparations for the First Syrian War. It is even possible that the prices of commodities already in high demand were additionally inflated as a result of to above-average minting activity.

As for the enigmatic 'copper coins of Ionia' it has to be noted that bronze coinage was already struck in Seleucia-on-the-Tigris during the reign of Seleucus I, in the first years of the third century.[87] Almost all of the bronze coinage found in the southern city of Uruk dating to the third and to the first half of the second century was minted in the atelier of Seleucia. It was only from the reign of Antiochus (IV?) onwards and especially in the Parthian period that Uruk minted its own small denominations.[88] As far as this limited evidence allows us to see, bronze coins from Seleucia circulated throughout Babylonia and it is thus quite likely that the city of Babylon also – located considerably closer to Seleucia than Uruk and without its own mint after 294/3 – was provided with coins from the mint in Seleucia. Bronze coinage was thus by no means a completely unknown phenomenon

[85] Houghton and Lorber 2002 I: 113–14 and II: 141. Although other cities had a comparable output in terms of different issues (Laodicea-by-the-Sea, Sardis), none of them could, according to Houghton and Lorber (2002 I: 113 and 139), compete with Seleucia-on-the-Tigris in total volume and range of circulation of its coins. Note again that the number of coin issues is not the most reliable indicator of total output of a given mint, but in the absence of die studies of Seleucia-on-the-Tigris remains the only viable means of obtaining a rough estimate.

[86] Houghton 2004: 53–4 identifies four distinct periods of minting activity, all of which can be connected to military campaigns. A telling hoard is the one listed in Houghton and Lorber 2002 II: 121–2 as 'Findspot unknown, 2003'.

[87] Between *c.* 300 and 296 in the so-called 'first workshop', see Houghton and Lorber 2002 I: 56–7. Another mint tentatively located by Houghton and Lorber in Babylonia ('Uncertain mint 8') also produced bronze coinage under Seleucus I but not the mint operating in the city of Babylon (which was in any case closed around 294): see Houghton and Lorber 2002 I: 51. Also all the other larger eastern mints (Susa, Ecbatana) produced bronze coinage under Seleucus I: see Houghton and Lorber 2002 II: 133–9.

[88] Leisten 1986: 316–30 for the Seleucid coins (337–51 for the activity of the Uruk/Orcha mint). The hoard contains also a handful of bronze coins minted at Susa from the reigns of Antiochus III, Seleucus IV and Antiochus IV. However, coins from Seleucia are clearly in the majority. From the reign of Antiochus IV, we have two *chalkoi* from Seleucia and one *chalkos* and one *hemichalkos* from Susa, as well as one *hemichalkos* from Uruk. The attribution of the latter to the reign of Antiochus IV is questionable, Houghton and Lorber (2003 II: 74) prefer Antiochus VII, a solution which lowers the beginning date of the Uruk bronze issues to Alexander I Balas. There is no bronze coinage found in the city of Babylon.

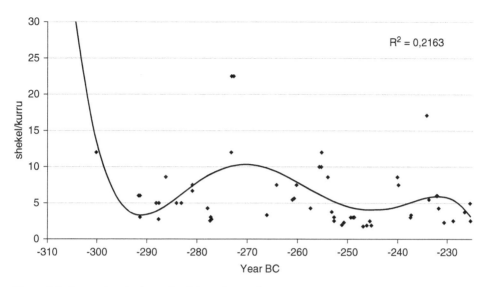

Figure 5.7 Cress prices in the earlier Seleucid period, *c.* 300–225

in Babylonia in the early Seleucid period although initially its use might have been largely confined to the Greco-Macedonian segment of the population as a means of payment.

The possible background to the comment of the author of the diary –as well as the reference to silver being sent to Transpotamia in the same diary – might thus be that in a period of 'high demand', or, less euphemistically, requisitions of precious metals, the Babylonian urban elites and the temples were also increasingly encouraged, or perhaps rather forced, to use and accept bronze coinage in commercial transactions. Whether the events narrated in the diary discussed here – especially the hypothesised confiscation of arable land in lines r36–8 – can be interpreted as part of the administrative reforms of Antiochus I, which were undertaken at precisely the same time, 37/38 SE (275–273), and which are visible so far only in the documentation of Uruk, must remain speculation, but is a certainly tempting scenario.[89]

Concerning the general price level of the period under discussion, it is often stated that the Seleucid epoch was an era of low prices in Babylon.[90] Although this view is essentially correct, it still needs to be modified. The

[89] On this reform see Doty 1977: 308–35, especially 330 for the possibility of a connection between the First Syrian War and the introduction of new taxes (*andrapodōn, epōnion*). See also Van der Spek 2000a: 306.

[90] See the succinct statement in van der Spek 2010: 381: 'The Seleucid period seems to have been a fairly prosperous period in comparison with the preceding period of Alexander and his immediate aftermath (330–300) and the succeeding Parthian period as far as the diaries go (141–61).' Similarly, Grainger 1999: 315 speaks of a high standard of living for the Seleucid period.

Table 5.6. *Commodity prices in the earlier Seleucid period*

Commodity	Mean price (shekels per *kurru*)[a]	Standard deviation
Barley	2.57	1.63
Dates	2.25	0.88
Kasû	0.93	0.73
Cress	6.19	4.84
Sesame	9.90	5.88
Wool	1.84	1.39

Note:[a] Wool price in shekels per 5 minas.

mean price of barley is at 2.57 shekels/*kurru* indeed significantly lower than in the preceding periods (during the Late Achaemenid period that value stood at 3.37 shekels/*kurru*), but for the other commodities, the picture is less straightforward. Dates, for example, cost on average 2.25 shekels/ *kurru*, which is considerably below the mean price of the Early Hellenistic period, but still above the value of the Late Achaemenid period of 2.02 shekels/*kurru*. *Kasû* similarly stood at a mean of 0.86 shekels/*kurru* and was thus slightly more expensive than during the Late Achaemenid period (0.75 shekels/*kurru*), as was sesame (9.90 compared to 9.67 shekels/*kurru* in the Late Achaemenid period). Similarly, wool was slightly less expensive in the Late Achaemenid period (1.54 compared to 1.84 shekels/5 minas in the first three quarters of the third century). Only cress with a mean of 6.19 shekels/*kurru* was cheaper in the period *c.* 300–225 than during the Late Achaemenid period (7.05 shekels/*kurru*).

It was thus mainly for barley and cress that the first seventy-five years of the Seleucid period constituted an era of low prices. Dates were as expected cheaper than barley, but the margin between the mean values of these two commodities had narrowed from 1.35 shekels/*kurru* in the Late Achaemenid period (and about 3 shekels/*kurru* in the last quarter of the fourth century) to 0.32 shekels/*kurru* between *c.* 300 and 225. It was only from the last decade of the third century onwards that the date price would return to a level more pronouncedly below the price of barley. This drop in the date price seems to constitute a return to the normal relationship rather than a surprising change.[91] Figure 5.17 comparing the price movements

---

[91] This finding is interesting because it sheds new light on an ongoing discussion in scholarship concerning the reasons for this sustained decrease in the date price, on which see, e.g.,

of barley and dates during the whole of the Seleucid period (*c.* 300–140) shows furthermore that during the first twenty years or so of the third century, dates were in fact on average more expensive than barley. This unusual finding can be explained by the fact that the date price recovered from the ravages of the wars of the Successors only progressively. Orchards destroyed (and also those abandoned) during these decades needed to be replanted, and it takes several years for a date palm to be fully productive.[92] Grainger (1999: 318) spoke of a delayed price decrease for dates, which according to him took place in the last quarter of the third century. However, this is not the whole story, since dates already in the first half of the third century were three times cheaper when compared to the Early Hellenistic period (*c.* 330–300). After these troubled decades, the price level fell again close to the Late Achaemenid level: the mean price of that period of 2.02 shekels/*kurru* aligns very well with that of the first half of the Seleucid period, which amounted to 2.25 shekels/*kurru*. The importance of date horticulture in and around Babylon during the Late Achaemenid period is unclear, but at least during the long sixth century northern Babylonia saw an intensification of agricultural production manifesting itself in a switch from extensive agriculture (barley production) to intensive horticulture (date gardening) in northern Babylonia. This practice is best attested in the town of Sippar, located some 30 kilometres north of Babylon.[93] Judging from the above and from the development of the price relationship between barley and dates, the same situation prevailed after our documentary sources thin out during the reign of Xerxes. However, the state of the documentation at our disposal does not allow us to investigate this question in greater depth. In any case, the Esangil archive from Babylon and the Brewers' archive from Borsippa attest to the ongoing prominent role of dates as a staple in the temple economy.[94]

A point of interest is that in spite of the lower general level of the date price, the lowest date prices were higher than the lowest barley prices in this

---

Aperghis 2004: 83–4, especially his fig. 5.6. This issue is treated more exhaustively in the following section on the latter half of Seleucid reign over Babylonia.

[92] It takes a date palm at least five to six years to bear fruit for the first time and even longer to be fully productive, see Volk 2003–5: 290–2; also Streck 2004: 263–74.

[93] Jursa 2010: 322–60. As the map of the Sippar countryside in Jursa 2010: 323 (fig. 4) shows, several estates of the Sipparean Šamaš temple were located halfway between Sippar and Babylon, or even closer to the latter city. Considering the general vicinity and the good connections via waterways (most prominently via the Euphrates) of the two places, it is certainly wiser to consider them one unified economic space rather than speaking of imports from Sippar into Babylon.

[94] Hackl 2013: 476–591 on the Brewers' archive.

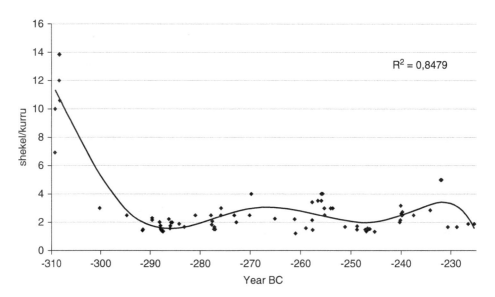

Figure 5.8 Date prices in the earlier Seleucid period *c.* 300–225

period, as can be seen in Figure 5.9 (taken from van Leeuwen and van der Spek 2014). The barley price could drop to a level below the 1 shekel/*kurru* mark – there are twenty such very low prices attested, the lowest of which amounts to 0.67 shekels/*kurru* in 278 – whereas the date price never fell below 1.2 shekels/*kurru*. This phenomenon explains the greater volatility of the barley price, and is a reflection of the fact that barley as the preferred main staple crop was particularly inelastic in demand. If the price of dates drops below a certain threshold, a demand shift towards the preferred commodity barley can be expected, but vice versa, no such substitution effect takes place.[95] The CV of barley for the period *c.* 300–225 with a value of 0.63 is indeed much higher than that of dates (0.39).

Figure 5.8 shows that dates indeed were less prone to producing outliers as compared to barley. After the very high prices during the period of warfare between the diadochi, the date price never attained a level above 5 shekels/*kurru* – this is markedly different from the barley data. The most notable outlier in the dataset of date prices, 5 shekels/*kurru*, dates to the winter of 233/2.

This point in time coincides with a period of high barley prices between *c.* 240 and 230, with a maximum price of 6.67 shekels/*kurru* in January 232. These years can be shown to be correlated to a period of both political unrest and natural disasters. The Classical sources are completely silent on

[95] See Huijs, Pirngruber and van Leeuwen 2015: 131 and fig. 7.2 for an illustration.

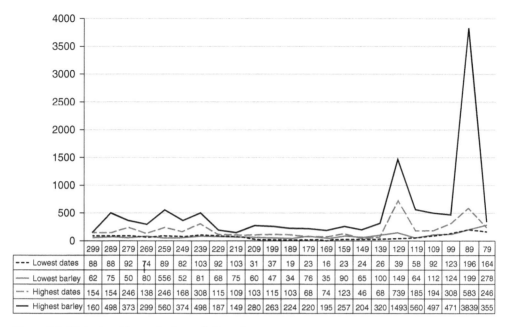

	299	289	279	269	259	249	239	229	219	209	199	189	179	169	159	149	139	129	119	109	99	89	79
--- Lowest dates	88	88	92	74	89	82	103	92	103	31	37	19	23	16	23	24	26	39	58	92	123	196	164
—— Lowest barley	62	75	50	80	556	52	81	68	75	60	47	34	76	35	90	65	100	149	64	112	124	199	278
—·· Highest dates	154	154	246	138	246	168	308	115	109	103	115	103	68	74	123	46	68	739	185	194	308	583	246
—— Highest barley	160	498	373	299	560	374	498	187	149	280	263	224	220	195	257	204	320	1493	560	497	471	3839	355

Figure 5.9 Highest and lowest barley and date prices

Babylon in this period, but the diaries provide us with several glimpses into the events in Babylon during those years.[96] The impression conveyed by these reports is one of a country in troubled times, afflicted by various difficulties: repeatedly, fighting in the city is mentioned (ADs -237, -234A, -30A+B? and -229A): for example, in September/October 235 it is explicitly stated that a general revolted from the central authority (AD -234A, 13). The royal palace was also somehow directly involved in one of these episodes (AD -229A), and one of these occurrences was accompanied by an elevated mortality rate (AD -237). Additionally, natural disasters aggravated the situation. A locust invasion is mentioned for 238 (but cannot be correlated directly to a specific price bump), and in spring 234 the country seems to have been afflicted by a severe drought which was followed by a 'great flood' in winter 233/2. Although none of these events can be directly identified as a cause for the above-average prices, it is highly likely that an interplay of all the factors listed above had some repercussion in the price data.

Not only barley was afflicted by the high prices, all other commodities also exhibit a peak price two or three times above the mean. Sesame cost

---

[96] Van der Spek 2006b: 298–301 provides a succinct summary of the events from the reign of Seleucus II (246–226), and notes *en passant* (301) the above-average barley prices prevailing after 239.

Table 5.7. *Commodity prices during the 230s*

Commodity	Mean price (shekels per *kurru*)[a] (Early Seleucid period)	Peak price (230s)
Barley	2.57	6.67
Dates	2.25	5
Kasû	0.93	1
Cress	6.19	17.14
Sesame	9.90	30
Wool	1.85	1.67

Note:[a] Wool price in shekels per 5 minas.

30 shekels/*kurru* in March 232, and frequently arrived at values of 20 to 22.5 shekels/*kurru* in the period between 238 and 233, compared to a mean price of 9.90 shekels/*kurru*. Equally, the cress price amounted to 17.14 shekels/*kurru* in October 235, a value almost three times its mean value (6.19) in the first three quarters of the third century. And, as argued above, the date price in winter 233/2 also amounted to 5 shekels/*kurru* and hence to more than double the mean of that commodity in the period 300–225. The enduring political crisis – or maybe rather a series of unconnected revolts – in interplay with natural disasters seems thus to have put strains on the supply of almost all commodities recorded in the ADs, with the exception of the notoriously stable wool prices. To judge from the dates of the price peaks, the second half of the decade was a particularly precarious period.

The relatively elevated number of outliers immediately visible in particular in Figure 5.6, which shows barley prices, conveys the impression that Babylonia during the Seleucid period was repeatedly afflicted by food crises.[97] Rather than constituting distinct peaks caused by specific factors, some of these summit prices can be more accurately described as extended periods of market instability (with occasional moments of relief) during which exogenous shocks had particularly severe impacts. The crisis period of the 230s in particular, but also the high prices in the mid-250s, are best interpreted in such terms. Such an approach takes better account of the longer-term

[97] Van der Spek 2014 lists seven periods of high barley prices for the half century between *c.* 280 and 230. This aligns remarkably well with the finding of Földvári, van Leeuwen and Pirngruber 2011 that throughout the whole period for which the ADs provide us with prices (*c.* 400–60), famines occurred approximately every seven years.

consequences of exogenous shocks in the region, such as higher prices in the ensuing harvest year also, caused by the phenomenon of autocorrelation: crop failure not only diminishes the availability of foodstuffs but equally of seed-corn, thereby increasing the chances of a smaller than usual harvest in the following year too. According to the economist Karl G. Persson (1999: 61), 'high autocorrelation is a property typical of almost all types of prices series'. In combination with the overall low level of consumption and the lengthy period taken for prices to return to normal,[98] these findings point to endemic problems in the supply of basic commodities.

On the other hand, during periods of relative political stability (and in the absence of other price-driving forces such as natural disasters), prices could also stay stable at fairly low levels, as happened for example in the early 270s or the late 240s. Slotsky's (1997a: 105) conclusion that 'the long-term trend in the prices of the six commodities … during the Seleucid period … is clearly downward' is thus in need of qualification. The trend-lines exhibit a decidedly more complex pattern than a universal downward trend. Already during the 290s, prices were at their lowest, and all commodities represented in preceding figures (barley, dates, sesame) show a first trough during this decade. The subsequent decades show a pattern of considerable price swings, with peaks in the barley data in the late 270s, the mid-250s and throughout the 230s. It is notable that date and sesame prices (Figure 5.9) follow the general pattern of barley, showing prices clearly above average during the latter two episodes.

The period of high prices during the 250s is also exhibited by the data for *kasû*, but this commodity seems not to have been afflicted to a significant extent by the crisis of the 230s, during which prices remained stable at a fairly low level, between 0.67 and 1 shekel/*kurru*. The two major peaks in the *kasû* price data, which date to November 301 and April 288, can not be connected to any known potentially disruptive incident (nor is it plausible to hypothesise one in the light of the fact that the price for both barley and dates was at a more than moderate level of 1.5 and 1.43 shekels/*kurru* respectively).

Overall, these findings support the notion of more general food crises afflicting the country than mere harvest failures, although these latter events also have to be reckoned with, despite the fact that (or especially because) they are never explicitly mentioned in the ADs.[99] A completely different

---

[98] Van der Spek and van Leeuwen 2014b.

[99] There are, however, occasional references to crop diseases, e.g., in AD -122, 8: 'That year, *samānu* seized the barley during the harvest' (ADART III, 291). The impact in this particular

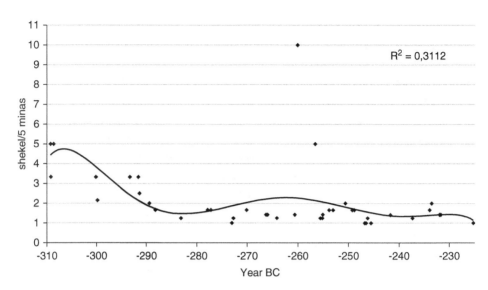

Figure 5.10 Wool prices in the earlier Seleucid period, *c.* 300–225

pattern in this period is exhibited by wool prices. Figure 5.10 shows that, unlike the other commodities discussed so far, this commodity was not, by and large, affected by any of the shortages driving up commodity prices.

Quite to the contrary, wool prices recovered even more slowly than those for dates and indeed show a fairly stable decline over time with minor fluctuations. Before 290, prices were persistently above a mark of 2 shekels of silver per 5 minas, whereas afterwards prices oscillated between 1 and 2 shekels/5 minas. This means that wool, unlike food commodities, did not participate in the considerable downswing which took place after *c.* 300. It is tempting to follow the model provided by date prices and hypothesise that after the protracted warfare which took place in the three decades after Alexander the Great's death, the number of ovine livestock was depleted to some extent. Consequently, wool prices needed quite some time to recover fully. An additional factor in the slow recovery might be attributed to the fact that in the Neo-Babylonian and Achaemenid period, the centre of wool production in Babylonia was Uruk in southern Babylonia.[100] If these circumstances did not change significantly in the (largely undocumented) Late Achaemenid period, the disruption of the network of trade

case seems to have negligible, the barley equivalent was above the level of the preceding years. In an earlier instance (AD -346) an occurrence of crop disease might have aggravated the effects of a locust invasion; see Pirngruber 2014.

[100] Jursa 2005b; Kleber 2008: 237–54; and Kleber in Jursa 2010: 595–616.

and commerce of the earlier period might additionally have had repercussions in the price data.

The only outliers in the wool dataset in the early Seleucid period (easily discernible in the figure) date to a very short period between October 261 (10 shekels per 5 *minas*) and May 257 (5 shekels per 5 *minas*), and, interestingly, there is not a single price extant between these two attestations. As far as the sparse documentation allows us to see, other commodities do not exhibit particularly high prices in this period. Barley, for example, stood at moderate 2 shekels/*kurru* in the pre-harvest period 259 (January/February), with the date price amounting to 1.59 shekels/*kurru* at the same time. For 262, an Astronomical Diary does report warfare in Babylonia (AD -261B), but it is very unlikely that this event caused only the wool price to rise, while the prices of both dates and barley, which is clearly the commodity most prone to fluctuations caused by exogenous impacts, remained stable at a level below average.

Summarising, one can say that prices in the first seventy-five years of Seleucid rule over Babylonia stabilised rather quickly after the havoc wrought by the wars of the Successors and on average levelled off below the Late Achaemenid values. The price data of dates and wool followed a very distinct pattern, showing a slower recovery than other commodities. Regarding wool, the particularly low level of volatility and the exemption from exogenous shocks affecting both barley and dates are notable. The other non-staple commodities, cress and sesame, on the other hand could be shown to have been affected by the periods of high staple crop prices in the mid-250s and the 230s. Moreover, and contrary to what one would expect, these non-essential commodities experienced on occasion stronger price rises than the staple goods barley and dates: the peak price for barley in the 230s was about two and a half times the average and dates did not even double in price, whereas for both cress and sesame the highest price in this decade was around three times the mean.

A general weakening of market integration – a failure to efficiently balance supply and demand – during these periods is the most plausible explanation of this pattern. Also taking into account the often substantial duration of these periods of higher prices, we can thus make the case for more ample ramifications of politically (or ecologically, etc.) troubled periods than mere supply shocks causing subsistence crises or famine. Also, natural variation in the harvest outcome always has to be taken into account.

A final consideration concerns the gaps in our knowledge: potentially strongly disruptive episodes such as the invasion of Babylonia by Ptolemy III in 246 are not accompanied by any price data. This should serve as a

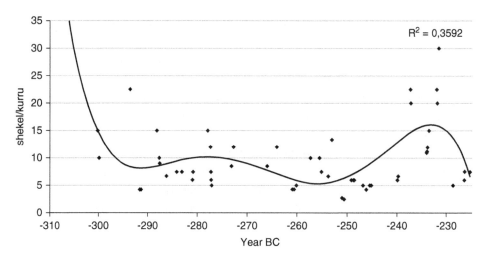

Figure 5.11 Sesame prices in the earlier Seleucid period *c.* 300–225

reminder that the trend-lines in our graphs are thus only of heuristic value
rather than conveying historical truth. Considering the conflict-laden history of the Seleucid Empire as well as the extent of natural harvest variation in antiquity, it is likely that several more peaks and troughs would
come to light with the discovery of more price data. This, at least, was
already the result of the publication of the Commodity Price Lists (Slotsky
and Wallenfels 2009) which brought to light hitherto unknown periods of
above-average prices of barley in the 280s and 260s (S/W 2 and 3).

The Later Seleucid Period, Antiochus III to the Parthian Conquest, *c.* 225–140: The Issue of Relative Prices

The latter half of the Seleucid reign over Babylonia is somewhat better documented than the preceding period; however, there are also larger gaps.
Whereas for example the reign of Seleucus IV (187–175) is still virtually
undocumented, the source material on the reigns of Antiochus III and IV
is abundant enough to have provided modern scholarship with data for
rather detailed biographies.[101] An important source for the fortunes of the
empire in the west is the Greek historian Polybius, whose focus is naturally
on the interaction of the Seleucids with the ever-growing Roman Empire.

---

[101] Schmitt 1964 on Antiochus III, and Mittag 2006 on Antiochus IV. A general overview and
synthetic discussion of the sources on Seleucid history kings after Antiochus IV is now
provided by Ehling 2008.

The conflicts of Antiochus III with Rome culminating in the extended warfare (192–188) and the severe defeat of the Seleucid king at Magnesia under Sipylos brought about substantial losses for the empire with the treaty of Apameia. Not only were the Seleucids forced to renounce all of Asia Minor west of the Taurus mountain range, but the size of the army was also severely restricted. Additionally, a huge war indemnity of 15,000 talents of silver was imposed upon them. This war indemnity is traditionally assumed to have been a severe blow to the empire, which, if it did not cause, at least accelerated its decline.[102] This claim will be kept in mind in our investigation of commodity prices in Babylon, one of the core provinces in terms of population size, level of urbanisation and agricultural productivity.[103]

The downfall of the empire, in which the loss of the province of Babylonia was but one episode, is, however, mostly attributed to political reasons. The relationship between the Romans and the Seleucids remained strained after the peace of Apameia was concluded. Exemplary is the story of the 'day of Eleusis' when Antiochus IV, after his conquest of Egypt, was forced to retreat under the threat of war by the Roman legate C. Popilius Laenas in 169. Although the Seleucid Empire was thus at times powerful enough to use force to intervene in neighbouring Egypt until the reign of Antiochus IV, the balance of power between these two empires shifted decisively, and Ptolemaic interventions in Syria occurred throughout the second half of the second century. Additionally, the dynasty was also afflicted by domestic troubles. The most prominent example is the insurrections in Judea under the Maccabees, lasting for several decades.[104] Another important factor in the decline of the Seleucid Empire is to be sought in the internecine conflicts for the throne between the different branches of the dynasty, notably between those who descended from Seleucus IV (Demetrius I and II) and those who descended, or professed

---

[102] The *locus classicus* is Will 1982[2]: 238–40, pointing out the combined effect of the indemnity itself and the loss of revenues from Asia Minor. His view is still largely shared by historians (it was recently stated that after Apameia 'Antiochus was in constant need of money' (Boiy 2004: 156)). Aperghis 2004 in his attempt at a quantification of the expenditure of the Seleucid state (259–60) likewise came to the conclusion that Apameia caused significant 'cash flow problems' (260) for the Seleucid Empire; similarly Grainger 2002: 347 (although his estimate of annual revenue of the Seleucid kings is clearly too low, cf. Aperghis 2004: 251). An important revision of the *opinio comunis* based on numismatic data was undertaken by Le Rider 1993, who claimed that overall, the financial situation of the Seleucid empire did not deteriorate to any noteworthy degree in the longer run ('une charge irritante, mais nullement aussi insupportable qu'on l'a souvent pensé', p. 62).

[103] See Aperghis 2004: 36–40 and 56–8 on population and urbanisation, and 60–3 on productivity.

[104] See, e.g., Fischer 1980, Bar-Kochva 1989 and now Honigman 2014 on this episode.

to descend, from his brother and successor Antiochus IV (Antiochus V and Alexander Balas).[105]

As was the case in the preceding period the eastern provinces, including Babylonia, are largely absent from the Classical sources. One of the few exceptions is constituted by the revolt of the Median satrap Molon, who in the early days of Antiochus III (222–220) defected from central authority and was even able to assert himself in parts of Babylonia for a short period.[106] Other episodes, such as the *anabasis* of Antiochus III into the Upper Satrapies (212–205), are hardly known beyond the fact that they happened.[107] There are, however, again historiographic cuneiform sources recording otherwise scarcely documented events, although these are perhaps less impressive than those of the first seventy-five years or so of Seleucid reign over Babylonia, such as AD -273B, the diary of the First Syrian War, or BCHP 11, the account of the invasion of Babylonia by Ptolemy III. One of the most intriguing documents from the later Seleucid period is BCHP 14, which refers to the settlement of Greek colonists under a king Antiochus (III or IV).[108] From the considerable number of Astronomical Diaries, AD -168A noting Antiochus IV's invasion of Egypt deserves special mention. AD -149A relates the victory of Alexander Balas over Demetrius near Antioch-on-the-Orontes, an event which is also narrated by Flavius Josephus in his *Antiquitates Judaicae* (13.58–61).[109] Frequently appearing *topoi* in diaries and chronicles of that period are judicial proceedings (e.g. AD -161A, BCHP 17) and cultic and religious matters, especially the performance of sacrifices to Bēl, Bēltiya and the Great Gods in the Esangila temple. AD -204A reports the participation of Antiochus III in the Babylonian New Year's festival upon his return from his *anabasis*.[110] Again there are several

---

[105] Ehling 2008: 279–84 attributes the highest importance to these struggles, playing down other factors (especially the impact of Roman foreign policy), which results in a somewhat unbalanced account. For an interesting approach to the Mediterranean East in later third and early second century and the rise of Rome informed by political theory, see Eckstein 2008. Several of the contributions in Erickson and Ramsey 2011 discuss the demise of the Seleucid Empire.

[106] Will 1982²: 17–23 and Schmitt 1964: 116–48.

[107] This undertaking and its few sources are analysed by Sherwin-White and Kuhrt 1993: 197–200. Antiochus' main aim seems to have been the reassertion of Seleucid suzerainty over the Eastern provinces, which had grown weaker in the previous decades.

[108] This chronicle is so far published only online as Greek Community Chronicle (BCHP 14) at www.livius.org/babylonia.html (accessed 22 October 2016). Van der Spek 1986: 71–8 argues for a date under Antiochus IV. However, the reign of Antiochus III cannot be entirely discarded: see the arguments advanced by Boiy 2004: 208.

[109] We follow here the interpretation of van der Spek 1997/8: 168–9. See also the alternative interpretation of Del Monte 1997: 91–4, who locates these events in the region of the Persian Gulf.

[110] Discussed in Pirngruber 2010: 535–38.

references to internal strife and also ethnic tensions between Greeks and natives in Babylonia (AD -162). The period August–November 145 in particular is densely documented thanks to the extensive historical sections of AD -144 covering months VI–VIII, conveying an interesting glimpse into the state of affairs in Babylonia in the years before the Parthian conquest.

Babylonia remained a province of the Seleucid Empire only until spring/ early summer 141, when it was conquered by Parthian troops under Mithridates I. AD -140A from year 170 of the Seleucid era (141/140) already dates according to a king Arsaces ([1]*Ar-šá-kám* LUGAL), the Parthian throne name all kings of the dynasty adopted. The Parthian takeover must consequently have taken place at some point after April 141 but before June/ July 141, since AD -141F, which records events between September 142 and April 141, is still dated to Demetrius II. In June/July 141, the highest echelons of the provincial administration seem to have been reorganised according to the agenda of the new king, who was staying in Seleucia-on-the-Tigris at this time (AD -140A, lines 3–9). Occasional Seleucid attempts at reconquest of the province did not meet with lasting success, and after the final failure of Antiochus VII in 130, Babylonia was to remain Parthian for centuries to come.[111]

Contrary to what one might expect in the light of mainstream scholarship declaring the treaty of Apameia a turning point in Seleucid history (see above), prices in Babylonia until the Parthian takeover were substantially lower for all commodities than during the first half of Seleucid reign.

Barley, for example, cost on average 1.59 shekels/*kurru*, compared to the mean value of the preceding period amounting to 2.57 shekels/*kurru*. It must be emphasised at this point that a difference of almost 1 shekel per *kurru* is indeed a noteworthy fluctuation: the scarce data at our disposal points to a monthly wage level for an unskilled worker between 1 and 4 shekels per month.[112] In the same period also the level of volatility as measured by the CV decreased from 0.63 to 0.41. In fact, there is not a single high price exceeding 4 shekels/*kurru* throughout the period between *c.* 225 and 140, whereas in the first seventy-five years of the third century prices on several occasions rose to a level between 4 and 6 shekels/*kurru* and even higher. The stunningly

---

[111] See Wiesehöfer 1993: 163–202 for an introduction to the Parthian Empire. The contributors to Wiesehöfer 1998 provide an excellent survey of the source documentation of this empire.

[112] The pertinent sources are briefly discussed in van der Spek 2006b: 291–3. See also Jursa 2010: 669–81 for comparative material from the sixth century: the data collected in his table 103 (674–6) results in an average monthly wage of 3.1 shekels of silver, indicative of quite a high standard of living for a pre-industrial society. See Pirngruber 2016 for a calculation of the welfare ratio based on the price data of the ADs.

Table 5.8. *Commodity prices in the later Seleucid period*

Commodity	Mean price (shekels per *kurru*)[a]	Standard deviation
Barley	1.59	0.65
Dates	0.82	0.44
Kasû	0.44	0.17
Cress	3.3	1.52
Sesame	6.9	2.35
Wool	1.42	0.42

Note: [a] Wool price in shekels per 5 minas.

high equivalents of October/November 188 (390 litres/shekel) and August–October 168 (372 and 378.5 litres/shekel in months V and VII respectively), on the other hand, appear less exceptional when expressed as *prices*: the all-time high equivalent of 390 litres/shekel reappears as 0.49 shekels/litre. This is still 1 shekel below the mean price of the period, but prices quite frequently rise to a level of 1 or more shekels above the average level.

In addition to a lower fluctuation in the data and the lower average price level, a third phenomenon which becomes evident from data shown in the figure is the very low coefficient of determination (R^2), amounting to only 0.09. The trend-line in Figure 5.12 in general moves slightly below the 2 shekels/*kurru* mark, with a great many small oscillations. The trend-line in Figure 5.6 depicting the development of barley price in the period *c.* 300–225 on the other hand oscillates considerably between below 2 and above 4 shekels/*kurru*. The data of that earlier period, however, is more clearly characterised by periods of peaks and troughs, which enables the trend-line to follow the available prices more closely. The conclusion is that in the later Seleucid period hardly any distinct trends are discernible in the data. Prices fluctuate more at random but within a rather narrow margin, whereas coherent periods of higher or lower prices do not occur with the frequency and intensity of the period between *c.* 300 and 225.

This is not to say that political events no longer have repercussions in the price data. However, their effects seem to last for briefer time spans only, and prices return much quicker to their base level compared to the preceding period. A good case in point is the mid-140s. In September/October 145, the barley price rose to 2.73 shekels/*kurru*, for the same period, AD -144 testifies to the (bellicose?) activities of a certain Aria'bu, the occurrence of various diseases in the country, as well as preparations made to ward off the impending invasion

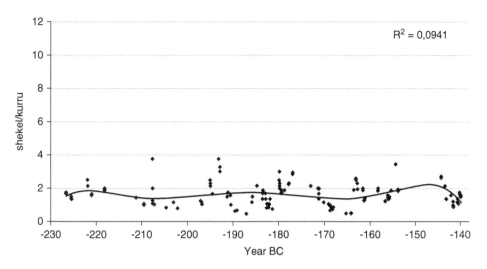

Figure 5.12 Barley prices in the later Seleucid period, *c.* 225–140

by the Elamite king Kamnaskires, which finally happened later the same year
(but, unfortunately, no prices from this later episode are extant).[113] However, in
the winter of the following year, prices are already back to a much lower level
of about 1.35 shekels/*kurru* (November/December 144). Both cress and sesame
show a similar pattern of a brief peak soon followed by relaxation, whereas dates
and *kasû* remained unaffected by this crisis.

Turning now to the price patterns of commodities other than barley, the
most peculiar trend-line is certainly shown by date prices. At a satisfactory r[2] of 0.41, prices show a steady decline from the 230s until well into
the 160s. After a rather unstable period with two particularly notable price
peaks in the later 160s and 150s – late summer 159 and late winter/early
spring 154 – prices are back to a fairly low level of around 0.5 shekels/*kurru*
and below in the second half of the 140s. The peak of late summer 159
is simply caused by the phenomenon of seasonal fluctuation as the two
highest prices of the year date to August and September respectively and
thus to the immediate pre-harvest period. The later and higher peak can be
shown to have occurred together with an increase in the barley price, but
the reason for this peak remains in the dark.[114] As was the case with barley,
the mean price of dates during the late Seleucid period, 0.82 shekels/*kurru*,

---

[113] See also Del Monte 1997: 98–100 on the longevity of the conflicts between Babylonia and
Elam in the decades to come.

[114] The historical section of AD -154A containing the high barley price also mentions the
presence of a general, but the precise context is unclear as the passage is badly broken. The

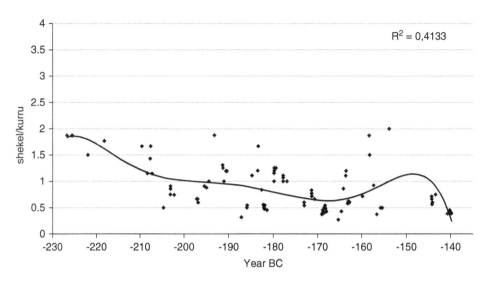

Figure 5.13 Date prices in the later Seleucid period, *c.* 225–140

is significantly lower than during the early Seleucid period (2.25 shekels/
kurru). The factor by which the price decreased was even larger, almost
threefold. The margin between the mean date and barley prices had now
widened again, to about 0.7 shekels/*kurru*. This was indeed below the level
of the mean price difference during the Late Achaemenid period, when that
value amounted to 1.35 shekels/*kurru*; however, in relative terms that picture changes. Barley was 1.67 times more expensive than dates during the
Late Achaemenid period. In the late Seleucid period, barley cost 1.94 times
more than dates, which were thus comparatively cheaper in the second
century than ever before. It was argued in the preceding section that the
widening of the gap between barley and date prices represents a return to
conditions before the Seleucid takeover rather than an unexpected novelty,
yet the magnitude is surprising.

Concerning this price decrease, several hypotheses have been put forward in the past. It has been interpreted as a sudden drop manifesting itself
in a year during the last decade of the third century by Aperghis (2004: 84
and fig. 5.6). The trend-line in Figure 5.13 seems to cast doubt on Aperghis'
interpretation of the price decline as an abrupt shock. It clearly shows that
prices decreased steadily from the 230s onwards, and especially that the

presence of such officials cannot be taken as an indication of some kind of local strife in
Babylonia. More often, such dignitaries appear in the context of regular visits from their
residence in Seleucia-on-the-Tigris, involving the performance of sacrifices in the Esangila
temple; see Pirngruber 2010.

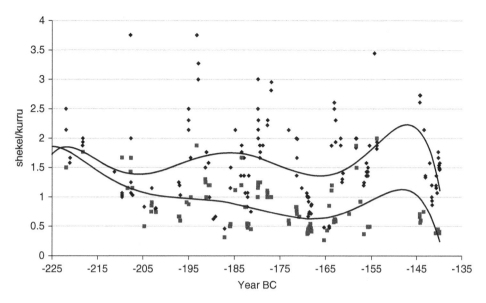

Figure 5.14 Barley and date prices in the later Seleucid period, *c.* 225–140
Note: top line/diamonds: barley; bottom line/squares: dates

deepest troughs were reached only in the 160s, when price regularly moved below the 0.5 shekels/*kurru* mark (whereas in the late 190s, for instance, the price returned consistently above the 1 shekel/*kurru* mark). Moreover, in the last decade of the third century, prices were very favourable for both dates and barley. After a high price of 3.75 shekels/*kurru* in the immediate pre-harvest season in 208, the barley price oscillated between 1.25 and 0.8 shekels/*kurru* between May 208 and March 197, hence at a level considerably below the average price of the period *c.* 225–140.

Consequently, it is most accurate to state that the relationship between barley and dates changed notably in the later Seleucid period. This phenomenon is observable only in the second half of the 190s. However, the reasons for this divergence are also to be attributed to the development in the barley price showing an upswing between 195 and 180, and not mono-causally related to the development in the date price. The question is best rephrased as to why the date price – unlike that of barley – continued to fall throughout the first half of the second century. The earlier explanatory approaches of van der Spek and Aperghis, respectively attributing the price decrease to a royal decree encouraging the plantation of new date palms or to a tax exemption on dates, both focussed exclusively on the supply side. However, as regards Aperghis' (2004: 84) hypothesis of the suspension of a tax of 50 per cent on dates, there is no historical evidence whatsoever, either for a 50 per cent tax on the date harvest in Babylonia or for an exemption thereof during the reign of Antiochus III.[115] Also the fact that the date prices kept falling until well into the 160s cannot be accounted for by this explanatory approach. Van der Spek's (1986 and 2006b: 302) idea of a royal decree by Antiochus III encouraging the planting of date gardens is based on a document first published by Sarkisian (1974), a rental agreement from Uruk dating to 221. According to Sarkisian's transcription the texts reads in several lines (10, 34, 42 and 44) *a-na al-lu za-qa-pu* [GIŠ]GIŠIMMAR, in one instance (line 34) the following line refers to a royal regulation (*di-'a-gi-ra-am ... ṭè-e-mu šá* LUGAL). Van der Spek translated the phrase as 'for the planting of additional date palms'[116] and suggested that Antiochus III attempted to stimulate the planting of date gardens by means of issuing a royal decree. However, this interpretation also has some problems, the first being that the reading *al-* is in all probability erroneous, the contract formulary would rather require a *dul-*, and thus read 'the work of planting date palms'.[117] Secondly, and more importantly, the text states nothing about the content of the royal edict. The passage concerning the planting of dates occurs several times in the text, and the only time it is juxtaposed with the royal decree is the passage specifying the modalities of the lease, immediately after the description of the property. It rather appears that the whole transaction is to be carried out under the regulations of a royal decree. In the light of Seleucid administrative praxis in Babylonia, it is for example conceivable the some kind of fee had to be paid for the transaction in order for it to be legally valid. Furthermore, a second reference to the royal *diagramma* is made in the same section in line 38 in connection with payments to be made to the temple (É DINGIR[MEŠ]). Hence, as rightly

---

[115] Aperghis 2004: 146. He obviously bases his case on the *a priori* implausible assumption that the magnitude of the tax exemption corresponds precisely to the price decrease (or increase of the equivalent), thus to about 50 per cent. Half of the harvest is a high, but by no means unreasonable estimate for a tax on agricultural produce, in particular fruit crops: see Aperghis 2004: 137–52, especially 146. At a conference in Amsterdam in May 2011, he reiterated his hypothesis by interpreting the difference in the date prices before and after 205 as a step function. Even if that were true on a formal level – the most important point is that a gap in the documentation of almost ten years during the 210s, hence precisely in the crucial years immediately preceding his watershed of 205, prevents us reaching a clear-cut solution (and note the low barley price in this decade) – such a structure of the price data could have equally come about under any other (e.g., van der Spek's) explanatory approach.

[116] The text is edited with translation in van der Spek 1995: 227–34. See also van der Spek 1986: 222–32, in particular the commentary to line 10 (230).

[117] A reading *dul-* (without closer inspection of the text) was suggested independently by Jursa and Hackl. This reading is difficult to reconcile with the traces according to the latter's collation; however, nor is *al-* entirely satisfactory. *Allu/û* is furthermore incongruent with the syntax of the remainder of the phrase.

recognised by Van der Spek (1995: 234) in a more cautious commentary to the text, what seems to be at issue in this passage are the modalities of the payment of the rent. From that angle, the edict in question seems to have also specified income rights of a temple leasing out land. Even the possibility that we are dealing with two different *diagrammai* cannot be entirely discarded. A third argument against the interpretation of this royal edict as decreeing an increase in the number of date plantations is textual. The lease contract in question bears strong resemblance to the lease contracts *ana zāqipānūti*, 'for the planting (of date palms)' which are well attested the Neo-Babylonian period. In these contracts, the lessee obliged himself to plant a date grove on formerly unproductive land; as compensation he was allowed to keep the full amount of the harvest for himself for a number of years.[118] A similar contract type – reclamation of barren land, *ana taptê* – existed also for agricultural land.[119] Furthermore, the subject matter was already an issue in the first half of the second millennium according to the Law Code of Hammurabi, which envisages in paragraphs sixty to sixty-three a scenario in which one citizen gives to another a field which is to be turned into an orchard (*eqlam ana kirîm zaqāpim*).[120] Hence, leases with the specific obligation for the lessee to plant date palms are by no means an unusual phenomenon in first-millennium Babylonia and even earlier. However, to what use a tract of land was put depended primarily on soil conditions, the availability of water, labour force and farming equipment (such as plough oxen) and the aims of the lessor, whether institutional household or private person. That kings attempted to generate additional income by means of regulating which crops were to be planted in a specific region of their empire is to the best of my knowledge an unknown economic strategy in Ancient Babylonia.[121] The specialisation in date horticulture of the Ebabbar temple in the sixth century came about through various structural and other factors – taxation, but also the availability of manpower required for the intensification of agricultural production – but was certainly not prescribed by the royal chancellery.[122]

---

[118] See Jursa 1995: 122–4, and 2005a: 22 for this type of contract. In his sample text (1995: 122, text 31), the lessee is exempted from rental payments for twelve years. The formulary of these contracts is described in Ries 1976: 67–72.

[119] Jursa 1995: 140–3.

[120] Edited in Roth 1995: 71–142, for example. See also van de Mieroop 2005: 99–111 on the monument. Paragraph sixty of the Law Code regulated the modalities of rental payment by the lessee in such cases.

[121] For the Seleucid Empire, see the discussion of the imperial revenue in Aperghis 2004: 137–79.

[122] Jursa 2010: 355–60, especially 359: 'The preference for intensive horticulture at the expense of extensive grain farming was inextricably linked to the requirements of the strongly monetised

The most recent approach focussing on the supply side was put forward by our research group (Huijs, Pirngruber and van Leeuwen 2015)[123] and explained the price decrease by an increase in the supply situation thanks to improved climatic circumstances during the second century. This is so far the only explanatory model also able to account for the price decrease observable in all other commodities, for example sesame, which dropped from 9.9 shekels/*kurru* in the period 300–225 to 6.9 shekels/*kurru* in the years 225–140. Regarding now the relative prices of dates and barley, it is expected that the date price would be more strongly affected since dates were, in comparison to barley, the inferior (i.e. less expensive) and hence less elastic basic commodity. Once the barley price fell below a certain threshold, people would substitute the inferior commodity dates with the more highly esteemed commodity barley.[124]

A second explanatory model can be adduced to complement the results of this approach focussing on climatic improvements, namely an investigation of the development of the prices in the light of the quantity theory of money. According to Irving Fisher's equation MV = PT, the money supply (M) multiplied by the velocity of circulation (V) equals the price level (P) multiplied by the level of transactions (T) (usually approached via an estimate of GDP).[125] In the later Seleucid period, which exhibits a lower price level for all commodities recorded in the ADs, one needs thus *ceteris paribus* to postulate a change in at least one other variable for the equation to hold. The first option is a concomitant rise in T, which is essentially the argument put forward by Huijs, Pirngruber and van Leeuwen (2015), who argued for an increase in the supply situation thanks to a more favourable climate. The second possibility is a reduction of the monetary supply. Historically, this is perfectly sensible. As is demonstrated in greater detail in the following section, the exceptionally low prices of barley (but also of other commodities) prevailing through the later 190s and the 180s can very well be explained in the context of Antiochus III's continuous war expenses culminating in the indemnity payment incurred with the peace treaty of Apameia in 188. In addition to the outlier caused by the temporal scarcity

economy and the gradual dissolution of the basic structures of the traditional redistributional household economy.'

[123] See also van der Spek and van Leeuwen 2014, where still another possibility, namely an increasing salinisation which would affect barley in stronger measure than dates, is briefly considered but judged unlikely.

[124] See Huijs, Pirngruber and van Leeuwen 2015: 131, fig. 7.2.

[125] A succinct account of the Fisher equation, also called the quantity theory of money, is provided by Mayhew 1995a: 239–43. Hollander 2008: 117–22 applied this approach in the context of the question of monetary supply in Late Republican Rome.

of silver as a result of the enforced immediate payment of a substantial sum (more than 5,000 talents of silver), it is possible that a general contraction of the amount of silver in circulation was another consequence of Antiochus III's campaigns. The consequences of a reduced amount of money would be similar to those of an increase in supply, and in both approaches the price of dates would decrease more strongly, because of a substitution effect.[126] Of course, the decrease in the price level may have been brought about by a combination of both factors, an increased supply of commodities and a concurrent lower level of monetisation. The observed decrease in price volatility in our period could in any case be taken as an indication that the latter factor outweighed the former. Contemporary Egypt displays the opposite scenario, as increased monetisation was argued to have been one of the causes for the higher price volatility prevailing in the second century.[127]

In contrast to the staple crops barley and dates, the non-staple goods clearly display a pattern of rising prices towards the end of Seleucid reign over Babylonia, as is shown in Figure 5.15 (cress prices) and Figure 5.16 (wool prices). These price rises already foreshadow the price increases that would affect barley and dates in the Parthian period after *c.* 130.

Wool shows a particularly clear pattern: after a period of roughly seventy years in which prices usually (but with occasional outliers) oscillated between 1 and 1.5 shekels per 5 minas, prices levelled off at a level of 2 shekels per 5 minas after 160. In the first decades of Parthian rule, prices remained at approximately the same level, before rising some more towards the close of the second century.

One factor influencing the price increases in cress, sesame and wool may be sought in the unstable political situation which affected the Seleucid dynasty after the death of Antiochus IV in 164. The reasons for the lag in changes to the prices of staple crop prices must remain elusive. One can for example hypothesise that in times of extended political instability, which, it has to be remembered, also entail a weakening of (the efficiency

---

[126] A decrease of the velocity of the circulation of money (V) as proximate cause of the price decrease is the most unlikely solution considering the short span of time during which the price drop occurred, and also because this scenario presupposes a substantial increase in the amount of money in circulation. The velocity of monetary circulation is usually held constant, but see Mayhew 1995b: 68–71 for its dynamic nature: the higher the level of monetisation of an economy, the lower the velocity of circulation will be. Note that also the calculations in van der Spek, Földvári and van Leeuwen 2015 point to a low level of silver in circulation, especially during the first half of the second century.

[127] Von Reden 2014: 275. Improving climate can account for the lower level of prices, but still does not preclude occasional harvest failures (and hence price peaks) due to crop diseases, etc., although fewer instances can be expected.

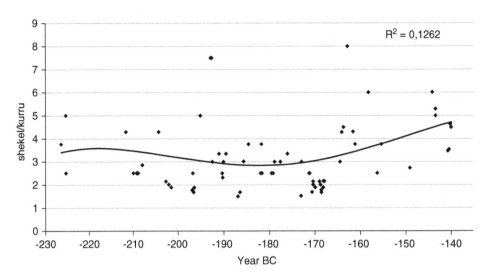

Figure 5.15 Cress prices in the later Seleucid period, c. 225–140

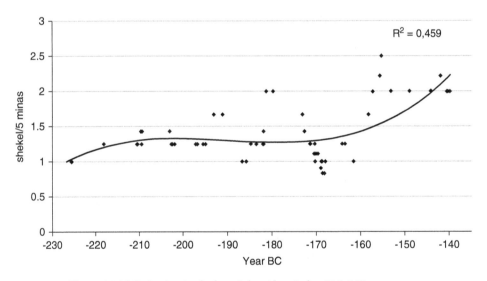

Figure 5.16 Wool prices in the later Seleucid period, c. 225–140

of) markets, producers of agricultural crops focussed on products with low demand elasticity as a means of risk aversion and also as a strategy to ensure one's own supply. This resulting imbalance in the supply of barley and dates (increasing) on the one hand, and cress, sesame and wool on the other (decreasing) would explain the stability of the former and the price increase in the latter commodities. On a side note, contrary to the decrease observable in the Late Achaemenid period, the price of wool is less affected than other commodities, which corresponds to its high elasticity of demand.

Overall, the troubled years preceding the Parthian takeover seem however to have had little repercussion in the price data compared to the political events of the third century. There are possibly bellicose activities of a certain Aria'bu in August/September 145,[128] and two months later in October/November of the Elamite king Kamnaskires, who is said to march plundering through the country, causing fear and terror (*hattu u gilittu*). Barley prices are unfortunately extant only from before this Elamite invasion, but already during the activities of Aria'bu they were at 2.72 shekels per *kurru*, a fairly high level when compared to 2.14 in August 144 (thus precisely one year later) or to 1.88 shekels/*kurru* in 156.[129] However, the even higher price of August 155 (3.43 shekels/*kurru*) – for which because of the absence of historical information no explanation can be offered – again casts doubt on the potential economic impact of this episode. The evidence of commodities other than barley is equally ambiguous. The date price during the harvest period amounted to 0.6 shekels/*kurru*, which is perfectly in line with the low date prices of this period, and the price for *kasû* is very low also, 0.25 shekels per *kurru*. This is indeed unexpected, as both prices stem from the very month of the Elamite invasion. The same month, on the other hand, shows that cress was significantly dearer in this year than it was five years earlier during the same period, at 6 shekels/*kurru* compared to 2.72 in July/August 150 and 3.75 in June/July 156. The price for sesame was oscillating between 9 and 12 shekels per *kurru* and thus was significantly above the price prevailing during the mid-150s, when it ranged between 5 and 6.93 shekels/*kurru*.

Finally, the near complete absence of major outliers in the price data of these decades deserves consideration. The figures in the section above show a fairly uniform picture for all commodities: in the period between the accession to the throne of Antiochus III and until the Parthian conquest in 141, outliers not only tend to decrease in magnitude but also in number. As explained above, the former phenomenon has its roots partly in the improved supply situation as a result of better climatic circumstances in these years (Huijs, Pirngruber and van Leeuwen 2015) and the lower availability and higher value of silver. The

---

[128] The passage in question is fragmentary, but two indications point to some kind of military action. Firstly, *illātu* (hostile) troops are mentioned. Secondly, the mention of canals in line 17 calls to mind a passage from the same diary, -144, in a later month, where the Elamite king Kamnaskires is said to 'march victoriously among the cities and canals of Babylonia' (r21).

[129] Before the prices of 145/4, there is a gap of almost ten years in the data; the prices from 156 and 155 have been included as the chronologically closest preceding data.

smaller overall number of outliers on the other hand is mainly to be sought in the, at least from a Babylonian perspective, tranquil political situation. There are for example no reports of foreign invasions or of internal conflicts, which were reported regularly in the third century until the years after the death of Antiochus IV, that is, the late 160s.

The peak barley price of the whole period, 3.75 shekels/*kurru* in 208, seems to have been simply the result of seasonal fluctuation. Even more frustrating is the case of the second time that the barley price reached its top price of 3.75 shekels/*kurru* in October 194. In that period, the price of dates was also considerably above average (1.88 shekels/*kurru* compared to a mean of 0.82). Similarly, during the same autumn of 194 cress stood at 7.5 shekels/*kurru*, and was thus more than twice its mean price, and sesame also was significantly above its average price (10.91 shekels/*kurru*). *Kasû* and wool were slightly above their average price, too, albeit to a very minor extent only. As was the case in the 230s discussed in the preceding section, a general price rise affecting all commodities seems to have taken place,[130] but as opposed to the earlier instance, there are no indications of domestic revolts or similarly disruptive events in Babylonia. The ADs provide hardly any historical information for the 190s, and the focus of the Greek sources is as usually on the western-most provinces of the empire. During those years, Antiochus III dedicated himself to large-scale military operations in Asia Minor and Thrace, which were brought to a successful conclusion in 192.[131] Afterwards he remained in the west, and his meddling in Greek affairs ultimately aroused the suspicions of the Romans and brought about the Roman War (192–188), which ended in an utter defeat for the Seleucids.

The one point of interest left to discuss for the late Seleucid period is the notably low prices occurring in October/November 188 and in the years 166 and 165. Table 5.9 shows that the two periods display somewhat different characteristics. For the former, the universal nature of the price decline cannot be doubted. All commodities attested (five of six) show a price level two to three times below the average of the period. Both the universality of

---

[130] The barley price already ranked above average prices in 196/5, and thus two years before the universal increases of 194/3. However, the prices in 196/5 were not only clearly below the level of autumn 194 – by 1 shekel and more – they also seem to have already recovered to a level at about the average price (1.67 shekels/*kurru*) with the harvest of 195. Unfortunately, the one and a half years between that harvest and the following peak in October 194 are not covered by any price data at all, precluding further analysis. However, considering the ubiquity of the price increase of 194, a connection to the higher barley prices of the harvest year 196/5 cannot be taken for granted and was at best indirect – if prices were high throughout the undocumented year 195/4 as well.

[131] Schmitt 1964: 262–95, and Ma 2000: 53–105.

the price decrease as well as the evenness as regards its magnitude strongly argue against either demand- or supply-centred approaches. Demand or supply shocks rather affect only individual commodities or groups thereof and also to different degrees (as in the case of the army convocation in the context of the First Syrian War in winter 274/3 driving up the price of barley and cress). A monetary explanation is thus more plausible, especially in the light of the likely decrease of silver in circulation described above, which took place in this very period. One event that immediately jumps to mind is of course the peace treaty of Apameia concluded in the same year of 188. The Romans obliged Antiochus III to make a payment of 15,000 talents of silver, of which 3,000 talents (plus a first annuity of 1,000 talents of the remainder, plus the first instalment of the rather insubstantial indemnity to the Pergamene king Eumenes II) had to be settled immediately. It is thus tempting to interpret the extremely low prices – high commodity equivalents for silver – as being caused by a temporary scarcity of silver, a consequence of the king tapping all resources available to him to come up with the considerable sum. It needs to be emphasised at this point that Babylonia had no silver mines of its own but was utterly dependent on the influx of precious metal – and vice versa in all likelihood disproportionately susceptible to monetary shocks. The impact of supply of precious metal and coins on price formation is in any case paralleled in Ptolemaic Egypt.[132]

The empire seems to have recovered fairly quickly from this silver drain and in the course of the following two years, prices returned to normal low levels. Both barley and dates were still below average in March 186 but already clearly above the level of 188 (barley stood between 1.15 and 1.5 shekels/*kurru* and dates at 0.5–0.55 shekels/*kurru*). Both commodities were back to their respective average levels (dates even above average) in spring 185. *Kasû*, cress and sesame were already back to an average level in 186. Wool was not attested in November 188, but was at a level below average – between 1 and 1.25 shekels per 5 minas – for the remainder of the 180s.

It should furthermore not go unmentioned that already in 190 the barley price was clearly below average, with the price oscillating between 0.63 and 0.67 shekels/*kurru*. This can be interpreted as first signs of a deflationary movement, and it is indeed possible that the expenses of the war of Antiochus III against the Romans left their mark in the Babylonian price data already before the indemnity stipulated at Apameia brought forth a further drain of silver resources. However, as there is no price data for any of the other commodities extant from that year, it is equally possible this movement was

---

[132] Von Reden 2014: 262[(+9)].

Table 5.9. *Trough prices in 188 and 166/5*

Commodity	Mean price[a]	188	166	165
Barley	1.59	0.46	0.48	0.475
Dates	0.82	0.32	0.27	0.43/0.86
Kasû	0.45	0.2	–	0.25
Cress	3.30	1.5	–	3/4.29
Sesame	6.90	2.73	–	–
Wool	1.42	–	–	1.25

Note: [a] All prices in this table are in shekels per *kurru*, with the exception of the wool price, which is given in shekels per 5 minas. The mean price refers to the period *c.* 225–140.

confined to barley and was caused, for example, by an exceptionally good harvest.

The price pattern of 166 and 165 is more difficult to explain. The barley price was already below average for the first half of the 160s and plummeted to an extremely low level in the period between autumn 166 and autumn 165. However, in the pre-harvest season of the same harvest year, in late winter 165/64, barley all of a sudden disappeared from the market, and in May 164, after the harvest, the barley price stood at an above-average level (1.88 shekels/*kurru*). Dates, on the other hand, were at an exceptionally low level only in October 166 (0.27 shekels/*kurru*), and in the course of the year 165, they rose from 0.43 shekels/*kurru* in spring (and contrary to the usual pattern of seasonal fluctuation) to 0.86 shekels/*kurru* in October, back to an average level. In the years between 170 and 165, dates were like barley at a level constantly below average. *Kasû* stood very low in October 165 (0.25 shekels/*kurru*), whereas the attestations for cress show prices at or above average (3 shekels/*kurru* in spring 165 and 4.29 shekels/*kurru* in October 165). The price for sesame moved in general below average for most of the 160s, and in October 165 the price stood at 4.29 shekels/*kurru*. Hence, as far as the evidence at hand allows us to tell, the main price trough for both dates and barley was reached in autumn 166, after which date prices slowly rose back to normal levels. Barley on the other hand seemed to have been on a very low level throughout 165, but disappeared from the market in February 164 and returned a few months later after the harvest at an above-average level.

Since again all attested commodities seem to have been affected – but alas, only prices for barley and dates are extant – and the magnitude of the decrease (about threefold) is about the same – and also similar to the trough two decades earlier – a monetary shock is again a likely solution. It is tempting but entirely speculative to connect the proposed silver scarcity leading to high equivalents to the festivities in Daphne taking place in the same year, which were to inaugurate the Eastern campaign of Antiochus IV.[133] Considering the amount of wealth displayed at the *pompē* and the number of military personnel participating,[134] requisitions of precious metals are not an unlikely scenario, especially if one considers that additionally the army to accompany the king on campaign had to be remunerated. That the finances of the royal treasury were somewhat strained after the Roman wars is indicated by various attempts at closer control of temple finances and episodes of outright plundering in various regions of the empire during the reign of Antiochus IV. The most famous event is certainly the enduring rebellion in Judea under the Maccabees,[135] but also the installation of a *zazakku* in the Esangila in Babylonia probably served the purpose of getting a tighter grip on the finances of the main Babylonian temple.[136] Antiochus IV even lost his life in an attempt to plunder the sanctuary of a female deity in Elam.[137]

The rising prices for dates and cress in 165 seem to constitute a rather quick – in the case of dates even contrary to the usual seasonal pattern – return to normal conditions. The main difficulty for that year is certainly the still extremely low barley price and its rapid rise in spring following a sudden collapse in January/February 164. Cress, sesame and wool are attested at average prices in the period between February and May 164, and it is thus only the data on barley that requires special explanation. Unfortunately, the historical sources are virtually absent for winter and spring of 164. Antiochus is known to have successfully campaigned in Armenia in early 165, and very likely visited the region of the Persian Gulf (Antiocheia-Charax) in October of the same year.[138] If this reconstruction

---

[133] Mittag 2006: 282$^{(+1)}$–95 provides an exhaustive overview of the earlier literature on this event, also Bunge 1976.

[134] Bar-Kochva 1989: 117 provides an estimated total of 45,500 soldiers for Daphne. To put this huge number in perspective, the size of the Seleucid army at the battle of Raphia 217 amounted to 68,000 troops; for the battle of Magnesia in winter 190/189, Antiochus III mustered 71,400 soldiers, the largest number ever convoked by a Seleucid ruler.

[135] On this episode see, e.g., Fischer 1980; Mittag 2006: 225–81; and Honigman 2014, all with additional literature.

[136] Dandamaev 1994 and Boiy 2004: 210.

[137] Mittag 2006: 307–10.

[138] The campaign is described in AD -164B+C; see Gera and Horowitz 1997, van der Spek 1997/8 and Mittag 2006: 296–307.

of events is correct, he very likely passed through Babylonia in summer/ early autumn of the same year, probably along the Tigris and thus bypassing the city of Babylon.[139] Events afterwards until his death roughly one year later are not recorded. What is striking in this scenario is that contrary to previous experiences, the presence of an army in Babylonia did not cause barley prices to rise, but was accompanied by some of the lowest prices throughout the period of the dataset provided by the ADs. Unfortunately, the reason for this unusual development – a market intervention in form of a royal edict prescribing artificially low prices for the sustenance of his troops leading to a depletion of all available stocks, for example – has to remain subject to speculation. However, what would suit this explanatory approach is the fact that barley prices reappear after the next harvest at a level above average, which can be interpreted as indicative of a still not fully recovered supply situation.[140]

Conclusions

Summarising the obtained results, I would like to briefly consider the price data from Seleucid Babylon in the longer run, in order to ascertain and refine some of the findings. In the preceding section, the movements of the respective trend-lines of barley and date prices in relation to one another have been discussed. The reason for their divergence after about 195 has been sought in a combination of a more favourable climate boosting supply of all commodities as well as a drain of silver, both phenomena bound to entail a lower price level, and in particular that of dates, the commodity less elastic in demand. Figure 5.17 shows this development in the context of the earlier attestations of the Seleucid period.[141] The gap between barley and date price was fairly narrow for roughly the first century of Seleucid reign over Babylon, with barley price ranging below the date price in the one and a half decades or so of the third century when date orchards had still not fully recovered from the wartime devastations

---

[139] Gera and Horowitz 1997: 247.

[140] The prices in this year are also mentioned in van der Spek and Mandemakers 2003: 529, where a confiscation of the barley stocks by the passing army is hypothesised. This would indeed explain the fact that barley disappears from the market, but does not account for the very low prices prevailing earlier in the same year. A short period of price controls in a very different context (stabilisation of prices in a period of high prices) has been also hypothesised by Slotsky and Wallenfels 2009: 168 on the basis of text S/W 14 for the mid-third century.

[141] The goodness of fit (r^2) is satisfactory for both commodities; 0.21 for barley, and even 0.60 for dates. The higher value for dates can be explained *inter alia* by their lower level of volatility.

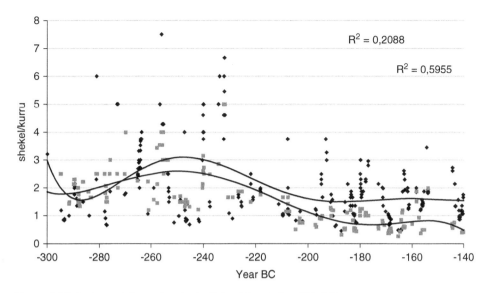

Figure 5.17 Barley and date prices in the Seleucid period, *c*. 300–140
Note: top line/diamonds: barley; bottom line/squares: dates

of the early Hellenistic period. The divergence, however, started to widen
shortly after the turn from the third to the second century. As already
briefly alluded to above (and as described more fully in the next chapter),
most crisis moments caused prices of both commodities to rise in uni-
son. However, at some point after 195, the barley price on the one hand
stopped its downward trend that set in for both commodities after the
troubled period of the 230s and stabilised at a favourable level of about
1.59 shekels/*kurru* (mean price), but the date price on the other hand continued to decrease. It has to be emphasised again that it is this diverging
pattern rather than an extreme drop in the date price (or a steep rise in
the barely price) that caused the widening of the gap between the two
commodities.

Of the remaining commodities, the trend-line of *kasû* follows that of dates
in that a sustained decline took place well into the second century. This is
also clearly shown by the difference in the mean prices between the early
and late Seleucid periods (0.93 shekels/*kurru* as opposed to 0.45). *Kasû* was
at all times the least expensive commodity, which probably reflects both
its biological nature – a parasitical plant rather than a crop that needed
cultivation – as well as its use as condiment rather than as a genuine foodstuff, meaning that it was purchased in small amounts only and additionally was very elastic in demand. The contemporaneity of the decrease in
the prices of date and *kasû*, the two main ingredients of Babylonian beer,

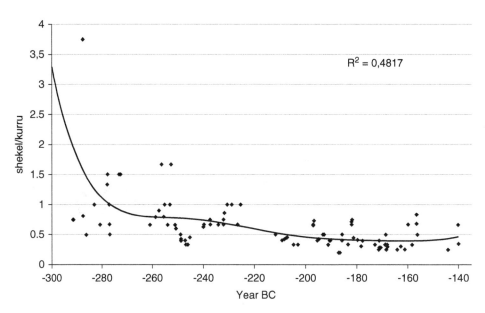

Figure 5.18 *Kasû* prices in the Seleucid period, *c.* 300–140

both in absolute and relative (compared to barley) terms is interesting.[142] It certainly favours the assumption of a substitution effect away from dates in their different forms and towards barley. One may also speculate about the impact of dietary habits of the Greek colonists on this price development, whose growing importance in the city of Babylon was recognised by the installation of a *polis* during the reign of Antiochus III or IV.[143] Greeks were after all not accustomed to rely on staples other than cereals (wheat and barley), and it is unlikely that they willingly adopted a Babylonian diet, based to a more or less equal extent on barley and dates, the latter mainly in form of beer seasoned with cuscuta (*kasû*).[144]

The graph for wool shows that the price for the only non-foodstuff is clearly the most stable price of the dataset. It constantly fluctuated between one and two shekels per *mina*, with the exception of the first decade or so

---

[142] On the manufacture and relevance of Babylonian beer, see Stol 1994.

[143] Boiy 2004: 207–8 argues for a date under Antiochus III, van der Spek prefers a foundation date during the reign of Antiochus IV, e.g., 1986: 71–8 and 1987: 66–70. On the Greek community in Babylon see also van der Spek 2005 and 2009 and Sherwin-White and Kuhrt 1993: 149–61

[144] See Poyck 1962: 68 and table 4.22. In the 1950s CE, dates accounted for about one quarter of daily caloric intake in the Iraqi countryside according to his sample. Total consumption of dates amounted to 60 kilograms per year, compared to 40 kilograms of barley (with additional 10 kilograms of wheat and almost 30 kilograms of rice, the latter commodity being absent from the diet in antiquity).

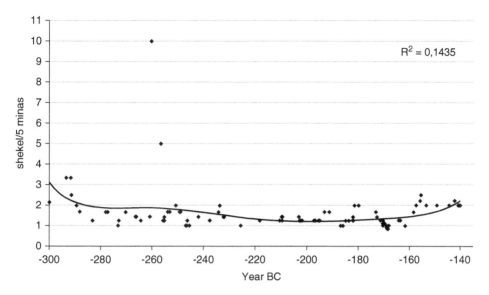

Figure 5.19 Wool prices in the Seleucid period, *c.* 300–140

after the warfare between Alexander's successors. In the first forty years of the second century prices tend towards the lower limit but after *c.* 160 they rise again and for the first time after about 150 years they regularly rech and even exceed the mark of 2 shekels per 5 minas. Moreover, wool, especially when spun and processed, is the only commodity of those recorded in the ADs for which long-distance trade is feasible, and indeed already attested in the early second millennium.[145] Whereas the raw wool was mainly traded regionally, high-value dyed cloth in particular was traded across long distances.[146] Indeed, still in the first century CE, Babylonian blankets were held in high esteem by wealthy Romans. A telling passage is Pliny *Nat. hist.* 7 74.196, stating that Emperor Nero paid 4 million sesterces for Babylonian *triclinaria*. The essential stability of wool prices throughout the period under discussion here can thus also be interpreted as reflecting its comparatively higher degree of integration in different markets.

What is also remarkable is the fact that outliers are very seldom only in the data for wool and *kasû*. For at least the most extreme outlier in the wool data (10 shekels of silver per 5 minas in October 261), which is more

[145] For the Old Assyrian trade connections to Anatolia see e.g., Dercksen 2004. Interestingly, already in this period, the bulk of textiles traded via Assur to Asia Minor originated from southern Babylonia; see Dercksen 2004a: 14 and Veenhof 1972: 98–103.

[146] On long-distance trade of wool in first-millennium Babylonia see Graslin-Thomé 2009: 187–205, see also Jursa 2010: 595–616 (contribution of Kleber) and Kleber 2008: 237–53 on the wool trade within Babylonia.

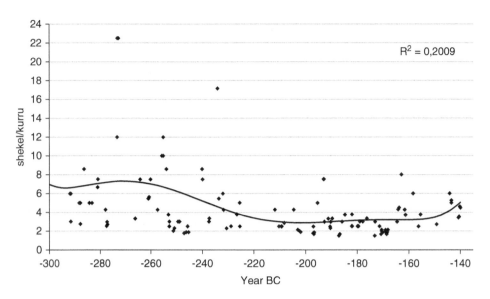

Figure 5.20 Cress prices in the Seleucid period, *c.* 300–140

than six times above the mean price of the whole period, the possibility of a scribal error should be considered. Such inaccuracies did occur;[147] on the other hand, unless there is good evidence to support doing so, it is methodologically unsound to simply delete inconvenient data which proves difficult to explain. What militates strongly against the possibility of a scribal error in this peculiar instance is the fact that the second outlier in the dataset (5 shekels per 5 minas) is constituted by the chronologically subsequent price in May 257.

As was the case with both barley and dates, cress prices are lower and less volatile in the period between *c.* 200 and 140. There is also a notable trough in the dataset in the late 250s/early 240s. There are several notable outliers scattered throughout the dataset, and we note that these again occurred mainly in the first half of the third century. Like the wool price, the price of cress shows an upward trend at the end of the Seleucid period, which is not the case for barley and dates.

The final commodity to be discussed is sesame, the most expensive crop. Sesame shows its most noticeable outliers during the crisis of the 230s, and like the other commodities its prices are clearly lower during the first half of the second century. This development is mainly due to the non-occurrence of large outliers in the later period; the general price level between both 290

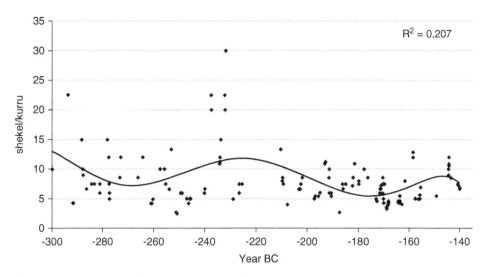

Figure 5.21 Sesame prices in the Seleucid period, *c.* 300–140

and 240 and 210–140 is between 5 and 10 shekels per *kurru*. Thus, the trend towards lower prices in the later period is much less pronounced than was the case with cress, let alone dates and *kasû*.

Two more points remain to be clarified, namely the question of the temporal distribution of the price data and the impact of seasonal volatility compared to exogenous shocks. To address the first matter, I should iterate that both the historical sections and the price sections become more detailed in the later diaries.[148] Until the middle of the second century, prices were most commonly recorded either for the whole month or for a tripartite division of a month into 'beginning – middle – end'. The latter formulation occurs especially with the staple goods barley and dates. After *c.* 145, there is an increasing number of cases of more precise – even daily – notations, a development which culminated in diaries such as AD -82B, r18 with separate barley prices for the morning and the afternoon of the same day.

Table 5.10 offers an overview of the price quotations of the Seleucid period and shows that in spite of the fact that the ADs tend to get more exhaustive over time, there is actually a decrease in the total number of the months for which barley prices are attested. There are 151 months with at least one barley price reported in the earlier half of the Seleucid rule over Babylonia (counted here as 300–225), whereas from the later half

---

[148] This development of the frequency and length of the historical sections is discussed in Pirngruber 2013: 200–2.

Table 5.10. *Distribution of barley prices in the Seleucid period*

Attestations[a]	300–225	Percentage	225–140	Percentage
January–March	40	26.5	35	25
April–June	39	26	30	21
July–September	32	21	33	23.5
October–December	40	26.5	43	30.5
Total	151	100	141	100

Note: [a] By 'Attestations' I mean the number of months that are represented by at least one price rather than the total number of prices attested.

(225–140), there are 141 months containing prices. This phenomenon can be attributed to the inclusion of the price data in the commodity price tablets.[149] If one were to consider only the price quotations from the diaries themselves, the years between 225 and 140 would indeed provide us with a higher number of barley prices.

A feature potentially influencing the results of any investigation is the distribution of prices within the year. Because of the phenomenon of seasonal fluctuation, a change in this pattern might bias prices and hence distort the analyses envisaged. Organising the data according to yearly quarters shows, however, that this is not the case. The most important finding is that the pre-harvest period January to March, which can be expected to contain the highest prices thanks to the phenomenon of seasonal fluctuation,[150] is represented in both periods by roughly one quarter of all attestations. *A priori*, one would thus not expect significant price differences between the earlier and later Seleucid period. The fact that the earlier period contains a slightly higher number of barley price attestations from the (immediate post-) harvest time of barley (quarter April to June) usually containing the lowest prices within the year is somewhat countered by the fact that in the later years more attestations from the period after the date harvest (quarter October to December), which is known to have lowered the barley price as well,[151] are extant.

---

[149] Slotsky and Wallenfels 2009. Four of these tablets (S/Ws 2, 3, 3A, 4) date to the earlier half of Seleucid reign over Babylonia, but only one (S/W 5) to the period 225-140.

[150] On which see most recently Földvári, van Leeuwen and Pirngruber 2011.

[151] See Vargyas 1997; also Földvári, van Leeuwen and Pirngruber 2011. Put simply, because of the increased availability of dates with the new harvest, their prices decreased strongly and hence it became more attractive to substitute the comparatively expensive barley with cheaper dates. This shift in demand in turn caused barley prices to sink as well.

Table 5.11. *Price volatility in the Seleucid period*

Commodity	CV: 300–225	CV: 225–140
Barley	0.63	0.41
Dates	0.39	0.54
Kasû	0.79	0.38
Cress	0.78	0.46
Sesame	0.59	0.34
Wool	0.75	0.29

In addition to lower average prices, the volatility of all commodities (with the conspicuous exception of dates) is also clearly lower in the later Seleucid period. Table 5.11 shows the coefficients of variation (CVs) for all commodities in the Seleucid period, revealing a substantial decline in volatility ranging between about one third in the case of barley and almost 75 per cent in the case of wool. The reason for the unexpectedly high volatility of date prices is to be sought precisely in the fact that this commodity shows a steady decline spanning a period of several decades.[152]

What can furthermore be shown is a significant decline in the seasonality of the barley price between these two periods. Figure 5.22 shows an index of seasonality derived from a regression analysis employing seasonal dummies. In both the Early and the Late Seleucid period, barley prices are clearly highest in the first two months of the year, hence the period preceding the harvest. In March and April, prices still increase but to a minor extent, maybe because of the harvest of some early barley varieties. In the months after the harvest, May and June, prices are clearly below their average in both periods. Interestingly, the pattern diverges between the two periods in the second half of the year. In the Early Seleucid period, prices continued to stay below average through summer and started rising from October onwards. In the Late Seleucid period on the other hand, the barley price started to rise in August but returned to below-average values in October and November. The period of the date harvest can thus be shown

---

[152] In such a pattern, prices continuously deviate to a significant extent from the mean. Contrast the graphs for barley (Figure 5.1) and dates (Figure 5.2): whereas the former shows an almost straight trend-line for much of the later Seleucid period with prices clustering in a narrow range around the mean, the graph for dates shows a significant price decline between *c.* 230 and 170, higher prices throughout much of the 170s and 160s and again lower prices in the 140s.

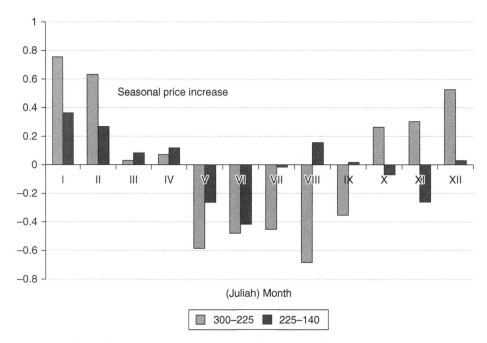

Figure 5.22 Seasonal fluctuation 300–225 and 225–140

to have had a stronger impact on barley prices after *c.* 230, when the prices of that commodity (and hence its demand elasticity) were lower.

However, the overall impact of seasonality is consistently higher in the earlier period. The index number of the price increase for January (which is the highest value for both periods) is 0.747 for the years 300–225, but only 0.359 for the years 225–140. Similarly, the negative growth rates in May amounts to −0.584 for the earlier period but only to −0.266 for the later. This finding complements the stronger impact of exogenous shocks in the earlier Seleucid period.

The graphs for the various commodities, and in particular barley, discussed in this chapter display a remarkable number of prices that diverge to a considerable extent from the trend-line, known as outliers. This chapter has investigated *inter alia* the reasons behind these deviations of commodity prices from the expected range by looking at their historical background. The basic reasoning behind this approach is fairly simple. Market prices such as the prices recorded in the ADs are set by the interplay of supply and demand, and various types of historical events are expected to have an impact either on the supply or on the demand situation of the individual commodities and thus to affect – increase or, less often, decrease – prices. Also, changes in the price level can come about by a decrease or an increase in the amount of money in circulation, which in antiquity was highly susceptible to the vicissitudes of history, too.[153] A simple (abstract) example of a demand shock would be a conscription of armed troops in the city of Babylon: in such a scenario, the presence of additional mouths to feed would put a considerable strain on the stocks of grain (and other foodstuffs) available, meaning that food prices would rise thanks to the increased demand. Supply shocks occur when, for example, during an episode of warfare, the city is besieged and cut off from its agricultural hinterland, or when crop failure as a result of bad weather or crop diseases reduces the availability of staple food.

Overall, this hitherto prevailing approach of elucidating price movements by reference to political history has shown good results.[154] The historical context of the prices often provided interesting – if occasionally tentative – explanations of oscillations in the price data. In the light of the sheer number of instances where it is possible to plausibly correlate history and prices, it would be highly unsatisfactory to explain away price peaks and troughs by 'intrinsic' factors, that is, mainly the harvest outcome. In order to strengthen the claim that historical events impact prices in Babylonia, I show in the next chapter by means of a regression analysis that such a correlation exists also on a formal level.

[153] In addition to the section on the Early Hellenistic Period and the minting of the Persian treasury above, see also, e.g., Jursa 2010: 734–53 for the long sixth century and van der Spek, Földvári and van Leeuwen 2015 for a comparison of the effects of a change in money supply between Seleucid Babylonia and medieval England. Note also the cautious discussion of commodity (grain) prices in the Greek Mediterranean by von Reden and Rathbone 2015: 167–8.

[154] For such approaches to the Babylonian prices, see, e.g., van der Spek 2000a and 2006b, as well as the comments of van der Spek 2014b and Slotsky and Wallenfels 2009 on the data discussed in their respective contributions. Von Reden 2014: 261 points to the potential relevance of political history in explaining price developments in Hellenistic Egypt (and Delos).

6 | Historical Events in a Quantitative Analysis

Prelude: The Flaws of Narrative History

In the preceding discussion of commodity prices from Late Achaemenid and Hellenistic Babylonia, price peaks and troughs have repeatedly been explained by reference to political events. For example, a cluster of high prices in the 230s immediately visible in several commodity graphs was shown to be correlated to a period of both political unrest and natural disasters. In addition, the two most notable price troughs in 188 and 166 are contemporary to events (the treaty of Apameia and the *pompē* at Daphne, respectively) that can reasonably be adduced as instances of a drain on precious metal temporarily depressing prices. In the present chapter, I will investigate the impact of historical events, political or other, on the price data of the ADs in more depth. Before substantiating the claim that it is indeed possible to link prices with extant historical information not merely by means of the traditional impressionistic method of a simple juxtaposition of historical data on the one hand with price data on the other, but via a statistical examination of the data, I will address the weaknesses of the former method.

By means of an example, I have discussed the one outlier in the barley price data from the Late Achaemenid period elsewhere (Pirngruber 2014), establishing a connection to a locust invasion damaging the harvest. The one price deviating from the pattern of low volatility in the Achaemenid barley price data between *c.* 350 and 330 dates to March 346, when the equivalent dropped from 120 litres per shekel at the beginning of month XII (*addaru*) – an equivalent which aligns very well with 117 litres per shekel at the end of the preceding month – to 69 litres only at the end of the month. As such sudden price jumps do not normally occur it is tempting to reckon with an unexpected exogenous shock behind this development. There is indeed one event which can explain the almost 50 per cent reduction of the equivalent, corresponding to a rise of 75 per cent of the (shekel per *kurru*) price from 1.5 to 2.61.

Table 6.1. *Barley equivalent in early spring 346*

Diary	Month[a]	Julian date	Price equivalent (in *qa*)
AD -346	IX	03.12.–22.12 347	102
	–TIL	23.12.–01.01 346	108+
	X	02.01.–21.01 346	114
	–TIL	22.01.–30.01 346	120
	XI–TIL	20.02.–01.03 346	117
	XII–SAG	02.03.–11.03 346	120
	–TIL	22.03.–30.03 346	69

Note: [a] SAG and TIL specify that the recorded price applies for the beginning (SAG) and the end of month (TIL) only.

An invasion of locusts is recorded in the same month (XII) and even in the same period (days 27–29) of the sudden rise in the price of barley. The pernicious impact of locust invasions, potentially obliterating entire harvests standing in the fields, was already known to the Mesopotamians as is clear from predictions such as 'If at the appearance of the moon (the star sign of) Scorpius stands by its right horn: in that year locusts will rise and consume the harvest.'[1] This locust invasion, as well as all other attestations of this type of event recorded in the diaries, has been discussed elsewhere in greater detail, with the result that in this instance the plague of locusts is indeed the most plausible explanation for the increase in prices.[2] Also, there are no other convincing explanations of the price movement. No internal strife or other events which may have caused this steep rise in prices are known from year 347/6. An assumption that this increase was merely connected to a more general shortage before the imminent barley harvest is not convincing. For such an explanation, the decrease in the equivalent in the same month is too steep. In normal years, the immediate pre-harvest period is characterised by a steady but smoother decline. To remain in the Late Achaemenid period, in AD -372 the equivalent is the same at the beginning and middle of month X (33 litres per shekel), declines then

---

[1] SAA X 364, r11–13. For more instances see CAD E (1958), s.v. *erbu* c. In particular, Neo-Assyrian kings occasionally compared the destructive impact of their army to a swarm of locusts, see, e.g., TCL 3 187 from the reign of Sargon II (721–705).

[2] Pirngruber 2014. In the majority of instances such a correlation could not be established, i.e., locust invasions do not automatically lead to price increases. This can be explained by the date of the invasions, which most often took place between the barley harvest and before the seeding when the crop was safe in the storage facilities.

to 28.5 at the end of that month and further to 24 litres at the beginning of the following month XI. Rather than a sudden drop of 50 per cent in the equivalent occurring within a period of ten days, we are dealing here with a decline in the equivalent in much smoother steps of about 15 per cent over a period longer than one month. AD -180D, from the reign of Antiochus III, shows an even more gradual decrease in prices over the period of the year in question, from 90 litres at the beginning of month XII to 84 in the middle and 78 at the end of the month. Several other instances distributed throughout the dataset confirm this pattern.

Such an investigation – if we indeed find solid instances of correlation between outliers in the price data and different kinds of exogenous shocks – is a straightforward way to make a case for the price-determining force of historical events. Some possible correlations between political history and peak prices have been discussed already in Chapter 5.[3] There is, however, a methodological problem also, and that is the positivist assumption inherent in such an approach. After all, it not only presupposes that all significant deviations from the mean price can be explained by recourse to historical events, but also to events that are documented in the extant sources. The highest outlier in the barley price data from the later Seleucid period – reign of Antiochus III onwards – helps to illustrate the danger. In April 208, the barley price rose to 3.75 shekels/*kurru*, which amounts to almost 2.5 times the period's mean price. However, already in the following month, the price dropped first to 2 and then even to 1.07 shekels/*kurru*. The best explanation for the high price is thus simply a supply crisis immediately before the harvest. Once new barley reached the market, the price even dropped to a level below average.[4] It is indeed tantalising that the highest outlier in the barley price data for the Seleucid period after 225 was caused by simple seasonal fluctuation rather than by an exogenous shock.

In addition to such methodological considerations, connections between price peaks and extant historical data often appear tenuous at best, with the interpretation being little more than an 'educated guess'. As an example, I would like to provide a brief discussion of whether the high barley prices in 257/6, up to 7.5 shekels/*kurru*, might again be explicable as caused by an exogenous shock. In autumn 256, there is a brief notice of skirmishes in the city of Babylon in an Astronomical Diary (AD -255A, r15), but only after the high prices which were recorded in February and April of the same year, and even in July 257. This leaves us with the tempting option to interpret

---

[3] See also the final paragraph there for earlier pertinent literature.

[4] On seasonal fluctuation, see, e.g., van der Spek and Mandemakers 2003: 527 and Vargyas 2001: 86–9.

the fighting as a kind of food riot, but excludes these disturbances as cause of the high prices.

The diary of the preceding year, AD -256, reports a locust invasion during the harvest period of 257 in Babylonia, a kind of event which about a century earlier in the Achaemenid period could be shown to potentially drive up prices to a significant extent.[5] The fact that prices also remained high the following year can be explained by the phenomenon of autocorrelation, a bad harvest entailing a lower availability of seed corn and resulting in similarly high prices in the following year also.

The supply situation might have been exacerbated by government strains put on the region in the context of the Second Syrian War (260–253). Then again, it is doubtful that this conflict had a major impact on Babylonian prices: it was fought exclusively in Asia Minor (Ephesus, Caria, Lydia) and on the east coast of the Mediterranean (Arados), and according to the reconstruction of John D. Grainger, the main part of the fighting took place in the earliest years, between *c.* 260 and 258.[6] Demands of the central administration might, however, have aggravated an already precarious situation. There is one brief reference in St Jerome's commentary on the Book of Daniel that refers to this period, stating that in the many wars fought between Antiochus II Theos and Ptolemy II Philadelphus, the former convoked troops from Babylon and other regions in the east (*In Danielem* 11.6: *totis Babylonis atque Orientis viribus dimicavit*). Hence, if we take the First Syrian War as a historical example, there might have been an additional increase in demand as a consequence of the convocation of an army in Babylon. Considering both the point in time as well as the location of the military operations, this is a somewhat implausible scenario, however. As stated above, the major manoeuvres had taken place before 257, and unlike in the First Syrian War, the Ptolemaic army did not, to the best of our knowledge, invade inland Syria, but confined its operations to the shores of the Mediterranean. Some negative impact in the form of financial contributions in cash or kind cannot, however, be discarded entirely in the light of the duration of the war.

Not only barley but also the other commodities exhibit above-average prices during these years. The date price stood at above-average values in the period between July 257 and May 256, fluctuating between 3.5 and 4 shekels/*kurru* compared to the mean of the earlier Seleucid period of 2.25

[5] The prices of these years have also been discussed in Pirngruber 2014.
[6] Grainger 2010: 121–7. On the war in general see also Will 1979[2]: 234–43, and Grainger 2010: 117–36. Grainger's dating of the secessions of the Bactrians and of Andragoras to 256 is more than doubtful, see Lerner 1999 and the thoughtful paper of Luther 1999.

shekels/*kurru*. There is thus a notable difference in the magnitude of the price increases between the two commodities dates and barley. Whereas the date price increased by a factor of about 150 per cent, the barley price rose to a level three times its mean. Considering that additionally the date prices either date to the pre-harvest period (July 257) or also to the months preceding the barley harvest at a time of already high barley prices (the prices in spring 256), a simple increase in demand for dates as a result of the limited availability (and costliness) of barley seems the most plausible explanation. Cress and sesame also show a similar pattern of above-average prices in spring 256. The sesame price, peculiarly, peaked for a second time in October 254, after it had already returned to more moderate levels in early 254. By then, the prices of barley and cress prices were similarly back to a normal (in both cases slightly below-average) level.

A reconstruction of the price history of that period could look like this: in spring 257, a locust invasion severely affected the barley harvest, driving up prices of both barley and, as a consequence of the shift in demand, to a lesser extent of dates. As a consequence of the ensuing dearth and possibly also government demands, local unrest was registered in Babylon in autumn 256, further destabilising the market situation: the highest sesame price and the episode of skirmishes in Babylon were recorded in the same month. There are also a few indications that already in the last years of the preceding decade all was not well in Babylon. The little information we have at our disposal conveys the impression of a rather tense and unstable political situation: AD -261B reports in a fragmentary passage the seizure of fields, mentioning a guard on a fortress as well as the verb GAZ, 'to kill, to murder'. Additionally, the commodity price list S/W 3 gives for the otherwise undocumented period 266–264 a barley price not only above average but also consistently increasing.

Such explanations are clearly not very satisfactory, and some past assertions are of dubious value at best. The high barley prices of 6 shekels/*kurru* and more prevailing in the winter of 286/5 are a good case in point. They were not recorded in an Astronomical Diary but on a commodity price list (S/W 2) and have been interpreted by editors of the tablet in connection with the final machinations of Demetrius Poliorcetes and his capture by Seleucus.[7] This solution seems highly unlikely. Demetrius had already been expelled from his Macedonian kingdom by Pyrrhus in 288, and

---

[7]   Slotsky and Wallenfels 2009: 53. Having been expelled from his Macedonian kingdom by Pyrrhus, Demetrius invaded Asia Minor at the head of a small army but was soon defeated and taken prisoner by Seleucid troops, see Will 1979[2]: 89–97.

spent the following years trying in vain to assert himself in regions held by Lysimachus in Asia Minor. The number of his troops cannot have been too impressive, given that Lysimachus did not deem it necessary to take up arms himself but rather sent out his son Agathocles to deal with the matter. Additionally, the comment of Seleucus' adviser Patrocles that 'the expense of maintaining the soldiers of Demetrius was a very small matter' points in that direction.[8] This whole episode, the duration of which was not longer than a few months, happened between the Taurus and Amanus mountain ranges and thus in Cilicia, far from Babylonia. There is no historical information on events in Babylonia this year; we know, however, that the crown prince Antiochus did not reside in the city in this year, but further to the east in Media (Diod. 21 20), which potentially relieved Babylonia from the expenses of maintaining the court. What is remarkable is the peculiar price pattern of the price development of the year in question, SE 26: the barley equivalent drops from a very moderate 84 litres/shekel in month I to 60 litres in month III and further to 36 and 39 litres in months VIII and IX respectively. This movement running counter to the usual pattern of seasonal fluctuation of falling prices in the period after the harvest, in combination with the rather low price still prevailing in month I, points to an unexpected harvest failure due to crop disease, adverse climatic conditions or similar. Of course, historical-political factors such as internal strife causing crop destruction cannot be excluded but, as stated above, the sources are silent about events in Babylonia in 286/5.

Finally, in some cases, there is simply no historical information at all extant, which could serve for an explanation of price peaks, tentative as it may be. The high price of 6 shekels/*kurru* prevailing in month IX year 30 SE (December 282) for example must remain enigmatic. In the light of the fact that in both month VIII and X of the same year prices are a rather moderate level (2.5 shekels/*kurru* and less) it is tempting to assume a scribal error – an option that always has to be considered.[9]

The reverse situation to the instances just discussed, that is, the absence of price data during known events which may have caused exogenous shocks

---

[8] Plut. *Dem.* 47.3. The context of Patrocles' statement was a petition of Demetrius to Seleucus for help and provisions. Obviously, his campaigns in Asia Minor were not going very well.

[9] As regards the possibility of explaining this high price with historical events, the chronicle BCHP 9 reports for 282 the mustering of the army by Seleucus I before the final confrontation against Lysimachus at Corupedium in early spring 281, which seems to have taken place in Babylon. However, as the convocation took place about six months before the high price under discussion, and prices were at an average level throughout the rest of the same year, this event can be ruled out as causing the outlier. See the commentary to line 3 of chronicle BCHP 9 at www.livius.org/babylonia.html (last accessed 15 September 2015).

to price levels, also often prevents us from obtaining a clearer picture of the impact of exogenous shocks. The best case in point is the campaign led by Ptolemy II into Syria (autumn 246) and Babylonia (early 245) following the accession to the throne of Seleucus II. This invasion, which started the Third Syrian War (246–241), was only short-lived because internal revolts in Egypt forced Ptolemy to retreat in the same year.[10] According to St Jerome, Ptolemy carried off booty to the immense value of 40,000 talents; this statement is, however, of uncertain historical value and might be dismissed as derived from Ptolemaic propaganda.[11] The writer of the fragmentary chronicle BCHP 11 does not mention any plundering or looting, but numerous references to battles and slaughter indicate the plight of the city of Babylon during this invasion. The date of the campaign – January and February – is also interesting, as the barley crop during these months is maturing in the fields and potentially exposed to destruction. The extant price data from that period is meagre: in August 246, 1 *kurru* of barley cost 0.7 shekels (258 litres per shekel); after a gap of three and a half years, the price stood at 0.88 shekels/*kurru* (204 litres per shekel) in January 242; and a few months later at 0.8, a decrease best explained by the usual pattern of seasonal fluctuation. The period of the actual invasion and its aftermath is not covered by any prices, and if there were any repercussions (which is very likely considering the impact of exogenous shocks in the period 300–225), prices had already recovered to about the level before the invasion in winter 243/2.

The situation in autumn 163 is similar. There are no prices extant from this year, during which some kind of conflict between the Greek population and the 'people of the land' took place, possibly in connection with the dispute over the regency for the minor Antiochus V between some of the highest officials of the empire, Philipp against Lysias and Timarchus.[12]

A Change of Method

In the preceding chapters, we have analysed the price data from the ADs in a diachronic perspective with the focus on outliers and possible explanations

---

[10] On the circumstances and course of events of this war, see Will 1979²: 248–61 and Grainger 2010: 153–70; also Hölbl 1994: 46–50. The main primary source is Justin 27 1.1–4.

[11] *In Danielem* 11.8: *quadraginta milia talentorum argenti tulit et uasa pretiosa simulacraque*. In the light of other quantifications of booties and indemnities occurring in the context of warfare between Hellenistic empires, the amount certainly seems exaggerated. Austin 1986: 485, however, raises no objection to this number.

[12] Del Monte 1997: 83–4, with a comment by van der Spek 2000b. See in general Ehling 2008: 111–30 on the period between Antiochus IV and Demetrius I.

for those anomalously high (or sometimes also low) prices. One conclusion was that certain events such as the extended period of domestic warfare in Babylonia in the last quarter of the fourth century, to name just a particularly influential one, indeed had repercussions on the price data.

In the pages that follow, I shall attempt to advance from an analysis of the correlation of individual historical events and outliers in the price data to an investigation of whether a systematic impact on prices of specific types of events can also be ascertained on a formal, statistical level. In order to attain this goal, a database of historical facts has been compiled from cuneiform documents – mainly Astronomical Diaries and the Hellenistic chronicle series BCHP – as well as Classical sources, and giving due consideration to the results of modern scholarship, containing events of a variety of different natures, from political episodes to ecological disasters. In a second step, these heterogeneous facts and events were classified and distributed among discrete categories.

These different classes of events will then be used as dummy variables in a regression analysis. This simply means that the presence or absence of each type of events in every year will be accounted for in an analysis of the oscillations in the time series of the commodity prices provided by the ADs. The aim of this procedure is to make statements about whether a given category of events systematically – rather than only selectively, as was shown in the preceding chapters – influenced prices, and to what extent. One methodological advantage of this approach over the discussion of outliers in the previous chapter is that all instances of a certain kind of event are considered, irrespective of the prices prevailing in the years of their occurrence. Thus, instances that seem to have had little or no impact on the price data can be included as well. This way, accusations that the investigation is marred by a confirmation bias, hence by an undue focus on events that show price-driving forces, can be effectively countered.

On the basis of the results obtained in the previous chapters, the first relevant category that jumps to mind is of course 'Warfare'. The historical discussion has shown that the underlying causes for price changes in the historical episodes of warfare can differ considerably from case to case: the presence of an army which needed to be supplied (demand shock); crop destruction or destruction of the agricultural infrastructure, most importantly the network of irrigation canals (supply shock);[13] influx or also drains of large amounts of silver in the form of plunder or indemnities due to won or lost campaigns (changes in the monetary base).

---

[13] Chaniotis 2005: 121–9 provides a discussion of the impact of warfare on agriculture according to classical authors and Greek epigraphic material.

Furthermore, an important issue that needs to be addressed at this point is the fact that several events could actually be interpreted as belonging to more than one category of events. A case in point is the indemnity payment amounting to a total of 15,000 talents of silver stipulated in the peace treaty of Apameia in 188. At first glance, the most logical interpretation of this event is to consider it under a heading 'Monetary shock': in particular, the initial payment of 3,000 talents (corresponding to almost 80 metric tonnes) of silver very likely put a severe – if only short-lived – strain on the precious metal resources of the empire. As the payment was due in coin,[14] an equivalent of 4.5 million tetradrachms was drained from the empire in a single year. However, there was more to this treaty than mere financial compensation: the loss of all territories in Asia Minor west of the Taurus mountain range and the compulsory reduction of the army's size, to name just two of the more grave effects. Historically speaking, the contract itself came about as the outcome of a lost conflict against the Romans.[15] There are thus equally good reasons to include the event under the heading of 'Warfare abroad'.

A more sophisticated approach is thus suggested to account for the qualitative differences between some of the categories. In a first step, the larger historical episodes consisting of a multitude of single facts, which can be classified as 'Domestic warfare' and 'Warfare abroad' are analysed *in toto*. Only then will the individual factors causing the price fluctuations, conceptualised as more abstract categories of events, be treated not only in their own right but also in relation to their cumulative effect on the price increases (and also decreases) throughout the historical episodes. As causal factors which occur mainly – but not exclusively – in connection with bellicose episodes, the following categories are sufficiently attested in order to qualify for further consideration:

- presence of an army in Babylon
- battles in and invasions of Babylonia.

It should be clear from the outset that these categories are not self-evident facts but rather are based on an interpretative reading of historical events.

[14] Le Rider 1992 and 1993: 51–2. The contract did not specify a denomination in which the payment had to be made, only that it was due in coins and in silver with a high degree of fineness. Fittingly, one third of the silver presented during the triumph of L. C. Scipio Asiaticus consisted of coins, whereas the usual proportion of coined silver was below 10 per cent; see Le Rider and de Callataÿ 2006: 179–84

[15] The short-term impact of this payment has been discussed at length in the previous chapter; for a brief discussion of the treaty see Sherwin-White 1984: 22–7. See also Grainger 2002: 328–49 on the negotiations preceding the conclusion of the treaty, especially 332–5 and 347–8.

It is thus apposite to discuss them briefly in order to elucidate by what rea-soning (other than the mere availability of historical information) they were compiled and which events were included therein. Rather than consti-tuting a mere simplification of factual history, this subsumption of related events under one common heading is an uncomplicated way of rendering historical information fit for a numerical analysis. After all, in the words of Hatcher and Bailey (2001: 13), 'If order is to be produced out of chaos, the modeller can only do so by abstracting common themes from the vast mass of seemingly unique and unrepeatable events of history.'

The focus in this section is of course on those kinds of events which are likely to have caused prices to rise or fall.[16] Unfortunately, there are also poten-tially interesting types of events that are difficult to model into a regression analysis. For example, the presence of the king and the royal court, which is occasionally attested in the ADs, would constitute an interesting category of a demand shock-type, considering the obligation of the province to sup-ply the Great King and his entourage with conspicuous amounts of various foodstuffs, as attested in the early Achaemenid period.[17] However, for several reasons this type of event is not a very suitable candidate to be employed as a dummy variable. First of all, the context of royal visits needs to be accounted for. For example, Antiochus III's visit to Babylon in 205, which included his participation in the Babylonian New Year's festival, also marked the end of his *anabasis* into the Upper Satrapies. He thus arrived at the head of a signif-icant number of armed troops, and we would expect this instance to have a stronger impact on commodity prices than, for example, a visit in a period of peace with a significantly smaller accompaniment.

More importantly, the status of the city of Babylon differed consider-ably during the various sub-periods between *c.* 400 and 140. In the Late Achaemenid period, the city was one of four imperial capital cities (along-side Persepolis, Susa and Ecbatana) and as such visited regularly by the Great King.[18] During the short-lived reign of Alexander the Great, the city

---

[16] For example, a category 'Cultic events' could have been established easily on the basis of the source material at our disposition. This category could have included *inter alia* the performance of sacrifices for the life (*ana bulṭi*) of the king or a high official to Bēl, Bēltiya and the Great Gods in the Esangila temple, which are so frequently described in the diaries, especially during the first half of the second century (see Pirngruber 2010). These irregular sacrifices, performed in addition to the daily rituals (Linssen 2005), consisted of small quantities of oxen and sheep from the temple herds, but they most certainly had no impact at all on the commodity prices.

[17] Kleber 2008: 84–94; Tolini 2011: 157–64.

[18] See Tuplin 1998 for a meticulous discussion of the sources. The pattern of seasonal migration between the four capital cities postulated by various Greek historians is according to him 'not in principle undermined' (89) by evidence from Persepolis.

also played an important role and was, *inter alia*, the seat of the financial administration of his empire and also the place where Alexander received various delegations upon return from his campaigns.[19] However, at quite an early point during the reign of the Seleucid dynasty, Babylon lost its position as capital city and was replaced as such by Seleucia-on-the-Tigris. The latter city was founded in the last decade of the fourth century, at some point after Seleucus' acceptance of the royal title, although it was populated on a larger scale only with some delay in the late 290s/early 280s.[20] This event clearly did not have the catastrophic consequences attributed to it by some Classical authors,[21] but from the early third century onwards, Babylon was only irregularly visited by the king and his retinue. Furthermore, with the foundation of the Syrian tetrapolis around Antioch-on-the Orontes as new imperial capital and a general focus of Seleucid foreign policy on the (often conflict-ridden) interaction with Ptolemaic Egypt and various minor powers in Asia Minor, the epicentre of the Seleucid Empire shifted considerably westwards. Hence, whereas Babylon was the capital city located in the heartland of an empire in the fourth century, it was degraded to a provincial town in the eastern half of the Seleucid Empire afterwards. It is thus only in this latter period, when royal visits became increasingly infrequent, that some discernible effect of the presence of the royal court can be expected. The main obstacle, however, is the whereabouts of the king, which are often difficult to ascertain. The sources at our disposal do not provide us with enough information to establish a sufficiently reliable database on a yearly basis. For all these reasons, a category 'Presence of the king' has to be discarded as inapplicable for regression analysis.

Similarly, locust invasions, although mentioned as price-raising force in previous chapters, are also a category not easily amenable to statistical analysis. This is mainly due to peculiarities in the price data in these instances. One of the outliers brought in connection with this kind of event, the high barley prices of up to 7.5 shekels/*kurru* in 257/6, actually dates to the year after the invasion; it was argued that there was an indirect connection to the invasion: autocorrelation caused prices to remain high also in the year after the event itself.[22] However, such an indirect relationship would not be

---

[19] Boiy 2004: 104–17 provides a convenient overview of the history of Babylon during the years between 331 and 323.

[20] For the elusive foundation date of Seleucia-on-the-Tigris see, e.g., Boiy 2004: 135–6. See BCHP 5 (r6–9 and commentary) at www.livius.org/babylonia.html on the settlement of Greeks from Babylon to Seleucia during the reign of Antiochus I as crown prince.

[21] Most prominently Strabo 16 1.5, but see van der Spek 2006a for a more balanced picture.

[22] Pirngruber 2014: 171–2.

accounted for by a simple regression analysis. The second and more solid case of locusts destroying the harvest, in March 346 is equally problematic because of the way the prices of this period were recorded by the scribes of the ADs: the price drop occurred suddenly at the end of a month with otherwise favourable prices, and our approach of taking a monthly average in case of multiple attestations would smooth out the impact of the invasion.[23]

Administrative measures such as the introduction of new taxes in the later 270s as attested in documents from Uruk[24] or the installation of a *zazakku* during the reign of Antiochus IV, possibly in order to gain better control of the finances of the Esangila, are even more difficult to gauge. In particular, such interferences in the province's economic life are more likely to have a gradual impact on prices rather than a one-time effect in the form of an exogenous shock.

The Impact of Warfare on Commodity Prices

The Different Categories of Warfare

As outlined above, historical instances of warfare will be treated in a different way from the single shocks (i.e. the individual battles) constituting the overarching episode. Two more qualifications are in order. First, a distinction is made between warfare in Babylonia and warfare outside that province. This procedure has been advocated by van der Spek[25] on the grounds of the potentially fundamentally distinct effects of the two scenarios: whereas domestic warfare almost certainly will drive up prices, the effect of warfare abroad is more ambiguous and can entail both rising and falling prices. A second distinction to be made is that between 'Warfare' and 'Rebellion', which seems to offer a useful way of accounting for the often notable differences in the extent and intensity of episodes of bellicose activities. The wealth of historical information at our disposition should provide us with the possibility of gauging, albeit crudely, the difference in magnitude of price increases between these two scenarios. It is of course a delicate task at this point to establish a firm distinction. Under 'Warfare', first and foremost armed conflicts involving at least one royal army (Seleucid or also invading royal armies, for example of the Ptolemies in 246), will be

---

[23] For the regression, it was chosen to consistently employ one price per month. In the case of several attestations per month, the arithmetic mean of all attestations was calculated.

[24] Doty 1977: 308–35.

[25] Van der Spek 2000a: 298–9.

included. This limitation to royal armies is taken as a convenient proxy for the dimension of the armed conflict. In absolute terms, as shown below, this means that usually an army consisting of an absolute minimum of 10,000 troops but more often substantially larger forces were involved: the Seleucid kings were able to muster armed forces of 50,000–60,000 soldiers when the need arose.[26] A final definition concerns geography. The term 'Babylonia' is here used to refer to the city of Babylon itself and its more immediate surroundings, including several smaller towns such as Borsippa, Kiš and Cutha, not the whole of the satrapy, including its distinct districts such as the Sealand in the very south or the trans-Tigridian Sittacene.

Warfare in Babylonia

Episodes of domestic warfare within Babylonia featured prominently in the preceding chapter as explanations for outliers in the price data of the diaries. Such warfare could affect both the supply and demand situation: the supply situation, because plundering and crop destruction were frequent phenomena in ancient warfare and were consciously employed as a military strategy to force the enemy to surrender,[27] but also because in times of war, spatial market integration – the possibilities for trade – deteriorates or suffers outright disruption, particularly when a city is besieged.[28] Additionally, one has to consider the secondary effects of warfare such as damage to the canal system so vital for Babylonian agriculture, and the reduced availability of manpower for seeding and/or harvesting as a result of conscription. The demand situation is affected when a more lengthy presence of an enemy army puts additional strains on the food supply. Furthermore, in the case that the army is abundantly supplied with silver, an inflationary effect because of an influx of money in addition to an increase in demand cannot be excluded. As mentioned above, periods of warfare are also periods of increased minting activity. An instructive example given by Aperghis (2004: 236–42) is the eastern *anabasis* of Antiochus III around 210, which

---

[26] See the assessment of Bar-Kochva 1976: 7–19.

[27] The most vivid descriptions stem (not surprisingly) from the Neo-Assyrian period. In the famous letter of Sargon II to the god Aššur (TCL 3) one reads for example (line 275) EBUR *tuk-lat* UN[MEŠ]-*šú* ... *ab-ri-iš a-qu-ud-ma*, 'the harvest on which his people relied, I burnt like a brush pile'. The experience of crop destruction is also reflected in omen apodoses such as EBUR KUR KÚR GU₇, 'the enemy will consume the harvest of the country' from the series *šumma izbu* (III 81, cf. Leichty 1970: 62). An example from the Hellenistic period is provided by the Diadochi Chronicle, BCHP 3, r25: SAR-*ut* URU *ù* EDIN SAR, 'he (probably Antigonus the One-Eyed) plundered city and countryside'.

[28] For siege warfare in Mesopotamia see Oppenheim 1955 and Eph'al 2009.

went hand in hand with increased activity at the mint in Seleucia-on-the-Tigris, the central mint of the province of Babylonia. It cannot, however, be excluded that some of the excess silver eventually found its way into the city of Babylon by means of trade, royal munificence upon return from the campaign when the royal court sojourned in the city or other mechanisms.

Both the ADs as well as Classical authors provide us with several reports of warfare in and around the city of Babylon, and sometimes even complementary accounts of the same events survive. More often than not these bellicose events can firmly be dated. The first episode considered, the battle of Cunaxa fought between the royal army of the reigning king Artaxerxes II and the mercenary troops of his rebellious brother Cyrus the Younger described most exhaustively by Xenophon (who himself participated in this battle), actually predates the beginning of the price series by several years. Although nominally an attempt at usurpation, the number of troops involved is closer to those deployed in the larger battles of the Hellenistic period than of a merely local rebellion and hence qualifies this event for the category of warfare. Although the numbers provided by Greek historians are grossly exaggerated – Cyrus alone is said by Diodorus (14 22.1 and 19.1) to have disposed of 70,000 troops, plus 13,000 Greek mercenaries, whereas for his brother the king even the minimum figure amounts to 400,000 troops[29] – more realistic estimates still oscillate between 40,000 and 60,000 troops for each of the armies of this battle.[30] As a point of reference, the Seleucid army defeated in the battle of Raphia (217) consisted according to Polybius (5 79) of 64,000 infantry and 5,000 cavalry, while the size of the victorious Ptolemaic army was somewhat larger (70,000 infantry and 6,000 cavalry).

The inclusion of the battle at Gaugamela in October 331, the decisive encounter between Alexander the Great and his opponent Darius III, within this category is even less disputable. Greek historians are at variance as to the numbers of troops involved (and their indications again have to be taken *cum grano salis*),[31] but this meeting of two of the largest royal armies

---

[29] Ctesias gave the same number of 400,000 troops according to Plut. *Art.* 13.2. The numbers produced in the eye-witness account of Xenophon are even higher. According to the Athenian general, 100,000 barbarian troops of Cyrus (plus 10,400 Greek hoplites) faced a 1,200,000-strong army of the Great King, of whom only 900,000 participated in the battle as one of the commanders, Abrocomas, arrived only when the battle was already over (Xen. *Anab.* 1 7.10–12). Plutarch, in his biography of Artaxerxes, sets the number of Greek mercenaries marching with Cyrus at 'nearly 13,000', whereas the total army of the Great King is said to have consisted of 900,000 men (Plut. *Art.* 6.4 and 7.3).

[30] Binder 2008: 184–8, especially 184–5.

[31] According to Justin (11 12.5), the troops of the Achaemenid king alone amounted to 400,000 infantry and 100,000 cavalry. The numbers in Diodorus (17 53.3) are even higher: he speaks

of the Ancient World is a most promising candidate for causing an exogenous shock. Both battle locations, Cunaxa and Gaugamela, are quite some
distance from the city of Babylon, however, in both instances the city had
to accommodate and thus also supply the armies both before and after the
battle, in the former instance the victorious army of Artaxerxes twice, in the
latter, first the Persian army under Darius and then, about three weeks after
the battle itself, the army of Alexander the Great.[32]

The period of continuous warfare following Alexander the Great's death
and the impact of the various armed conflicts between the different protagonists – in the main those of the ultimately victorious Seleucus against
Antigonus the One-Eyed and his son Demetrius Poliorcetes, but also minor
characters such as Docimus or Eumenes of Cardia – on Babylonian prices
has already received quite some attention in the scholarly literature.[33] During
the course of a decade and a half (*c.* 323–309), from the suppression of a
revolt of the Macedonian infantry instigated by Meleager in the aftermath
of the succession arrangement for Alexander the Great until Antigonus'
(involuntary) renunciation of the satrapy of Babylonia and Seleucus' final
triumph, the province was devastated almost yearly by bellicose episodes
on a different scale. As regards the former episode, the account by Diodorus
(18 2.4) does not mention bellicose action. According to him, reconciliation
was achieved already during the preparatory actions. However, the fuller
account by Q. Curtius not only mentions skirmishes in the city of Babylon
(e.g. 10 716–20) but also refers explicitly to the economic repercussions of
some of the actions undertaken. The blockade of Babylon by the infantry,
who had left the city as a consequence of the uprising led by Meleager, is
said to have caused dearth and famine (Curt. 10 8.12).[34]

---

of 800,000 infantry and 200,000 cavalry. In the accounts of both Arrian (*Anab.* 3 8.6) and
Plutarch (*Alex.* 31.1), the troops of Darius including his allies even surpass 1 million infantry.
As regards the veracity of the numbers of Greek historians, note that Bar-Kochva 1976: 72
and Bosworth 2002: 67 apparently judge at least Arrian's (*Anab.* 3 12.5) quantification of
Alexander's army (40,000 infantry, 7,000 cavalry) plausible. See also the comment of Bosworth
1988: 78, according to whom '[T]he Persians certainly had a numerical advantage, probably a
great advantage, but it cannot be quantified.'

[32] The entry of Alexander into Babylon is described in AD -330A+B, r9–15, see also Kuhrt 1990
on this episode. His activities in the city are recorded by Diod. 17 64.4–6; the same author
alludes to an army conscription of Darius III in Babylon preceding the battle (17 53.3).

[33] Most prominently in van der Spek 2000a: 299–305, but see also, e.g., Grainger 1999: 317–19
and Temin 2002: 55–6.

[34] The contestation of the Babylon settlement is analysed in detail by Bosworth 2002, in
particular 45–9. As for total numbers, Bosworth (2002: 81) seems to reckon 8,000–10,000
Macedonian infantry in the royal army (now under the supreme command of Perdiccas) in the
east at the time of Alexander's death.

Whereas the replacement of the satrap Archon *manu militari* by Docimus in 320 is to be counted as a minor episode (thus under 'Rebellion'), the tenacious fights between the armies of Seleucus and Antigonus between 311 and 309 and also the invasion of Babylonia by Eumenes and the *argyraspides* (silver-shields) under his command in 318/17 and his pursuit by both Seleucus and Antigonus qualify as warfare.[35] All of the three protagonists had considerable resources in terms of military power at their disposal. At the battle in the region of Gabiene fought in winter 317/16, Antigonus' 22,000 infantry and 9,000 cavalry defeated the numerically superior army of Eumenes (36,700 infantry, 6,000 cavalry); the army sizes in the slightly earlier battle of Paraetacene were roughly similar.[36] The final conflict between Antigonus and Seleucus starting in 311 also involved army sizes exceeding 10,000 infantry. Additionally, this time the city of Babylon itself was at the heart of the contention and suffered siege and destruction.[37] The Diadochi Chronicle reports that the city itself and the surrounding countryside as well as smaller towns in its vicinity, of which Cutha is mentioned explicitly, were repeatedly plundered. The tenacity of this struggle is also indicated by the partial success of Antigonus in the south of Babylonia (Uruk, Larsa and Ur), where he seemed to have prevailed over his opponent at least until summer 309.[38]

The final victory of Seleucus and his establishment of a monarchy, with the province of Babylonia playing an important role as centre point of the empire during its formative period,[39] marked a return to a more tranquil state of affairs. A longer period of relative quiet for the whole province commenced, lasting for almost half a century. It was only in 246 with the

---

[35] For the chronology see Boiy 2007a. The most important source for Babylonia during these years is ABC 10, known as the Chronicle of the Successors or Diadochi Chronicle. The most recent edition is found online as BCHP 3 (= ABC 10) with extensive commentary at www.livius.org/babylonia.html (accessed 21 October 2016).

[36] See Diod. 19 37–44 (Gabiene) and 27–31 (Paraetacene) for the fullest accounts of these battles. They are discussed at length in Bosworth 2002: 98–168. The victorious Antigonus co-opted the survivors from Eumenes' army and thus returned to Babylon with a total force of *c.* 60,000–70,000 troops, the cavalry amounting to about one fifth of that amount (Bosworth 2002: 92 and 159).

[37] Antigonus sent his son Demetrius with 15,000 infantry and 4,000 cavalry to reconquer the city from Seleucus. The latter, who according to Diodorus (19 90–1) had wrested the city from Antigonus' control with a minor force of only 800 infantry and 200 cavalry in the aftermath of the battle at Gaza in 312, is thought by Bosworth 2002 (236–8) to have replenished his ranks during the campaigns against Nicanor and his sorties into the eastern satrapies.

[38] The predominance of Antigonus is reflected in the different date formulas used in administrative documents in these cities, see table 2 in Joannès 2006: 132, and also Boiy 2007a: 22–7.

[39] On this point see Capdetrey 2007: 35–8 and 52–9.

invasion of Ptolemy III that the province suffered again military operations on a larger scale.[40] The most detailed account of this episode is now provided by the Babylonian chronicle BCHP 11,[41] which reports the attack on both Seleucia-on-the-Euphrates – the identification of this city is elusive – and Babylon by Ptolemaic troops, containing quite detailed descriptions of several skirmishes taking place in the city of Babylon in winter 246/5. Unfortunately, there are no attempts at quantification of the troops involved by the ancient historiographers (the source documentation for many of the Syrian wars is notoriously meagre), but the involvement of at least one royal army, the Ptolemaic one, is certain. Babylon was defended during the invasion by local troops and garrisons under the commands of the *rab sikkati* and the *pāhātu* of Seleucia according to BCHP 11.[42] As mentioned earlier, St Jerome (*In Danielem* 11.8) also reports of a massive booty of 40,000 talents of silver captured by Ptolemy III. This incident is a good case of domestic warfare in which economic repercussions are very likely to have occurred. This cannot, however, be ascertained, given the complete absence of price data during these years.

This incident was the only time that Babylonia suffered an invasion from a foreign army during the Seleucid period until the 140s. In the second half of that decade, at a time when Seleucid power was waning in all different parts of the empire, Babylonia suffered a quick succession of invasions of different regional powers. In autumn 145, the Elamite king Kamnaskires marched through the Babylonian countryside plundering and even defeated a Babylonian army under the *stratēgos* Ardāya (AD -144, r20–2). Already before this event, a band of marauders under a certain Aria'bu seems to have afflicted Babylonia (AD -144, 16–17). Finally, not even four years after these events, the Parthians under their king Mithridates I wrested Babylonia from the Seleucids in early summer 141. For more than a decade to come, Babylonia remained a bone of contention between the Seleucids and the Parthians, with regional rulers such as Hyspaosines of Mesene and nomadic tribes, most notably Arabs, additionally contributing to a precarious political situation.[43] Although possibly on a smaller scale than the

---

[40] On this Third Syrian (or Laodicean) War see Will 1979²: 248–61 and Grainger 2010: 153–70.

[41] Published online as Ptolemy III Chronicle at www.livius.org/babylonia (accessed 21 October 2016).

[42] Seleucus II, who had just ascended to the throne earlier the same year, seems to have been in Sittacene at the time of the invasion (see BCHP 10, r5–6, at www.livius.org/babylonia). About his activities during the period in which the Ptolemaic army stood in Babylonia nothing is known.

[43] Del Monte 1997: 102–44 provides brief comments to the historical passages of the Astronomical Diaries in the troubled period between 140 and 124.

invasion of Ptolemy III, the Elamite incursion is included in the category of 'Warfare in Babylonia' in order to adhere to the definition given above, namely the involvement of a royal army. Unfortunately, there is no information available on the size of the Elamite army. However, as that episode was accompanied by small-scale pillaging of other groups, it can be argued to have been larger than uprisings on a strictly local level discussed below under 'Rebellion'.

The Parthian takeover on the other hand is more difficult to gauge, as it is mainly known from the changed date formula in the Astronomical Diary of -140A referring to the Arsacid king.[44] Whether the takeover was accompanied by hostilities or even full-fledged warfare is uncertain; however, the perpetual struggles for the throne in Antioch will have greatly limited the capacity of the ruling king to intervene with a sizeable force. Indeed, it took the Seleucid Empire under its ruler Demetrius II about three years to attempt a reconquest of the province, which ended with the defeat and capture of Demetrius in summer 138. The price data of the years 141 and 140 in any case does not point to any major interruption of the economy: both barley and dates were less expensive in these years than throughout most of the 150s. Our interpretation will thus be one of a relatively peaceful takeover.

Warfare outside Babylonia

As already noted by van der Spek (2000a: 299), the effects of warfare in another region of the empire are more difficult to gauge. More specifically, he pointed to the possibilities of a decrease in demand due to military conscription in the province and to silver requisitions with a deflationary effect: both of these consequences of external warfare would drive down prices. However, as the discussion of the high barley and cress prices in 274 in the preceding chapter has shown, warfare abroad could also cause a demand shock and thus entail a period of increased prices in Babylon in the event of the royal army – or rather a part thereof – being convoked in the city.[45] The outcome of wars fought abroad also potentially exerted an influence on prices. Like requisitions, high indemnity payments for example can

---

[44] AD -140A, line 1: [MU 107.KAM *šá ši-i* MU 171.KAM ¹*Ar*]-*šá-kam* LUGAL; see Del Monte 1997: 102. See also the succinct account of these years in van der Spek 2010: 380.

[45] See also the discussion of the episode in van der Spek 2000a: 305–7. He explains the high prices by outright confiscations of grain (see also his interpretation of lines 34–9 of AD -273B at 305) rather than by an increased demand due to the presence of troops; but cf. above Chapter 5. He also points to the fact that over-taxation and/or confiscation of precious metals must have considerably worsened the financial situation of the locals.

Table 6.2. *Summary of the instances of domestic warfare*

Year	Event
401	Campaign of Cyrus the Younger against his brother Artaxerxes II, culminating in the battle of Cunaxa and the former's death. After victory, Artaxerxes led the army to Babylon to bestow honours upon his bravest generals. Artaxerxes gathered his troops at Ecbatana; before battle they pitched camp at the Euphrates in the 'plain of Babylonia'.
331	Battle at Gaugamela east of the Tigris in northern Babylonia on 1 October. Darius III gathered his troops at Babylon, which he reached after the defeat at Issus in 333. After Alexander the Great's victory, the Persian troops disperse, whereas his army marches towards Babylon. The city is taken peacefully after negotiations. Alexander and his troops sojourn for a period of *c.* 30 days.
323–322	Return of the Greco-Macedonian army to Babylon. Alexander the Great dies on 11 June 323 without a suitable heir. The Babylonian settlement is contested by the infantry troops under Meleager, with the result that the city is besieged. Indications of further upheavals, e.g., troops are sent from Babylon under the command of Peithon to quell rebellions in Bactria. Presence of royal court in Babylon until 319.
318–316	Silver requisition of Seleucus, the satrap of Babylonia. Eumenes invades the province and spends the winter of 318/17 in the 'Carian villages' in Babylonia; he is pursued by Antigonus, to whom Seleucus grants his support. Various references to destruction of the landscape and of scarcity of food. Eumenes is defeated in two battles by Antigonus in Paraetacene and Gabiene. After the latter's return to Babylon discord between Antigonus and Seleucus, who flees to Egypt.
311–308	After Antigonus' and Demetrius' defeat at Gaza, Seleucus reconquers Babylonia and also regions further to the east. Tenacious attempts by Antigonus and Demetrius to regain the province. Several military encounters between the two factions, leading to plundering of the countryside.
246–245	Ptolemy III invades Babylonia; prolonged warfare between Seleucid and Ptolemaic troops.
145–144	Bellicose activities of a certain Aria'bu and the Elamite king Kamnaskires in Babylonia. The province is defended by a general Ardāya, who is defeated. References to looting.

cause a drain of silver and thus deflation by reducing the amount of money in circulation. Annexations or loss of territory also potentially affect the state's finances by expanding or reducing the income generated by taxation. These latter effects are, however, not amenable to the current investigation as their effect becomes palpable in the long run only. Overall, one expects a weaker correlation of this category to price fluctuations in Babylon with respect to the previous category of domestic warfare. One reason for this expectation is that over time, the different types of events causing price decreases and increases respectively might cancel each other out (which incidentally strengthens the envisaged approach of treating causal factors of price increases separately from historical episodes). Additionally, the relative marginality of some of the cases – campaigns against insubordinate mountain peoples – will undoubtedly contribute to this pattern by having no repercussions at all on the local economy.

A useful guide to whether an impact on Babylonian prices can be reasonably expected for a given episode of warfare is the occurrence of at least one of the causal factors established above, namely 'Presence of an army' (i.e. convocation of troops in Babylon) or 'Monetary shock' (large indemnity payments or requisitions of silver). Regarding the latter, the only instance that comes to mind in combination with warfare abroad is the treaty of Apameia (and discussed in greater detail in the preceding chapter). A useful benchmark for the former factor is again the size of the forces deployed for battle by the Seleucid king. As the discussion below shows, major encounters (the battle at Raphia in 217, to name just the most conspicuous example) were regularly preceded by army convocations in the city of Babylon also, independent of where the actual battle was to take place. This possibility has to be allowed for even when not mentioned explicitly in the sources, especially when the number of troops deployed is substantial.

Before discussing individual cases of warfare, two other issues need to addressed, the first being the sheer number of instances of varying magnitude that can be argued as belonging to the present category, particularly in the Seleucid period. This problem becomes especially clear during the reign of Antiochus III (223–187), an exceptionally dynamic king who, to put it bluntly, spent his whole life on campaign.[46] After his suppression of the revolt of Molon, an official in charge of the Upper Satrapies between 222 and 220, he fought the Fourth Syrian War (219–217), subdued the usurper Achaeus in Asia Minor (216–213) and went on an *anabasis* into the Upper

---

[46] On his life see in particular the biography by Schmitt (1964), and the chapter dedicated to his exploits in Sherwin-White and Kuhrt 1993: 188–216.

Satrapies (212–205). After his return, he again waged war on Egypt, but this time more successfully (Fifth Syrian War, 202–195), before invading Asia Minor and Thrace (from 197 onwards) and eventually becoming entangled in that fateful war against Rome (192–188). The case is similar with other Seleucid kings. A good example is the first decade of the Seleucid era. After the founder of the dynasty, Seleucus I (311–281) established undisputed rule over Babylonia in 308, he campaigned as far as India, signing a peace treaty with the local king Chandragupta (Sandracottas) before again turning to the west, inflicting a decisive defeat upon Antigonus the One-Eyed at Ipsus in Phrygia in 301. After a period of relative quiet of almost two decades he again mustered a large army for the battle against Lysimachus at Corupedium in Lydia in 281.

The second problem is the definition of the category of 'Warfare'. If, for example, a dividing line is to be established between warfare against external enemies, which will be considered, and the suppression of local rebels, which will be excluded from the analysis, how shall usurpers be categorised? Do we count them as rebels against authority on a local scale and dismiss them from this analysis, or shall we accept their claims to independence and count them as external enemies and include the conflict between them and the Seleucid kings in this category of 'Warfare abroad'? The problem is still more complex as even temporarily successful attempts at usurpation in one or another region in the empire are not necessarily and immediately connected with armed conflict on a significant scale. The case of Achaeus in Asia Minor during the reign of Antiochus III[47] is exemplary. His insurgence against the central authority dates already to *c.* 220 but it was only several years later, in 216, that Antiochus III launched a campaign with the aim of disposing of the rebel (who was finally captured in Sardis in 213). The rebellion of Antiochus Hierax in Asia Minor against his brother and king Seleucus II[48] is not dissimilar. Seleucus II tried at once to subdue his rebellious brother, but had to retreat from Asia Minor after the defeat of the royal army at Ancyra in 239. Antiochus Hierax was later ousted from Asia Minor by the Pergamene king Attalus in the early 220s and exiled from the Seleucid Empire after a final defeat in northern Mesopotamia at the hands of his brother.

Similarly ambivalent and difficult to evaluate are instances of secessions of whole regions from the empire, also because often the sources are meagre.

---

[47] On his career see Schmitt 1964: 158–75 and 264–8.

[48] The most exhaustive account of this conflict and its elusive chronology is still Will 1979²: 294–301; see also Capdetrey 2007: 295–7.

Loss of royal control over a given territory is not by definition relevant to the category presently under discussion; however, attempts at reconquest of these regions possibly are. A prime example is the secessions of Parthia and Bactria, which took place without any large-scale fighting; hence, neither qualifies as warfare abroad.[49] In connection with these secessions the *anabasis* of Antiochus III into the Upper Satrapies (212–205), equally a border case, also has to be mentioned. The first two years of this enterprise are unproblematic as they were dedicated to a reorganisation of affairs in the province of Armenia and hence hardly qualify as warfare abroad. After 210, a journey further eastwards to Bactria and India at the head of an army of significant size served to reaffirm Seleucid sovereignty over territories which were either – and often only nominally – still under Seleucid control (Persis, Arachosia, Carmania, also Failaka) or had defected from central authority (Parthia, Bactria).[50] The Bactrian king Euthydemus proved to be a particularly tough opponent, and it was only after several years besiegement of his capital city Bactra that he agreed to acknowledge formally the suzerainty of the Seleucid king. Hence, at least in this last instance one could arguably speak of a case of warfare. Then again, the question arises whether the whole campaign – and similarly the campaign of Alexander the Great into the eastern provinces of the Achaemenid Empire after Gaugamela – constitutes an instance of actual warfare, or whether it is better characterised as display of power in somewhat neglected areas, including attempts at pacification of noncompliant provinces and potentates.

In the light of these difficulties of definition, and the fact that it is possible to find an instance of an armed conflict somewhere in (or also outside) the empire in most years of the Seleucid period, it has been decided to focus under the heading of 'Warfare outside Babylonia' exclusively on the conflicts with other major powers, hence the wars against Egypt (including the seven Syrian wars, and the attempts at reconquest of the province during the Late Achaemenid period) and the other Hellenistic dynast(ie)s, as well as the confrontation with Rome. If every event that could be considered in some way as military activity were to be considered independent of its magnitude or plausible impact on Babylonia, the almost yearly occurrence of the category would render any analysis meaningless. This finding is of course grounded in the prevailing ideology of kingship during the Hellenistic period, which very much emphasised the importance of military prowess

---

[49] The chronology of these separatist movements in also quite unclear; see Lerner 1999 and Luther 1999.
[50] Will 1982[2]: 51–69 and Sherwin-White and Kuhrt 1993: 197–200.

as a royal attribute, exerting a 'constant compulsion on the kings to prove themselves active and successful military figures'.[51] The Seleucid Empire is hardly an exception, and most of its kings did not die a peaceful death. The fate of the founder of the dynasty, who was assassinated in the aftermath his victory over Lysimachus at Corupedium in 281 by Ptolemy Ceraunus, a son of Ptolemy I and refugee at Seleucus' court, is instructive here. Many of his successors did not fare any better: Seleucus III was murdered by his courtiers during a campaign against Attalus of Pergamum, Antiochus III was killed while plundering a temple in Elymais and his son Antiochus IV died of an illness during a campaign into the eastern satrapies.[52]

The impact of some of the other, 'minor' kinds of campaign – the subjugation of usurpers and the repression of rebellious cities or tribes – will then be considered only if a direct connection to Babylon can be established from the sources. For instance, and as shown below, 'Army convocations' also often took place in the city of Babylon when the actual aim of the campaign was a region as far away as Sidon, to pick one random example.

This minimalist approach centres thus on those conflicts which owing to their scale are most likely to have exerted some kind of influence in more distant regions also. However, even with this restricted focus on major wars, some examples of campaigns that are not very likely to have influenced commodity Babylonian prices at all can still be found. These instances need of course to be retained in order not to convey a wrong impression of the potential of warfare abroad to influence Babylonian prices, and make for a more balanced assessment. A good case in point is the Seventh Syrian War (147–145). This conflict brought about an utter defeat for the Seleucid Empire, ending in the loss of Coele-Syria and a brief interregnum with Ptolemy VII Philometor on the throne in Antioch. However, the whole episode only affected the far west of the empire, the region along the shores of the Mediterranean. Ptolemy met little resistance on his way northwards, there were no major battles fought. The whole war is maybe best characterised as only one episode of the ongoing struggles for the Seleucid throne between various contestants, in this specific case between Alexander Balas

---

[51] Austin 1986: 464, see also 456–9 on the importance of the role of the king as military leader. See also Bosworth 2002: 246–78 for a wider discussion of Hellenistic kingship.

[52] See van der Spek 2010 for short biographies of the Seleucid kings until Demetrius II, who likewise found his end under bellicose circumstances: he was murdered on the run near Tyre after losing a battle near Damascus against the rival king Alexander II Zabinas; see Ehling 2008: 205–11. The subtitle of the chapter on Antiochus III in Sherwin-White and Kuhrt 1993, 'Imperialist and Warrior', is equally telling.

and Demetrius II.[53] However, none of the contestants seems to have been able to draw on the resources of the province of Babylonia in this conflict.

Other instances within these perpetual conflicts with the Ptolemaic Empire are more promising as candidates of warfare outside of the province of Babylon which still had repercussions in the Babylonian price data. The possible consequences of the First Syrian War in 274 – a demand shock due to army conscription in Babylon – have already been discussed at length in the previous chapter, whereas the Third Syrian War (246–241) only partly belongs into the category of warfare abroad as it was the province of Babylonia itself which suffered an invasion during the first year of this conflict.[54] However, after Ptolemy III's withdrawal as a result of domestic problems, fighting continued in Syria, especially around the city of Seleucia-in-Pieria, as well as in Asia Minor, and peace was only made in 241.

The Second Syrian War was fought between 259 and 253, mainly in the regions of Asia Minor and coastal Syrian and Cilicia. The first year or so of the conflict seems to have entailed a particularly precarious situation for the Seleucids, with invasions of Ptolemaic troops as far as Tarsus and Arados.[55] This may have had indirect implications for Babylonia, in the form of levies or tax impositions to finance the war. Convocations of military troops in the city are not attested during this conflict, and are rather unlikely considering the absence of larger battles once the initial threat was warded off. Coincidentally, Babylonia suffered from internal unrest throughout the late 260s and early 250s according to the evidence of the ADs. As these local skirmishes started some time before the war, any connection between these events seems unlikely. The Second Syrian War ended with an armistice confirming minor gains of territory for Antiochus II from Ptolemy, which were, however, largely offset by the emergence of independent kinglets in Asia Minor such as Cappadocia. A major influx of booty is thus also not to be expected. However, considering its duration and relative importance (compared to, for example, the punitive expeditions of the Achaemenid kings on Cyprus alluded to below), one should be cautious not to discard *a priori* the possibility of repercussions in the price data.

The Fourth Syrian War, which can be succinctly described as an abortive attempt of Antiochus III to reconquer and annex Coele-Syria (219–217),

---

[53] Grainger 2010: 337–50.

[54] This episode is described at length in BCHP 11. This document was not considered in the account of Grainger 2010: 153–70, who erroneously assumes (162) that Ptolemy crossed the Euphrates but did not reach the city of Babylon.

[55] Grainger 2010: 117–36, and Will 1979²: 234–43; against the idea of a longer Ptolemaic occupation of Arados based on numismatic evidence see also Duyrat 2005: 226–9.

also took place relatively far from Babylonia. The possibility of an army convocation in Babylon in the run-up to the battle of Raphia following the pattern of the events in the First Syrian War in 274/3 is, however, not unlikely, in particular during the four-month truce in winter 219/18 which both sides used for extensive preparations. Polybius (5 79.6–7) explicitly mentions the presence of eastern contingents including Persian bowmen and slingers, Medians, Cissians, Cadusians and Carmanians among the 65,000-strong army of Antiochus III, but how these troops made their way westwards is alas not specified.[56] Babylon is certainly the most logical meeting point for these eastern auxiliaries for a campaign in the west, in which case an increase in demand may have driven up prices. Be that as it may, the absence of any price data from the decade 220–211 reduces the impact of this instance in any case to theoretical speculation.

The Fifth and Sixth Syrian wars were more successful for the Seleucid dynasty. The latter campaign (170–168) constituted certainly a brief moment of glory – the conquest of Egypt by Antiochus IV in early 169 – already turned to naught the following year by the brusque intervention of the Roman legate, C. Popillius Laenas.[57] A passage in Polybius points towards the capture of a substantial booty during this campaign[58] but whether these gains led to an increase of the monetary base also noticeable in Babylon is doubtful. The Seleucid Empire seems to have struggled with financial difficulties throughout the reign of Antiochus IV: the installation of a *zazakku* in Babylon, the attempts at interventions in the temple in Jerusalem culminating in the revolt of the Maccabees, as well as Antiochus IV's ignominious death during an attempt at a temple raid rather point towards chronic shortage in precious metal in the years following the Egyptian campaign.[59] Against this background, the reduction in the weight of bronze coins during these years is best interpreted as an attempt to increase revenue from seignorage.[60] Again, we do not expect this campaign to have had to great an impact on prices in Babylon. The Fifth Syrian War (202–195)[61] met with more enduring success and brought with it the conquest of Coele-Syria for

---

[56] The events during this period of ceasefire are discussed in Grainger 2010: 202–8.

[57] Mittag 2006: 159–81 and 209–24; Grainger 2010: 291–308.

[58] According to Polyb. 30 26.9, the *pompē* at Daphne in 166 was financed to a large part by means of the spoils of the Egyptian campaign. In modern scholarship, a substantial booty in precious metal is also tacitly assumed, e.g., Mittag 2006: 198 and 222.

[59] See Mittag 2006: 198–201, 235–81 and 328–31 for a discussion of these factors, with additional literature.

[60] Le Rider 1994: 27–28, who also provides (less convincing) alternative explanations of this weight reduction such as an adjustment to a distorted exchange rate between bronze and silver. See also Mittag 2006: 182–98.

[61] Grainger 2010: 245–71.

the Seleucid Empire. Especially for the decisive battle at Mount Paneion in 200, the convocation of an imperial contingent including Babylonian troops can again reasonably be hypothesised. Grainger goes so far as to postulate the conscription of an army even bigger in size than the one that had unsuccessfully fought the Ptolemaic army at Raphia about two decades earlier.[62] The incorporation into the Seleucid Empire of vast parts of Asia Minor in the period between the Fifth Syrian War and the Roman War – with a few exceptions only (such as Smyrna and Lampsacus) most cities readily accepted Antiochus III's claims to suzerainty[63] – was achieved by a much smaller force, with estimates of the Seleucid troop size ranging between 20,000 and 30,000 soldiers.[64]

In addition to these conflicts between Seleucids and Ptolemies, the Roman War of Antiochus III (192–188) has to be considered, as it was equally fought on a grand scale. At the decisive battle at Magnesia (ad Sipylum), more than 70,000 troops fought on the Seleucid side according to Livy.[65] Again one has to consider the possibility that at some point during the campaign reinforcements were mustered in and sent from Babylon. In addition to an eventual convocation, the harsh conditions of the treaty of Apameia following the Seleucid defeat in terms of indemnity payment and reduction of the army size have been noted above.

Most conflicts outside Babylonia dating to the Late Achaemenid period were fought against relatively minor enemies in a location far from Babylonia, and no repercussions in the commodity price data of the ADs can plausibly be postulated in relation to these. A prominent case in point is the campaign to subdue the rebellious Cypriot king Evagoras in the 380s, which factually amounted to little more than the subjugation of a minor ally, although the Great King was probably involved in person in this conflict at the head of his army.[66] As established above, campaigns like this are not considered here. More demanding in terms of manpower and military

---

[62] His figure of 70,000 troops in Grainger 2010: 257 constitutes an educated guess only. Polyb. 16 18–19 is the only ancient account of the battle; see also Grainger 2010: 256–61.

[63] Schmitt 1964: 269

[64] Grainger 2002: 36–7 and 124; see also 191–2 on the small size of the army which he sent over to Greece in 192 (in the words of Grainger 'a nominal force only' (191)).

[65] Livy 37 44. His number for the Roman strength, 30,000 soldiers in total, is rather a propagandistic understatement. Grainger 2002: 322–3 estimates a force level of approximately 50,000 for both sides. In the context of the battle at Magnesia (ad Sipylum), he expressly points to Babylonia as one of the more important regions for recruitments in case of larger battles (271).

[66] See van der Spek 1998a: 240–51 for the chronology this conflict. See also Briant 1996: 666–71 and 1011 (including a brief discussion of AD -381C) for the wider context of the campaign.

Table 6.3. *Summary of the periods of warfare abroad*

Year	Event
373–372	Artaxerxes II launches an abortive campaign against pharaoh Nekhtanebo. Famine in Babylon.
351–350	Another unsuccessful campaign against Egypt.
343–342	Reconquest of Egypt.
274–271	First Syrian War, beginning with an army convocation in Babylon.
259–253	Second Syrian War.
244–241	Continuation of Third Syrian War after Ptolemy's retreat from Babylonia.
219–217	Fourth Syrian War, battle of Raphia.
202–195	Fifth Syrian War.
192–188	Roman Wars of Antiochus III. Treaty of Apameia including payment of a huge indemnity and territorial losses.
170–168	Sixth Syrian War.

operations required for victory was the tenacious reconquest of Egypt, which only after several abortive campaigns (in spring 373 and 351/50) was brought to a successful close around spring 342.[67] For this last campaign, Diodorus (16 51.3) explicitly makes a connection with Babylon, writing that the city was the destination of the army (carrying with it 'many possessions and spoils') upon its return. A reference to the failure of 373 is probably contained in a fragmentary diary.[68] The same diary also reports the occurrence of famine in Babylonia, but whether there was a direct causal relationship between the campaign in Egypt and the unfavourable supply situation in Babylon is open to doubt. On the other hand, it is not implausible to assume that an eventual army convocation earlier in this year for the impending Egyptian campaign aggravated a pre-existing scarce supply situation.

Rebellion in Babylonia

An attempt has been made to account for the fundamental differences in the extent and intensity of the episodes of bellicose activities by distinguishing

---

[67] These campaigns of Artaxerxes II against the pharaohs Nekhtanebo I and II (30th dynasty) are discussed by Briant 1996: 671–4, 700–6 and 1030–1. See now also Ruzicka 2012 for the vicissitudes between Persia and Egypt.

[68] AD -373B, see van der Spek 1998a: 251–2.

between warfare on the one hand and rebellion on the other. It should be clear from the outset that only instances of rebellion in Babylon are likely to have had repercussions in the Babylonian price data and hence be of interest here. Rebellions in other parts of the Achaemenid or Seleucid empire are not considered. This definition thus excludes for example the so-called 'Great Satraps' Revolt' from the reign of Artaxerxes II[69] and also the well-documented episode of the protracted revolt in Judea under the Maccabees, which started in the last years of the reign of Antiochus IV. Interestingly, in this latter conflict the battles seem to have been fought by local and at the most regional troops only,[70] suggesting that the involvement of the imperial army is rather unlikely. The documentation of this conflict incidentally provides us also with some order of magnitude for the troops needed to quell local revolts. Most numbers given in the Books of Maccabees were rejected by Bar-Kochva as certainly too high; the only one he was inclined to accept were the 20,000 infantry of the force of Bacchides at the battle of Elasa in 160. He also assumes that for this battle a larger force compared to previous combats was raised because it followed several Seleucid defeats;[71] however, the difference in number from the forces gathered for the decisive encounters in the major conflicts with the Ptolemies amounting to up to 70,000 soldiers is noteworthy. The size of the army mustered for the battle at Elasa was even slightly below the numbers provided by Grainger (2002: 36–7) for the size of the regular field army of Antiochus III (as opposed to the enormous contingents mustered for important battles, such as Raphia), which he puts at about 30,000. Accepting the 20,000 infantry thus as an exceptionally high number for the subduing of a local revolt, we assume that usually fewer than 10,000 troops were involved in the conflicts described below.

Unfortunately, a quick look at the material at our disposal already reveals that quite often instances of rebellions in Babylon are not accompanied by adequate price data. The revolt of Molon during the reign of Antiochus III[72] is a prominent example. No diaries are extant for the period during which it affected Babylonia (spring 221–February 220); only for the period between Molon's defection in Media and his invasion of Babylonia in autumn/winter

---

[69] This revolt has been (convincingly) interpreted by Weiskopf 1989 as a series of at best loosely interconnected instances of insubordination of medium- to high-ranking officials and local dynasts. AD -366A possibly refers to one episode during this revolt, but the events take place in 'Mesopotamia', i.e., Assyria in modern terminology; cf. van der Spek 1998a: 253–5.

[70] Mittag 2006: 268–77. Among the Seleucid military officials charged with the subjugation of the insurgents were Nikanor, the *meridarch* of Samaria, and Gorgias, the *stratēgos* of Idumea.

[71] Bar-Kochva 1989: 44 and 1976: 13–15. The troops under the command of Nikanor and Gorgias were for example defeated near Emmaus in summer 165.

[72] Schmitt 1964: 114–50.

222 do we have some prices. Also the clash in 320 between the future satrap of Babylonia appointed by Perdiccas, Archon, and the satrap he was to replace, Docimus, from which the former emerged victorious,[73] dates to a period for which no prices are documented: from the years between 322 and 309, not a single diary survives. A similar or rather even worse case is constituted by the events narrated in AD -362,[74] which mentions armed conflict and an episode of plundering in Babylonia in the vicinity of the town of Sippar in the winter of 363/2. A son of the king is involved, as well as royal troops, leading the editors of the tablet to suspect that the diary describes a revolt of an Achaemenid prince in connection with the struggles for the succession of king Artaxerxes II. However, there is not a single diary with price data extant from the period between autumn 367 and winter 347. In spite of the troubled history of the last Achaemenid kings – the murder of Artaxerxes III and several of his sons, including the short-lived Arses/Artaxerxes IV at the instigation of the eunuch Bagoas as well as the violent accession to the throne of Darius III – no other revolts are attested from the satrapy of Babylonia.[75]

Interestingly, instances of rebellion against the central authority in or around Babylon, or of strife between different fractions in the city, occur with a somewhat higher frequency during the Seleucid period. An exemplary case is provided by the events in 262/1. Fragmentary diaries mention the seizure of fields (AD -261B, 2), the evacuation of precious objects (gold and silver, but also garments) into the royal palace for safeguarding against an enemy (AD -261C, r11–12) and the carrying out of the death penalty (AD -261C, 11). Unusually for the diaries of the Seleucid period, two officials are called by their name (Paini and Thērōn), and the garrison in the city of Babylon was also involved in these events.[76] Only a few years later, there was again unrest in the city. According to AD -255A, the 'people of the land' entered the centre of the city under arms, but, unfortunately, nothing more is preserved in this document.

Another potential case dates to spring 278, when according to an Astronomical Diary, 'fear and panic' (*hattu u gilittu*) occurred in the land (AD -277A, 6). The word *hattu*, fear, is often employed to characterise the atmosphere in the country during periods of warfare. A quite close parallel is provided by

[73] On this event see Schober 1981: 38–40 and more recently van der Spek 2014a.
[74] This diary came to light only after the publication of ADART I (to which it belongs chronologically) and was published by Hunger and van der Spek 2006.
[75] See Briant 1996: 789–800 for a critical discussion of the Greek sources on the eventful transition from Artaxerxes III to Darius III.
[76] The passages are briefly discussed in van der Spek 2006b: 297 and in Boiy 2004: 143.

AD -144. In the account of the invasion of the Elamite king Kamnaskires following his victory over the Babylonian troops under the *stratēgos* Ardāya, just as in 278, 'fear and panic' afflicted the country. The chronicle BCHP 3 (=ABC 10), dating to the period of warfare between the Diadochi, twice uses (r24 and r37) a different expression, 'weeping and mourning' (*sipdu u bikītu*) to describe the impact of warfare. One might thus speculate that also in January 278 all was not well in Babylon; however, there are good arguments that militate against a bellicose background in this instance. First of all, the same diary (AD -278) reports in unfortunately very broken passages that later the same year thieves who had removed cultic paraphernalia from the storehouse in the juniper garden were put to death by burning. The fear mentioned in this diary could thus be explained as religiously motivated. Another approach would be to focus on the unusual position of the remark among the astronomical day-to-day observations – as was also the case in AD -309, but not so in AD -144, where fear and panic are at the end of the historical section, after the description of the destructive effects of Kamnaskires' invasion – and conclude that the fear was triggered by a particularly unfavourable celestial constellation occurring on that day or similar. In any case, as this diary can be satisfactorily reconstructed (months I to VII recorded in AD -277A did not have historical sections) and the extant historical sections do not refer to bellicose actions, but only to judicial matters concerned with sacrilegious actions, we will not infer the presence of armed conflict in Babylonia on the meagre basis of the occurrence of fear in the country.

About two decades after the events of 262/1, a major crisis seems to have erupted as during the 230s, since several diaries allude to warlike activities. As was discussed in greater detail in the previous chapter, the decade or so between *c.* 240 and 230 was marked by repeated occurrences of skirmishes in the city involving military officials on the local level.[77] Actual moments of revolt are attested in the diaries for the years 238, 235 and 229, with an additional more doubtful (because of the fragmentary state of the tablet) instance in 231.

After a period of relative quiet during most the reign of Antiochus III (with the exception of the revolt of Molon discussed above), the next potential attestation of a domestic crisis in Babylon dates to 178. However, as all that is extant in the AD of that year is a reference to the troops of the king, we deal again with an at best questionable case. The case is similar for 157, when a skirmish of unknown dimensions is reported in another very

---

[77] See also van der Spek 2006a: 299–301 and Boiy 2004: 150–2. See also the discussion in the previous chapter for additional adverse factors (droughts, locusts) at work during these years.

Table 6.4. *Summary of rebellions and civil unrest in Babylonia*

Year	Event
363–362	Military conflicts in the vicinity of Babylon with involvement of the royal offspring.
320	Docimus replaces Archon by order of Perdiccas as satrap of Babylonia. He had to conquer the province by force.
262–261	Unrest in Babylonia. Evacuation of valuables into the royal palace.
256	Armed conflict in the city of Babylon, in the central city quarter Eridu.
238	Fighting in Babylonia between two different groups of troops.
235	Revolt of a general against the central authority.
231	Troops mentioned in the broken diary AD -231, possible reference to fighting.
229	Again armed conflict in the city of Babylon, in the quarter around the royal palace.
222–220	Revolt of Molon, who occupies Babylonia in 221. He is defeated only after several abortive attempts.
(177)	Royal troops and a military commander are mentioned in the broken diaries AD -176A+B.
163	Episode of ethnic strife in Babylonia, the Greek part of the population evacuates the city. Conflict between various officials.
157	Skirmish mentioned in a broken passage in AD -156A.

fragmentary diary (AD -156A, r20). An instance from 161 is again more certain, AD -162 describes (ethnic?) strife between the Greek residents of Babylon and the 'people of the land'.[78] The conflicts dragged on for several months, and it seems that the whole affair was brought to a conclusion in the spring of the following year by means of a judicial trial.

Regression Results

Before discussing the results of the regressions for the Late Achaemenid and Seleucid periods (*c.* 400–140), an apparent contradiction needs to be

---

[78]   Van der Spek 2005 and 2009 (especially 108), who also discusses the parallel evidence provided by the chronicle BCHP 14.

addressed. The prices in the Astronomical Diaries are most often indicated for periods of one month and less – usually beginning, middle and end of the month – whereas the instances of warfare in the preceding section have been dated according to years only. Theoretically, it would of course be possible to date at least some of the instances more precisely; however, there are good arguments not to do so and stick to a cruder method of dating. Firstly, what is most often recorded in the diaries or reported by a Greek or Roman historian is not an entire war campaign but rather single episodes thereof, such as a particular battle, a mustering of a larger or smaller part of the army or otherwise. Secondly, as opposed to the causal factors discussed in the following section (such as 'Presence of an army'), the impact of warfare is not strictly punctual. As already mentioned in the introduction to the present chapter, an episode of warfare in antiquity (as well as today) usually consists of a multitude of single events spread irregularly over time. Hence, importantly, almost every single type of event that potentially occurs during a war, be it a period of siege, a gathering of an army or a battle fought in the vicinity of Babylon entailing crop destruction and or even damages to the canal system, exerts a detrimental impact on prices not only at the precise moment of its occurrence but also in the weeks and months after or even before they actually take place.

The drawback of using two different yardsticks – namely, months for prices but years for the events – on the other hand is comparatively small. The main risk of this method is that the error term of the regression will increase, providing us with insignificant results (as expressed in low *t*-values). However, as the sample employed is comparatively large this is in general not the case here. A second risk is that the magnitude of the impact of the categories analysed will be underestimated as a result of the potential inclusion of prices from stable periods which in theory should be lower than during periods of warfare. However, as this effect concerns all three categories under discussion here, the more important relative magnitudes should (and in fact do) remain unaffected. In the light of all these facts, and also for the sake of internal coherence, the historical episodes to be analysed will thus be dated by year only.

A final word of warning pertains to the conclusions derived from this analysis. The aim of a regression is to demonstrate whether there exists a relationship between two or more variables, and if so, to make a statement about the strength of that relationship.[79] Regression does not say anything about causation. The best way to exemplify this is the category of

---

[79]　See Feinstein and Thomas 2002: 94–5.

rebellion in Babylon. Usually one would expect rebellions to drive up prices because of bellicose actions entailing crop destruction, market interruption and similar phenomena. However, the opposite can equally hold true and throughout the course of history, high prices are a widely attested cause leading to riots and unrest.

For both barley and dates, a pattern of a seasonal fluctuation – low prices in the months after the harvest, high prices in the period preceding the harvest – has been established beyond doubt.[80] Consequently, it has been judged useful to include for these two commodities monthly dummies to control for the more regular pattern of intra-annual volatility (variables 1 to 12 on the regression sheets). For barley especially this method yielded good results in line with earlier research on seasonality. A proportionally high growth rate in its price (at *t*-values above 1) is shown in the months from December to February. The month with the highest price increase was January, thus the month when the price-alleviating effect of the date harvest in autumn dwindled and the new barley harvest (usually in April/May) was still about three months away. January was incidentally also the only month to yield a result significant at the 5 per cent level. For dates, the results of the seasonal regression in combination with the political events were not significant, with the *t*-value in all cases clearly below 1.

As for the impact of political history, the results are similar for barley and dates. Domestic warfare (variable 13; see also Table 6.5) undeniably exerts a very strong impact on both commodities. The partial regression coefficients amounted to 6.90 and 3.71 respectively, and both results were clearly significant at the 5 per cent level, with the *t*-value exceeding 10 in both cases. The higher coefficient for barley indicating stronger price increases in cases of warfare can furthermore be interpreted as underlining the lower demand elasticity of the country's most important staple crop.

The regression for warfare abroad (variable 14) did not yield significant results for both commodities, whereas the smaller armed conflicts such as rebellions or civil strife (variable 15) are significant for barley at the 5 per cent level (*t*-value of 1.897), the partial regression coefficient amounting to 0.85. Hence, as expected, the magnitude of price increases correlated to this category of events is significantly smaller than with warfare. For dates, the results are less pleasing. The results are significant only at the 20 per cent

---

[80]   Temin 2002, especially 57–8; van der Spek and Mandemakers 2003: 525–8 (in a review of Slotsky 1997a, whose analysis of the price data of the Astronomical Diaries did not show a pattern of seasonal variation thanks to a somewhat flawed methodology); Földvári, van Leeuwen and Pirngruber 2011.

Table 6.5. *The impact of warfare and rebellion on commodity prices*[a]

Commodity	n[b]	R^2[c]	Domestic warfare (t-value)	Warfare abroad (t-value)	Rebellion (t-value)
Barley	349	0.37	6.90 (13.49)	0.15 (0.49)	0.85 (1.90)
Dates	300	0.30	3.71 (10.33)	0.06 (0.27)	0.39 (1.30)
Cress	260	0.11	5.73 (5.16)	1.86 (2.57)	1.48 (1.81)
Kasû	221	0.01	0.16 (0.99)	0.06 (0.56)	0.07 (0.58)
Sesame	257	0.29	13.54 (9.07)	−1.65 (−1.63)	0.67 (0.58)
Wool	232	0.22	1.80 (6.87)	−0.46 (−2.48)	0.98 (3.48)

Notes: [a] For the full results (for barley, dates and wool) see the regression sheets in the Appendix; [b] n: Number of observations; [c] R^2: Coefficient of determination.

level (t-value of 1.298), hence still of some relevance, but again the regression coefficient is smaller than that for barley.

The coefficient of determination (R^2) is satisfactory for both regressions, amounting to 0.37 for barley and to 0.30 for dates. The conclusion is thus that price fluctuations of staple crops in Babylonia can indeed be explained to a considerable extent by the vicissitudes of political history, which take clear precedence over seasonal variation as regards impact on prices. The efficacy of the dummies for domestic warfare and rebellion supports the notion that barley and date price in Babylon are subject to a supply-and-demand-based price-determining mechanism. The insignificance of the dummy for warfare abroad on the other hand can be interpreted as militating against any claims of over-regional market integration in the Seleucid Empire. Possible dearness of basic commodities elsewhere in the empire did not influence the prices of staple crops.

The outcome of the regressions for commodities other than barley and dates are of very variable explanatory power. The regression for *kasû* has for all dummies employed such a low value for the coefficient of determination (and also for the regression coefficients and t-values) as to be meaningless; there is thus no relationship between the price of *kasû* and the different types of warfare. The explanation for this abnormality may reside in the nature of this commodity, usually identified with the dodder plant (cuscuta), which is a parasitical plant rather than a cultivated crop.[81] Furthermore, cuscuta is

---

[81] The case for an identification of *kasû* with cuscuta was made most exhaustively by Stol 1994. Slotsky 1997a accepts his argumentation (but sticks to the translation mustard used by Hunger and Sachs in primary edition of the diaries), see Slotsky 1997a: 31–4, with a succinct summary of the alternative suggestions of identification.

not a foodstuff but was mainly used as spice to season date beer, the typical beverage in first-millennium Babylonia. Cuscuta was thus not only immune to crop destruction but also had a very high level of demand elasticity. It is not surprising that both these characteristics combined led to an absence of any discernible effect of political history on its prices.

Cress has also a rather low R^2 (0.11), hence only a comparatively small amount of the overall price fluctuation is explained by the regression. However, the results of all three dummies are significant at a 5 per cent level and conform to expectations. Again, warfare has by far the strongest impact and yields the most solid result. Interestingly, and as opposed to both barley and dates, warfare abroad also has an impact on the price of this commodity, roughly at the same magnitude of rebellions in Babylonia. This can be tentatively explained by the fact that cress was often stronger than other commodities affected by army convocations in Babylon (e.g. in 274/3 during the First Syrian War), perhaps owing to its suitability to be used as a travel ration, a well-established use during the sixth century.[82]

Sesame (at 10 per cent only) and wool (at 5 per cent) were also affected by warfare abroad, but in a positive way: the price of both commodities decreased during these episodes. The pattern exhibited by these commodities thus lends weight to van der Spek's caveat (2000a: 299) that warfare abroad can also lead to falling prices in Babylonia as a result of a decrease in demand. A corollary of this line of interpretation is that export possibilities seem to have been rather limited. This is not to say that trade did not take place, but at least in politically difficult periods the additional supply that accrued because of the fall in demand could not be easily disposed of. Nor can a deflationary effect as a consequence of silver requisitions be excluded, but it is difficult to reconcile with the notable increase in the price of cress.

For wool, all three regression coefficients are significant at a 5 per cent level, with domestic warfare causing the largest price increases. The explanatory power of the regression is clearly better than that for cress, the R^2 amounting to 0.22. The decrease in the wool price during periods of warfare abroad was clearly on a lower scale than the increase caused by rebellions (−0.46 and 0.98, respectively). For sesame, the coefficient of determination is slightly better than that for wool (0.29). The impact of warfare abroad can be compared to the values obtained for cress (only with a negative sign),

---

[82] See the discussion of the outlier of winter 274/3 in the preceding chapter and also the regression of the dummy 'Presence of an army' on cress prices in the next section. On travel rations see Janković 2008: 445.

but the coefficient of regression of domestic warfare is somewhat odd as it is double the value of that for the staple crop barley (13.49). There is no ready explanation as to why this particular commodity is so greatly affected by warfare, whereas for the category of rebellions the results are statistically not relevant.

Overall, the results of the regression are encouraging. For all commodities, domestic warfare clearly exerted the strongest price-driving influence and also yielded the most solid results from a statistical point of view. The category was usually followed by rebellions in Babylonia, with a smaller degree of correlation to the price data and occasionally (with dates and sesame) statistically insignificant results. The effects of warfare abroad are more variegated: such episodes increased the price for cress but drove down prices for sesame and wool. Overall, these results are more tenuous in their statistical reliability, and insignificant for both barley and dates. The absolute values of the regression coefficients are somewhat surprising at times. The ranking order barley (6.90) – dates (3.71) – wool (1.80) for warfare in Babylonia very much conforms to expectations when considering the demand elasticities of the individual products, but the high values for cress (5.72) and especially sesame (13.49) are puzzling. Here, clearly other, more elusive factors come into play, such as the impact of wartime destruction on the different crops, nutritional requirements of the armies standing in the country, etc. For example, one might argue that the higher level of perishability put disproportionately high strains on the demand for cress, one of the most important suppliers of essential vitamins (especially vitamin C) in Babylonia.[83]

The Causes Underlying Price Rises

Warfare-Related Factors

In this section, two types of price-driving forces that seem particularly effective during periods of warfare, both in Babylonia and abroad, are analysed, namely military operations in Babylonia and army convocations. The former category consists to a large extent of instances also contained in the categories of domestic warfare and rebellion in Babylon discussed in the preceding section, the latter includes certain cases also listed under warfare in Babylonia and warfare abroad, but with several instances of

---

[83] On cress see Stol 1983/4 and Janković 2008: 445[(+71)].

army convocations for the purpose of subjugating internal enemies hitherto not considered. Also, not all instances of warfare in Babylonia comprise occurrences of armed conflict, as was for example the case in 317/16, when the imperial army under the leadership of Antigonus the One-Eyed merely passed through Babylon in its pursuit of Eumenes while the actual battles took place at a considerable distance from Babylon in Gabiene and Paraetacene. However, in this section the focus is less on the full historical episodes but rather on the selective events that are part of them, hence the recorded instances of battles, of popular unrest or of plundering. From a different angle, military operations can generally be said to affect the supply side (looting, crop destruction, etc.), whereas army presence puts strains on the demand side. We will not only calculate the direct effects of these two factors but also their cross-effect, since they can be active simultaneously. This procedure provides us with an indication of the extent to which the total price increases during the various episodes of warfare are to be explained by the occurrence of military actions and army presence alone. The remaining residual will give us an idea of the extent to which the price increases must be attributed to other factors not yet taken into consideration. Again, the regression analysis is preceded by introductory remarks elucidating in more detail which events are to be considered and the rationale for their inclusion.

Military Operations in Babylon and its Countryside

As seen in the preceding section, armed conflict in the city of Babylon and its immediate surroundings are encountered quite frequently in both classical and cuneiform sources, sometimes even for the same period as in the case of the warfare between Alexander's successors. The aim of the current regression is to measure the total impact of armed conflicts within Babylonia. After all, warfare and rebellion are characterised by similar phenomena albeit on a different scale. Additionally, the concern here is not with armies merely passing through Babylon in the course of military operations but only with genuine instance of armed conflicts in and around Babylon. By this definition, neither the battle at Cunaxa to the north of Babylon nor the battle at Gaugamela is included in the regression as neither was fought in the immediate vicinity of the city.

Among the wartime phenomena which potentially affect prices, occurrences of plundering stand out in a number of attestations. The terse style of Babylonian historiography unfortunately hardly ever provides us with more precise details, as can be illustrated by a few lines from the so-called

Diadochi Chronicle, BCHP 3 (r25–6)[84] dating to the final period of conflicts between Antigonus the One-Eyed and Seleucus in winter 309/8 which
read: '[… Antigonus (?)] came out from Babylon and plundered city and
countryside […] he went down to Cutha and plundered […].' In a similar
vein, AD -144 (r20–2) reports the plundering of the countryside by the
Elamite army under Kamnaskires, while in a defensive reaction the inhabitants of the countryside around Babylonia seem to have sought to safeguard their possessions. Likewise, allusions to protective measures against
plundering also occur in episodes that have been qualified as rebellions.
Exemplary is the case documented by AD -261C, when various commodities (among them precious metals) were brought into the palace as a protective measure in spring 261.

Greek authors also report several episodes of pillaging. Diodorus in
his description of the campaign of Cyrus the Younger reports that his
troops seized 'booty from foraging' near Thapsacus on the Euphrates (14
21.6). He also mentions in the course of the hostilities between Seleucus
and Eumenes that the latter was forced to cross the Tigris in 317 because
his troops could not find provisions as the countryside lay plundered (19
12.4).[85] Similar actions are also attested directly for the city of Babylon, for
example in autumn 311, when Demetrius, having recaptured part of the
city from Seleucus and his *stratēgos* Nicanor, plundered the country before
returning to the shores of the Mediterranean.[86] Plutarch (*Dem.* 7 2) furthermore mentions a siege laid to one of the city's citadels that could not
be captured immediately in the course of these hostilities. Siege warfare
is of course a particularly effective means of cutting one's enemy off from
supplies and a well-known cause of dearth,[87] and cuneiform documents
also attest instances in which the city of Babylon or its fortifications suffered a siege. The chronicle BCHP 11 reporting the invasion of Babylonia
by Ptolemy III in winter 246/5 states (lines 7–8) that after the capture of
Seleucia-on-the-Euphrates 'battle equipment and numerous siege engines'
were transferred from there to Babylon.

Often, Astronomical Diaries and chronicles simply refer to a 'battle', *ṣaltu*,
taking place without specifying further details (e.g. ADs -237 and -234 or
BCHP 14), or to kings 'marching around victoriously', *ṣaltaniš atalluku*

---

[84] Also published as ABC 10 in Grayson 1975; see also Del Monte 1997: 183–94, and Glassner
   2004: 242–7.
[85] In the context of the same campaign Diodorus specifies (19 13.6) that Eumenes had to
   distribute rice, sesame and dates to his soldiers because of a lack of grain.
[86] Plut. *Dem.* 7 3 and Diod. 19 100.7.
[87] See Eph'al 2009 for a recent discussion of siege warfare in the Ancient Near East.

(e.g. AD -144). Occasionally, as for example in the report of Gaugamela in AD -330A+B, troops are said to 'cause a defeat' (*dabdû šakānu*) of their enemy. It is only on rare occasions that destructions within or around the city potentially affecting commodity prices are described in more detail. One of the few instances is again provided by BCHP 3, which relates in r27 the destruction of a storehouse of the temple of Nergal at the hands of the troops of Antigonus.[88]

Another unfortunately fragmentary passage in the same chronicle (r6–7) points to even more severe damage to the city when Seleucus seems to have tried to employ the Euphrates as means of combat by diverting the course of the river in order to blow a breach into some defensive rig. This incident of course raises the question of damage to Babylonia's canal system, so vital for its economy, but the sources are not very informative on this issue. In particular Seleucus seems to have had little hesitation in taking advantage of Babylonia's landscape. In addition to the ruse above, Diodorus (18 73.3)[89] reports that in his pursuit of Eumenes in 318 he tried to inundate the camp of his opponent by breaching a canal (a stratagem which was successfully warded off by Eumenes). That battles taking place in Babylonia potentially affected both crops and the canal system can also be inferred from a passage in Xenophon[90] which describes the digging of a trench of substantial dimensions around the royal camp near the battle field of Cunaxa as a defensive measure by Artaxerxes II.

In addition to the phenomena listed thus far putting strains on the supply side, one has to reckon with other more general disruptions of economic life caused by episodes of armed conflict. A prominent example are the evacuations of the city which occurred for example in summer 163, when according to AD -162 the Greek part of the population left the city together with their households in a period of civil unrest. Additionally during Demetrius' attempt at reconquest of Babylon from Seleucus in 311, Seleucus' general in charge, Nicanor, ordered the inhabitants of the city to leave for their own safety (Diod. 19 100.3–7).

---

[88] Line r30 in the hypothetical but plausible completion by van der Spek and Finkel at www. livius.org/babylonia.html reports additionally the destruction of houses in the city in the course of hostilities.

[89] For a similar passage in the context of the same campaign see Diod. 19 13.1–4.

[90] Xen. *Anab.* 1 7.14–16; see also the parallel account of Diod. 14 22.4. According to the latter, the trench around Artaxerxes' military camp was 60 feet wide and 10 feet deep, whereas Xenophon puts the dimensions at 5 fathoms wide by 3 fathoms deep, hence 30 by 18 feet, running over a length of 12 parasangs (60 kilometres!).

Table 6.6. *Summary of the instances of military operations in Babylonia*

Year	Event
363–362	Military conflicts in the vicinity of Babylon with involvement of the royal offspring.
323–322	Return of the Greco-Macedonian army to Babylon. Alexander the Great dies on 11 June 323 without a suitable heir. The Babylonian settlement is contested by the infantry troops under Meleager, with the result that the city is besieged. Indications of further upheavals, e.g. troops are sent from Babylon under the command of Peithon to quell rebellions in Bactria. Presence of royal court in Babylon until 319.
320	Docimus replaces Archon by order of Perdiccas as satrap of Babylonia. He has to conquer the province by force.
318–317	Eumenes invades the province and spends the winter of 318/ 17 in the 'Carian villages' in Babylonia; he is pursued by Antigonus, to whom Seleucus grants his support.
311–308	After Antigonus' and Demetrius' defeat at Gaza, Seleucus reconquers Babylonia and also regions further to the east. Tenacious attempts by Antigonus and Demetrius to regain the province. Several military encounters between the two enemy factions, plundering of the countryside.
262–261	Unrest in Babylonia. Evacuation of valuables into the royal palace.
256	Armed conflict in the city of Babylon, in the central city quarter Eridu.
246–245	Ptolemy III invades Babylonia, prolonged warfare between Seleucid and Ptolemaic troops.
238	Fighting in Babylonia between two different groups of troops.
235	Revolt of a general against the central authority.
231	Troops mentioned in the broken diary AD -231, possible reference to fighting.
229	Again armed conflict in the city of Babylon, in the quarter around the royal palace.
222–220	Revolt of Molon, who occupies Babylonia in 221. He is defeated only after several abortive attempts.
(177)	Royal troops and a military commander are mentioned in the broken diaries AD -176A+B.

Table 6.6. (*Continued*)

Year	Event
163	Episode of ethnic strife in Babylonia, the Greek part of the population evacuates the city. Conflict between various officials.
157	Skirmish mentioned in a broken passage in AD -156A.
145–144	Bellicose activities of a certain Aria'bu and the Elamite king Kamnaskires in Babylonia. The province is defended by a general, Ardāya, who is defeated. Reference to looting.

Army Presence

The most obvious instances of army presence are of course the instances of domestic warfare as defined in the preceding chapter. Moreover, we have seen that also during campaigns in other parts of the empire or even beyond, army convocations occasionally took place in Babylon, with at least one certain case (during the First Syrian War in winter 274/3) and other hypothetical instances (e.g. in 219/18 in the run-up to the battle at Mount Paneion). Additionally, we also include campaigns which were led against rebels within the empire and which directly involved Babylonia as meeting point of substantial army contingents. In these cases it has to be kept in mind that the numbers given by Greek historians for the army size of the Achaemenid Great Kings (usually 300,000 infantry) for such expeditions are wildly exaggerated.[91] The first instance to be mentioned is the campaign against the land of Razaunda led by Artaxerxes II described in AD -369,[92] when the conscription of the army took place in the city of Babylon. Another episode in this context was the revolt of the Sidonians under their king Tennes in 346 or 345 supported by the Egyptian pharaoh Nectanebo II. Despite initial successes against the Persians troops mustered by the satraps of the Transeuphratene, Belesys and Mazaeus, the city was forced into surrender rather rapidly: the Babylonian chronicle ABC 9 reports the arrival of deportees from Phoenicia in October 345. Since Diodorus (16 41.1) explicitly mentions that after the initial setback troops were sent from

---

[91] Binder 2008: 322; 300,000 infantry seems to have constituted 'bei vielen griechischen Autoren die Normgrösse der Standardheeresgruppe'.

[92] The land of the Cadusians against which Artaxerxes II led his troops according to Plutarch (*Art.* 24.1) has been tentatively identified by van der Spek 1998a: 249 with the Razaunda of AD -369, r8. His hypothesis was contested by Binder 2008: 316–21.

Babylonia to quell the revolt, it is also included in this investigation. Not to be considered here on the other hand is the campaign against the Cypriot king Evagoras mentioned in AD -381C, for which campaigns troops were mustered according to Diodorus (15 2.2) in Phocaea and Cyme. These punitive campaigns against the Phoenician coast and the island of Cyprus are best placed into the wider context of an envisaged reconquest of Egypt,[93] meaning that those certainly larger operations (starting in 373, 351 and 343 respectively) are retained here as at least possible cases in which an armed force was assembled in Babylon. From the Seleucid period, one might add the short-lived and abortive attempt at reconquest of Parthia and Bactria under Seleucus II as a possible instance of the presence of an army. However, this campaign is difficult to treat as a dummy because its date is known only very approximately. Will hypothesises a date between 230 and 227,[94] but Seleucus II with his sons was still west of the Euphrates in spring 229 (and thus not on campaign) according to AD -229B. As the following years are not documented (either in terms of price data or of historical information) – there are no diaries extant for the years -228 and -227 – it is maybe the safest solution not to consider this campaign here at all.

The effect of an army presence is an increase in demand due to the presence of a larger number of people than usual, whose the needs had to be satisfied. The provisioning required for a longer campaign journeying possibly through uninhabited or even hostile territory further entailed a higher than usual demand from these army troops. There is ample evidence that the officials in charge did not hesitate to resort to confiscation as a means of procuring foodstuffs as well as money when the need arose. A famous example is provided by BM 68610, a judicial record concerning a dispute over a tract of temple land between the Šamaš temple of Sippar or Larsa and the royal official Iltalimatu. The latter seems to have had laid claim, wrongly, to the land in question, the ownership of which was subsequently returned to the temple but tellingly not without having satisfied royal demands to the amount of one half of that land's harvest in the year of the trial.[95] Also in the ADs one can find occasional references to sequestrations of fields (AD -261B) and confiscations of foodstuffs (AD -309: this diary inserts the note *ina piš-ki* TI-*qé*, 'he took illegally', in the price section, line 12. The commodity in question is very likely dates). Additionally, AD -273B, when

---

[93] See Briant 1996: 700–9 and Ruzicka 2012: 68–70 and 84–98.

[94] See Will 1979[2]: 308–13 on the meagre sources at our disposal and an assessment of this campaign.

[95] The text is known as Porter Travels II (originally published in 1877), and discussed by van der Spek 1986: 202–11 and 1993b, 65–6 and most recently Joannès 2006: 112–15.

Table 6.7. *Summary of the instances of army presence*

Year	Event
373	Egyptian campaign.
369	Razaunda (Cadusians?).
351	Egyptian campaign.
346	Preparations for warfare in Phoenicia.
343	Egyptian campaign.
331	Alexander the Great conquers Babylon.
323–322	Alexander the Great returns from India.
318–316	Eumenes, Antigonus and Seleucus.
311–308	Antigonus and Demetrius versus Seleucus and Nikanor.
274–273	Run-up to First Syrian War.
246–245	Presence of Ptolemaic army.
219–218	Run-up to Fourth Syrian War.
145–144	Elamites, etc.

describing the military preparations for the Seleucid counter-attack against Ptolemy's invasion of Syria, refers to what seems to have been a withdrawal of tax privileges on arable land (AD -273B).[96]

Classical sources provide us with a good number of additional examples of the ways the presence of an army constituted a burden for any province. An interesting attempt at quantifying the needs of the imperial army of Antigonus the One-Eyed is given by Diodorus (19 58.2), who puts its annual consumption in the context of the arrangements for the siege of the city of Tyre in Phoenicia at 4.5 million *medimnoi* (237,000 metric tonnes) of wheat.[97] Diodorus specifies that this amount had to be provided by the local allies, the harvest of whose countries was thus probably to a significant extent put at the disposal of the army which they were hosting.[98] Hence,

---

[96] See van der Spek 1993b: 67–70 for this interpretation.

[97] Assuming that the size of his army amounted to some 40,000 men (including allies and craftsmen), this would result in a daily ration of slightly over 16 litres of wheat per soldier per day. In the light of the numbers given by Diodorus (19 27.1 and 28.4; cf. the discussion above) for the respective army sizes of Antigonus and Eumenes during the campaigns in winter 317/ 16, 40,000 seem a reasonable 'educated guess'. The daily ration thus obtained is certainly too generous but one has to take into account also the considerably higher allowances for the various higher ranks of the army as well as for the royal commander himself and his *philoi*.

[98] The same author (17 64.3–6) has a similar episode (albeit without an attempt at quantification) for the aftermath of the battle at Gaugamela, when the victorious army of Alexander the Great found 3,000 talents of silver and foodstuffs in abundance in the nearby city of Arbela.

it was not exclusively the presence of a hostile, conquering army that put strains on the country's economy, but in this latter case, plundering and destructions have to be reckoned with in addition to an increase in demand.

Regression Results

Splitting up the effects of warfare on commodity prices between military operations and army presence shows a pattern that is not unexpected. Just as was the case in the preceding analysis, barley prices were more strongly affected than date prices, which in turn were more strongly affected than wool prices (the regression coefficient for this latter commodity is also statistically insignificant for the category of army presence). Hence, the respective demand elasticity of the commodities can be shown to determine the magnitude of the price increases. Cress is less affected than dates by military operations, but disproportionately strongly affected by army presence, a phenomenon that has been tentatively explained above by the high perishability of this supplier of vitamins and its traditional usage as a travel ration. The coefficients for *kasû* are again insignificant, whereas sesame is the commodity that is affected most strongly by both dummies (and as was already the case in the domestic warfare category). The R^2 is for all commodities except for *kasû* at around 0.2, in most cases slightly higher.

With the conspicuous exception of cress, military operations reveal themselves a stronger price-increasing force than the mere presence of an army, particularly for barley and dates. This result can be interpreted as indicating that whereas the Babylonian economy was better able to cope with an increased demand, it was more susceptible to supply shocks. Such a reading aligns well with the finding that inter-annual storage was not practised as a means of price stabilisation and risk reduction on a significant scale, discussed in more detailed in Chapter 4. It also underlines the strong impact that armed conflict had on commodity prices in the Ancient World and is moreover a typical pattern for pre-industrial societies at large. To further assess the impact of the factors under discussion here, the cross-effect, meaning the impact of simultaneous occurrences of military operations and army presence, should be also considered.

What Table 6.9 shows is that the contemporary occurrence of both factors for the same dataset causes a shock that is more than the mere sum of the constituent parts. For barley, that difference amounts to an additional increase of *c.* 20 per cent and somewhat less for dates. The cross-effect is strongest for sesame, but curiously turns negative for cress. This means that the cress price is higher when only one of the factors is present. This at first

Table 6.8. *The impact of military operations and army presence on commodity prices*

Commodity	n [a]	R^2 [b]	Military operations (*t*-value)	Army presence (*t*-value)
Barley	349	0.24	3.00 (7.47)	1.05 (3.44)
Dates	300	0.21	1.67 (6.41)	0.76 (3.69)
Cress	260	0.22	1.42 (2.13)	5.32 (7.31)
Kasû	221	0.015	0.09 (0.83)	0.16 (1.36)
Sesame	257	0.19	4.97 (4.85)	4.54 (4.60)
Wool	232	0.20	1.54 (7.14)	0.06 (0.35)

Notes: [a] n: Number of observations; [b] R^2: coefficient of determination.

Table 6.9. *The cross-effect of military operations and army presence on commodity prices* [a]

Commodity	n [b]	R^2 [c]	Cross-effect (*t*-value)
Barley	349	0.38	6.33 (8. 79)
Dates	300	0.34	3.65 (7.49)
Cress	260	0.23	−2.2 (−1.47)
Sesame	257	0.33	14.49 (7.24)
Wool	232	0.25	1.5 (3.65)

Notes: [a] As all relevant values for *kasû* (coefficient of determination and coefficient of regression) were at about 0.0, the results have not been reported in the table. Again, seasonality has been accounted for in both barley and dates by means of monthly dummies. It is not surprising that the regression coefficients of Table 6.5 (column 'Domestic warfare') and Table 6.7 often bear great similarity to one another as the parameters considered are very similar.
[b] n: Number of observations; [c] R^2: coefficient of determination.

glance curious pattern can, however, be explained by the disproportionately strong price increases of cress in cases of army convocations in Babylon for campaigns fought elsewhere, the best example being the cress prices in winter 274/3.

A final remark pertains to the way the regression analysis was carried out in this chapter, namely in two separate steps distinguishing between historical episodes and underlying causes. If both calculations were carried out in a single regression, the results for barley would still be a very strong and significant price-increasing impact for the category of domestic warfare (regression coefficient 7.07, *t*-value 8.01) and a more moderate effect for the category of internal rebellion (regression coefficient 1.46, *t*-value 3.49). However, the underlying factors of army presence and military operations are already considered in these values, and it is precisely this overlap that causes the coefficients of these latter categories not only to decrease but moreover to become statistically meaningless, with *t*-values around and below 1.0 only. This problem is commonly referred to as multicollinearity (see Feinstein and Thomas 2002: 322).

Conclusion

Regression analysis, where applicable, provided us with a simple means of quantifying the repercussions of political history in commodity prices in Babylonia. The quantitative aspect is twofold. First of all, the *t*-values of the single regressions confirm that the results thus obtained are unlikely to be accidental. Indeed, most of the regressions were significant at 95 per cent, meaning that there is only a 5 per cent chance that each of the results is coincidental.

Secondly, the impact of distinct categories of events (episodes of warfare, army convocations, etc.) on the price observations of the ADs can be expressed as percentile price increases. Considering elasticity of demand, it hardly comes as a surprise that the price of barley was usually more strongly affected than that of dates, and the latter more strongly than that of wool. This sequence is the same for the categories 'Warfare' and 'Military presence'. As for the remaining commodities, the results for *kasû* are normally statistically clearly insignificant (and also the regression coefficients tend towards 0), the cause of which pattern is to be sought in the nature of this commodity as parasitical plant rather than as a crop to be cultivated. At the other end of the scale, sesame proved to be the commodity most strongly influenced by the vicissitudes of history. The fact that cress was disproportionately strongly affected by the category 'Army presence' has just been adduced as explanation for the odd value of the coefficient of the cross-effect, and it also explains why this commodity is also the only one affected by the category 'Warfare abroad' on a significant level.

In the concluding remarks that follow, I contextualise the Babylonian price data in a wider framework, by means of a comparison with various other regions from world history of the pre-industrial period.

Conclusions and Outlook

Performance ...

In a very critical reaction to Temin's *The Roman Market Economy* (2013), Peter Thoneman notes concerning the scarcity of ancient data amenable to statistical analysis: 'This is not just the banal point that no statistical evidence (price-sets, population numbers, changing interest rates) happens to survive, nor even the slightly less banal point that these data never existed or were never collected in the first place.'[1] If taken *cum grano salis*, his statement may be justified in a Greco-Roman context,[2] but for Babylonia, the situation is clearly different. Over the span of several centuries, thousands of commodity prices were collect in a text genre known as Astronomical Diaries, and a non-trivial proportion of these prices (*c.* 3,000 overall) are still extant today. The interest in these price data was triggered by the fact that Babylonian astronomers-astrologers recognised commodity prices as a cyclical and consequently potentially foreseeable phenomenon.[3] The prediction of price developments still eludes economists today, as the remark usually attributed to J. K. Galbraith that 'the only function of economic forecasting is to make astrology look respectable' reminds us. Sadly, the joke would certainly have been lost on the Babylonian *ṭupšar Enūma Anu Enlil*. However, their penchant for data collection provides the historian of the Ancient Near East with the unique opportunity to gauge the performance of the Babylonian economy, rather than having to confine oneself to descriptions of the economic structure.

The preceding pages have shown that commodity prices in Late Achaemenid and Seleucid Babylonia were indeed heavily influenced by historical events. Among the factors causing price increases, warfare and armed conflict in and around Babylon stand out in efficacy. Another quantifiable event category is constituted by the presence of the army, both in periods of warfare in Babylonia and simply because of convocations of

---

[1] In the *Times Literary Supplement*, 9 August 2013: 11.

[2] The most recent exhaustive survey of prices for grain in the Greco-Roman Mediterranean is von Reden and Rathbone 2015.

[3] Pirngruber 2013: 199.

army contingents as a consequence of conflicts in other provinces. In the former case, a significant cross-effect between the categories of 'Warfare' and 'Presence of the army' could also be established. In addition to these types of events, which proved to be quantifiable in a relatively uncomplicated manner, additional factors not easily amenable to statistical analysis, such as locust invasions, could be identified. However, not only do such exogenous shocks – hence one-time effects – have repercussions in the price data. An important role regarding the determination of the price level was also played by changes in the amount of money in circulation and climatic change. Unsurprisingly, demand elasticity played a crucial role in relation to the magnitude of the impact of historical events: the staple foods barley and dates (in this order) were more strongly affected than cress, *kasû* or wool.

What are the implications of these results? Most obviously, they further corroborate the by now common opinion that prices in first-millennium Babylonia were to a significant extent set by the interplay of supply and demand, with an additional important role for the level of monetisation. After all, the exogenous shocks discussed in the preceding chapters drove up or depressed prices by affecting one of these factors. At the very least, the results discussed in this book indicate that a characterisation of the Babylonian economy during large stretches of the first-millennium as a 'more elaborate form, mediated by a monetary equivalent (usually silver, but not always), of the command economy' (Bresson 2016: 107) clearly underestimates the importance of market forces at work.

The economy of Late Achaemenid and Seleucid Babylonia displays a rather high degree of market efficiency when compared to roughly contemporary economies. The value of intra-annual volatility of *c.* 15 per cent given by Földvári, van Leeuwen and Pirngruber 2011 compares favourably with the intra-annual wheat price variation in Egypt ranging between 20 per cent and 30 per cent given by von Reden 2010: 155. The higher values of Egypt compared to Babylon can be readily explained by its single-crop structure; however, both values are still low by the standards of pre-industrial societies. Compared with the rather scanty data on grain prices for the island of Delos, integrated into the regional Cycladic economy, these figures are very moderate indeed, as the latter show a much higher level of volatility. During the year 282, the wheat price on the island more than doubled from 4.5 drachmae per *medimnos* in the immediate post-harvest period to 10 drachmae/*medimnos* five months later.

It hardly comes as a surprise that Egypt and Babylonia, two exceptionally fertile regions by ancient (Mediterranean) standards, fare comparatively

Table 7.1. *Price volatility in comparison*

Region	Commodity	Time period	CV
Babylon	Barley	620–484	0.99
Babylon	Barley	573–549	0.42
Babylon	Dates	620–484	0.6
Babylon	Barley	305–230	0.63
Babylon	Barley	230–140	0.41
Babylon	Dates	305–230	0.39
Cairo	Wheat	1260–1512 CE	0.79
Syria	Wheat	1260–1512 CE	0.65
Calcutta	Wheat	1764–1794 CE	0.79
Calcutta	Wheat	1870–1910 CE	0.18
Calcutta	Rice	1764–1794 CE	0.38
Calcutta	Rice	1870–1910 CE	0.18
(Central) Europe	Grain	1500–1799 CE	0.15–0.25

well as regards price stability. More interestingly, it is now also possible to gauge the performance of the Babylonian economy in a wider comparative perspective. A convenient yardstick of market performance is price volatility as expressed by the coefficient of variation. The lower the CV, the more an economy is capable of handling unexpected supply or demand shocks by various means such as spatial market integration (hence trade), storage, technical innovations and suchlike.

As Table 7.1 clearly shows, Babylonia does not fare particularly well when compared to early modern Europe, which displays a significantly lower level of price volatility.[4] The most representative values for the CV in Babylonia amount to 0.6–0.4 (the very high value of 0.99 in the period 620–484 was caused by the inflationary tendencies in the last quarter of the sixth century; see Jursa 2010: 745–53), whereas volatility in early modern Europe was only at about half this level and less. On the other hand, the level of volatility in Babylonia during the sixth century and then during the Seleucid period is comparable to the medieval Near East (Cairo and Syria), the values obtained are even slightly more favourable than in these regions.

[4] The data in this table is culled from the data in Jursa 2010 (sixth-century Babylonia), Söderberg 2004 (Cairo and Syria), Studer 2008 (Calcutta; see also his table 6 (417) for the low CVs of 0.15–0.2 of various European cities in the period 1764–94 CE), and Bateman 2010 (early modern Europe). For the CVs of barley and dates during the Seleucid period see Chapter 5. See also Földvári, van Leeuwen and van Zanden 2011 for more data.

Another suitable point of reference in terms of price volatility is constituted by India in the eighteenth century CE, before the country's economy made a giant leap in the late nineteenth century CE.[5] Not unlike Babylonia, India had a kind of dual-crop economy (rice and wheat) with a notable difference in the volatility of the two main cops, similar to barley and dates in Seleucid Babylonia.

This comparatively high level of price volatility is hardly surprising in the light of the strong repercussions which historical events could be shown to have exerted on Babylonian commodity prices. The topic is all the more important as a high level of price volatility hampers further development of market efficiency, for example.[6] The overall result is that although the Babylonian market worked in a fairly efficient manner – prices indeed behaved like market prices and moved in a perfect random walk, see for example Temin 2002 – the performance of the economy, hence its capacity to balance exogenous shock, was very limited. Temporary shortages caused by intrinsic reasons such as seasonality or by exogenous shocks having an impact on demand or supply, were difficult to balance. Seen in this light, it is all the more remarkable that there is almost no evidence from Babylon for price controls through the state and similar measures so amply attested in the Greek world and in particular Classical Athens.[7]

... and Structure

So what were the causes behind these substantially fluctuating prices? After all, there were several factors conducive to price stability present in first-millennium Babylonia. First of all, a highly productive agriculture in terms of seed/yield ratio benefiting from a sophisticated system of irrigation ensured a constant and relatively abundant supply.[8] A second characteristic was the dual-crop regime mitigating intra-annual seasonal fluctuation (Földvári, van Leeuwen and Pirngruber 2011) and thus also the overall level of volatility. Some aspects of the institutional framework, such as the stability of the system of measuring units – the *kurru* of 180 litres subdivided

[5] See Studer 2008: 400–7 for a quick overview of India's economic development in the colonial period. Note also the considerable numbers of outliers – caused by harvest failure – in his data for western India in fig. 2, 397–8.
[6] Van Zanden 2004: 1029.
[7] Bresson 2016: 254–9.
[8] See Jursa 2010: 48–53 (and table 2) on agricultural productivity in Babylonia.

into *pānu* (36 litres), *sūtu* (6 litres) and *qa* (one litre) – in spite of the frequent regime changes (from the Achaemenids to Alexander the Great to the Seleucids and later to the Parthians) is also remarkable.

However, on the negative side, several key factors outweigh these beneficial traits. Thanks to prohibitively high transport costs, Babylonian farmers were not able to trade their surplus in staple goods supra-regionally. It is hence misleading and a rather infelicitous analogy with Roman Egypt or Sicily to tag Babylonia as 'the granary of much more extensive realms'.[9] Rather, a bumper harvest would simply cause prices to dwindle because of the prevailing glut but not necessarily entail larger profits for farmers – which in turn constituted a major disincentive for any investments in agriculture. Vice versa, in times of harvest failure, the supply situation was likely to remain strained for extended periods, as additional supplies were hard to come by. The same trait also explains the susceptibility of pre-industrial economies to display autocorrelation. The absence of storage as one means of risk aversion and price stabilisation has been amply discussed in Chapter 4. Another aspect to be considered is the pattern of urbanisation in first-millennium Babylonia. As the research of Földvári, van Leeuwen and van Zanden (2011) has shown, price volatility tends to be higher in regions with one dominant city, for example Babylonia and Babylon or also twelfth-century CE Egypt and Cairo compared to less centralised regions (in which often a different political economy prevailed) such as Tuscany or the Low Countries. Another factor contributing to unstable prices was the shifting monetary supply. As we have seen, inflation in the last quarter of the fourth century can be attributed to a considerable extent to an increasing amount of silver in circulation. In the second century, a reverse movement, a drain of silver in the later reign of Antiochus III, seems to have been instrumental in causing troughs of extremely low prices and likely also played a part in the pattern of decreasing prices in the first half of the second century. Finally, in particular for the high level of volatility during the Late Achaemenid period, the analysis of internal power structures in Chapter 3 proved rewarding. In particular, the interlinkage of the markets for capital, means of production and commodities favouring a few powerful entrepreneur-type businessmen – best known is the Murašû clan in the

---

[9] Adams 1981: 176. The major difference was of course that Sicily and Egypt were located at (or in the case of Egypt rather connected via the Nile with) the shores of the Mediterranean and had hence access to cheap waterways. On the grain market of the Roman Empire see Erdkamp 2005: 175–205; see in particular his ch. 5, 'Rome and the Corn Provinces' (205–57), for a discussion of the supply of the city of Rome by means of the surplus generated in Sicily and Egypt.

region around Nippur – constituted a major impediment for markets to work efficiently.[10]

Not only is price volatility considered a major impediment to economic growth and improved standards of living. The subject matter is also relevant in so far as price volatility is a valid proxy for the degree of efficiency of the market segment in an economy.[11] The pattern of prices during the Late Achaemenid period indicates that market forces were working only very imperfectly (which in turn also raises the question of alternative forms of economic integration), and it is in this sense that the price data of the Astronomical Diaries sheds light also on the nature of the Babylonian economy. In this context, Garfinkle's warning that 'it is a mistake to assume that proving the existence of a price-setting markets amounts to proving the predominance of such a market over other contemporary modes of exchange'[12] is an important reminder of the possibility of the persistence of non-market mechanisms, especially in the more rural regions. I have already referred to the fact that some of the dependent labour forces (*šušānus*) on royal/state-owned estate in the Late Achaemenid period were provided for by means of rations. Further, the modalities of payment of various professionals in the ambiance of the Esangila temple in Babylon in the form of 'salaries in kind', most often dates, which persisted well into the Seleucid period, further complicate the picture.[13]

It should be self-evident by now that the employment of the methodologies and the parlance of the science of economics does not necessarily entail a 'modernist' stance: such instruments can equally by used to highlight deficiencies and weaknesses of (not only) pre-industrial economies (as seen from a modern vantage point). This claim can best be substantiated by reference to the institution of agricultural entrepreneurs. The activity of people like the Murašûs was certainly at no point an efficient solution in the sense that it benefited the wider economy. The case of Late Achaemenid Babylonia is thus also an excellent illustration of recent economic theory that postulates that institutions do not only or even primarily exist because they provide efficient solutions to specific economic needs in a society, as was the point of departure of the

---

[10] See van Zanden 2004: 1040–2 on the harmful impact of Chinese moneylenders on market efficiency in Java during the nineteenth century CE.

[11] Persson 1999, especially 103–6 on market integration and price volatility; see also 23–39 on price volatility and standards of living. Ogilvie 2011: 393–4[(+15)] provides a succinct overview of factors conducive to a high level of volatility.

[12] Garfinkle 2012: 9.

[13] For the terminology 'salaries in kind' see Jursa 2008. Pertinent texts are referred to by Boiy 2004: 17–18; Hackl 2013: 256–9 provides an update of the discussion.

New Institutional Economics school of thought with its roots in the work of the Nobel laureate Douglass C. North. Quite the contrary, much recent research has been dedicated to explanations of the persistence of economically inefficient institutions by acknowledging the crucial role of culture on the one hand, and of conflicts over distribution of key resources within past societies on the other.[14] This latter approach is certainly a good match with what we see in the sources at our disposal: economically inefficient extractive institutions reigned supreme in Late Achaemenid Babylonia because these best suited the needs of those in political power.

It is in this sphere, at the interface between the economic and the political, that the New Institutional Economics has much to contribute to studies of ancient economies both in the Middle East and in the Mediterranean.[15] It is not merely that commodity prices in Babylonia during latter half of the first millennium reacted to individual events. The Late Achaemenid period shows that the relationship between the political and the economic is located on a deeper, structural level. Although the absence of pertinent sources makes it difficult to analyse this process in detail during the Seleucid period, it is telling that the decades displaying the highest number of price outliers, *c.* 280–220, correspond to a peak period in a recently devised instability index for the Seleucid Empire.[16] The impact of empire was thus fully felt in Seleucid Babylonia.

---

[14] The original claim that institutions that persist are necessarily efficient was also abandoned by North himself (e.g., North 1990). Ogilvie 2007 provides a concise overview of different approaches to institutions.

[15] See in particular North, Wallis and Weingast 2009 for a most useful framework applied, e.g., in Pirngruber forthcoming A.

[16] Monson 2015: 188, fig. 5.3.

Appendix: Regression Sheets for Barley,
Dates and Wool

Barley

SUMMARY OUTPUT

Regression Statistics

Multiple R	0.607775084
R Square	0.369390553
Adjusted R Square	0.33996381
Standard Error	2.206356805
Observations	349

ANOVA

	df	SS	MS	F	Significance F
Regression	15	952.4085206	63.49390138	13.97474022	1.84279E-27
Residual	334	1625.915457	4.868010351	–	–
Total	349	2578.323978	–	–	–

	Coefficients	Standard Error	t Stat	P-value	Lower 95%	Upper 95%
Intercept	1.53660464	0.468246293	3.28161624	0.001141184	0.615521152	2.457688129
X Variable 1	1.265751057	0.623173603	2.031137152	0.043032624	0.039911314	2.491590801
X Variable 2	0.923041959	0.605232687	1.525102624	0.128179816	-0.267506354	2.113590272
X Variable 3	0.640205116	0.612968598	1.04443379	0.297040052	-0.565560444	1.845970676
X Variable 4	1.0157876	0.627274439	1.619367118	0.106312098	-0.218118864	2.249694063
X Variable 5	0.508930877	0.611828015	0.831820159	0.406104772	-0.694591053	1.712452807

X Variable 6	0	0	65535	—	0	0
X Variable 7	0.424822636	0.652087863	0.651480667	0.515184253	−0.857894114	1.707539386
X Variable 8	0.176519511	0.642459458	0.274755876	0.783673672	−1.087257281	1.440296304
X Variable 9	0.690786168	0.594860379	1.161257655	0.246366374	−0.479358861	1.860931197
X Variable 10	0.517813431	0.57535011	0.8999971	0.368770224	−0.613953108	1.649579969
X Variable 11	0.09780194	0.626168464	0.156191098	0.875976755	−1.133928969	1.329532849
X Variable 12	0.711537538	0.622003738	1.143944152	0.253465981	−0.512000973	1.935076048
X Variable 13	6.895439367	0.511182583	13.48919073	2.10256E-33	5.88989625	7.900982483
X Variable 14	0.151997332	0.309855012	0.490543405	0.624071531	−0.45751595	0.761510614
X Variable 15	0.846192507	0.445955058	1.89748382	0.058626315	−0.031042073	1.723427087

Dates

SUMMARY OUTPUT

Regression Statistics

Multiple R	0.54395089
R Square	0.295882571
Adjusted R Square	0.257785575
Standard Error	1.522005584
Observations	300

ANOVA

	df	SS	MS	F	Significance F
Regression	15	277.4288623	18.49525749	8.554430724	3.54482E-16
Residual	285	660.2027843	2.316500998	–	–
Total	300	937.6316466	–	–	–

	Coefficients	Standard Error	t Stat	P-value	Lower 95%	Upper 95%
Intercept	1.637385233	0.334979439	4.888017118	1.70303E-06	0.978037652	2.296732814
X Variable 1	-0.04004992	0.449045755	-0.089188952	0.928994387	-0.923916803	0.843816962
X Variable 2	-0.082307798	0.455703716	-0.180616911	0.856796648	-0.979279694	0.814664099
X Variable 3	0.100975714	0.464833343	0.217229928	0.828184592	-0.813966233	1.0159766
X Variable 4	0.111264287	0.460424336	0.241655965	0.809220534	-0.794999311	1.017527885
X Variable 5	0.25582109	0.455704979	0.56137436	0.574983501	-0.641153291	1.152795472
X Variable 6	0	0	65535	—	0	0
X Variable 7	-0.198772424	0.459638032	-0.432454258	0.665738329	-1.103488323	0.705943475
X Variable 8	0.085821514	0.440550486	0.194805175	0.845684266	-0.781323937	0.952966966
X Variable 9	0.082485229	0.436087412	0.189148383	0.850111151	-0.775875454	0.940845911
X Variable 10	-0.096463191	0.429381335	-0.224656229	0.822407701	-0.941624151	0.748697768
X Variable 11	-0.275298522	0.460447418	-0.597893508	0.550385787	-1.181607555	0.631010511
X Variable 12	-0.081706947	0.464337162	-0.175964695	0.860446643	-0.99567225	0.832258356
X Variable 13	3.711940091	0.359405205	10.32800871	1.89333E-21	3.004514724	4.419365458
X Variable 14	0.059734483	0.220606317	0.270774128	0.786760756	-0.374489904	0.49395887
X Variable 15	0.389831378	0.300390275	1.297749661	0.195422729	-0.201433572	0.981096327

Wool

SUMMARY OUTPUT

Regression Statistics

Multiple R	0.473138546
R Square	0.223860084
Adjusted R Square	0.213647717
Standard Error	1.078894822
Observations	232

ANOVA

	df	SS	MS	F	Significance F
Regression	3	76.54727013	25.51575671	21.92048885	1.64774E-12
Residual	228	265.3952004	1.164014037	–	–
Total	231	341.9424705	–	–	–

	Coefficients	Standard Error	t Stat	P-value	Lower 95%	Upper 95%
Intercept	1.674289947	0.084400799	19.8373707	1.48334E-51	1.507984658	1.840595235
X Variable 1	1.796198738	0.261509831	6.868570608	6.10218E-11	1.280913715	2.31148376
X Variable 2	−0.459399445	0.185573461	−2.475566515	0.014030554	−0.825057687	−0.093741204
X Variable 3	0.984651408	0.282606047	3.484183785	0.0005918	0.427797912	1.541504904

Note: Variables 1, 2 and 3 correspond to variables 13, 14 and 15 in the preceding sheets.

Glossary

The entries below explain a few selected technical terms that are recurrent throughout the book, in particular in the discussions of the graphs and in the statistical analyses. They aim to provide historians who are not familiar with economists' and economic historians' parlance with a convenient point of reference. The explanations are based on Feinstein and Thomas 2002 and Black, Hashimzade and Myles 2009.

Coefficient of Determination (r^2/R^2): The coefficient of determination describes the goodness of the fit of a regression (line), that is, how much of the variation of the dependent variable (on the y axis) is explained. Its value is always between 0 and 1, and the higher it is, the more variation is accounted for. In our case, the coefficient indicates how much of the variation in the price data is explained by the regression. The R^2 of 0.37 for barley in Table 6.5 summarising the regression results for the impact of warfare on commodity prices means that about 37 per cent of total price variation is explained by the *dummy variable 'Domestic warfare' (and the remainder by other factors: seasonality, harvest stocks, etc.). See further Feinstein and Thomas 2002: 103–6.

Coefficient of Variation (CV): In the context of this book, the CV is used as an indicator of price volatility. A measure of dispersion, the CV is simply the *standard deviation of a data sample divided by its arithmetic mean. A CV of 0.2, for example, means that prices deviate on average 20 per cent from the mean. It gives an idea of percental, rather than absolute, oscillations around the mean value. Consequently, it is better suited than the standard deviation for comparative purposes between different datasets of data.

Dummy Variable: A dummy variable can be employed in a quantitative analysis to account for factors that are not easily measured – such as historical events. Qualitatively different scenarios are assigned a different number. The procedure thus enables us, albeit to a limited extent, to transform historical information into mathematical form (Feinstein and Thomas 2002: 12). In the context of this book, dummies are only employed as explanatory variables; moreover, only two categories (yes/no) are considered. Thus, a process of twofold abstraction is involved. First, specific instances (e.g. of warfare waged in Babylonia) are subsumed into a larger category ('Domestic warfare', in our case). Second, in order to measure the impact of this category on the Babylonian price data, a year in which warfare was waged in Babylonia is given the number 1 (yes), whereas years without warfare are assigned the number 0 (no). The result (expressed as R^2, see *Coefficient of Determination) explains not only whether but also to what extent the category had indeed an impact on prices.

Regression: A regression summarises the relationship between different variables in a given dataset. In this book, the focus is on the relationship between prices and historical events (the latter modelled as *dummy variables). A dependent variable (prices) is thus expressed as a function of one or several explanatory variables (historical events). A regression establishes only whether and to what extant there is a relationship between variables; importantly, it conveys no information regarding causality. The calculations in Table 6.5, for example, show the relationship between prices and dummy variables. The coefficient of regression of the variable 'Domestic warfare' of 3.72 for dates means that date prices more than treble (rise by 372 per cent) during episodes of domestic warfare on average.

Standard Deviation: The standard deviation is a measure of dispersion. Mathematically speaking, it is the square root of the variance, or 'equal to the square root of the arithmetic mean of the squared deviations from the mean … It is measured in the same units as the data series it refers to' (Feinstein and Thomas 2002: 50). Hence, in Table 5.2 the standard deviation of 0.75 for wool prices means that the single wool prices deviate on average 0.75 shekels/*kurru* from the mean value of 1.54 shekels/*kurru*.

t-value: Obtaining a satisfactory *t*-value means that the results of the regression are not likely to be the product of chance. In that case, the outcome is said to be statistically significant. The higher the *t*-value, the more probable it is that the results obtained are actually meaningful. In more technical terms, the result of the *t*-test, or Student's test, indicates that the null-hypothesis postulating the opposite of the anticipated outcome can be rejected. In economic history, a 95 per cent confidence interval is usually adopted, which means that there is only a 5 per cent chance that in spite of a seeming falsification the null hypothesis still holds true. For the purposes of the regressions in Chapter 6, it can be stated that if *t* amounts to *c*. 2.0, the results are valid at a 95 per cent level. The *t*-value of 13.49 for barley in Table 6.5 means thus that is absolutely unlikely that the finding that the category 'Domestic warfare' has a strong impact on barley prices is mere coincidence: the chance that the null-hypothesis 'domestic warfare has no impact on barley prices' holds true is less than 0.01 per cent. On the other hand, it is quite uncertain whether the observed weak impact of the category 'Warfare abroad' on barley is not mere chance. The *t*-value of 0.66 means that there is a good chance, about 25 per cent, that in this case the null-hypothesis (again, no impact) holds true. For further explanations, see Feinstein and Thomas 2002: 131–8 and 160–9. The distribution of t – the t(est) statistic – is similar to a normal probability distribution, the reference employed in this book is table 5.1 in Feinstein and Thomas 2002: 135–6.

Bibliography

Abraham, K. 2004 *Business and Politics under the Persian Empire. The Financial Dealings of Marduk-nāṣir-apli of the House of Egibi (521–487 BCE)*. Bethesda, MD: CDL Press

Adams, R. McC. 1965 *Land behind Baghdad: A History of Settlements on the Diyala Plains*. University of Chicago Press

1981 *Heartland of Cities. Surveys of Ancient Settlement and Land Use on the Central Floodplain on the Euphrates*. University of Chicago Press

Adams, R. McC. and H. Nissen 1972 *The Uruk Countryside. The Natural Setting of Urban Societies*. University of Chicago Press

Adamson, P. B. 1985 'Problems over storing food in the Ancient Near East', *WdO* 16: 5–15

Andreau, J., P. Briant and R. Descat (eds.) 1997 *Économie antique. Prix et formation des prix dans les économies antiques*. EAHSBC 3. St.-Bertrand-des Comminges

2000 *Économie antique. La guerre dans les économies antiques*. EAHSBC 5. St.-Bertrand-des-Comminges: Musée archéologique départemental

Anson, E. 2007 'Early Hellenistic chronology. The cuneiform evidence', in Heckel, Tritle and Wheatley (eds.): 193–8

2014 *Alexander's Heirs: The Age of the Successors*. Malden, MA and Oxford: Wiley-Blackwell

Aperghis, G. G. 2000 'War captives and economic exploitation. Evidence from the Persepolis Fortification tablets', in Andreau, Briant and Descat (eds.): 127–44

2004 *The Seleukid Royal Economy. The Finances and Financial Administration of the Seleukid Empire*. Cambridge University Press

Archibald, Z., J. Davies and V. Gabrielsen (eds.) 2005 *Making, Moving and Managing. The New World of Ancient Economies, 323–31 BC*. Oxford: Oxbow

Austin, M. 1986 'Hellenistic kings, war, and the economy', *Classical Quarterly* (NS) 36.2: 450–66

Baker, H. D. 2008 'Babylon in 484 BC: the excavated archival tablets as a source for urban history', *ZA* 98: 100–16

Baker, H. D. and M. Jursa (eds.) 2005 *Approaching the Babylonian Economy. Proceedings of the START Project Symposium held in Vienna, 1–3 July 2004*. AOAT 330 = Veröffentlichungen zur Wirtschaftsgeschichte Babyloniens im 1. Jahrtausend v. Chr., Band 1. Münster: Ugarit Verlag

2014 *Documentary Sources in Ancient Near Eastern and Greco-Roman History. Methodology and Practice*. Oxford and Philadelphia: Oxbow

Bar-Kochva, B. 1976 *The Seleucid Army: Organization and Tactics in the Great Campaigns*. Cambridge University Press

1989 *Judas Maccabaeus: The Jewish Struggle against the Seleucids*. Cambridge University Press

Barjamović, G. 2004 'Civic institutions and self-government in southern Mesopotamia in the mid-first millennium BC', in Dercksen (ed.): 47–98

Basu, K. 1997 *Analytical Development Economics. The Less Developed Economy Revisited*. Cambridge, MA: MIT Press

Bateman, V. 2010 'The evolution of markets in early modern Europe, 1350–1800: a study of wheat prices', *Economic History Review* 64.2: 447–71

Beaulieu, P.-A. 1988 'An early attestation of the word *hadru*', *NABU* 1988/54

2005 'Eanna's contribution to the construction of the North Palace at Babylon', in Baker and Jursa (eds.): 45–73

2006 'De l'Esagil au Mouseion: l'organisation de la recherche scientifique au IVe siècle avant J.-C.', in Briant and Joannès (eds.): 17–36

2013 'Arameans, Chaldeans, and Arabs in cuneiform sources from the Late Babylonian Period', in A. Berlejung and M. Streck (eds.), *Arameans, Chaldeans, and Arabs in Babylonia and Palestine in the First Millennium B.C.* LAOS 3. Wiesbaden: Harrasowitz: 31–55

Bedigian, D. 1985 'Is še-giš-ì sesame or flax?', *BSA* 2: 159–78

Bedford, P. 2007 'The Persian Near East', in Scheidel, Morris and Saller (eds.): 301–29

Bergamini, G. 2013 'Babylon in the Achaemenid and Hellenistic period: the changing landscape of a myth', *Mesopotamia* 48: 23–34

Bikerman, E. 1938 *Institutions des Séleucides*. Paris: Geuthner

Binder, C. 2008 *Plutarchs Vita des Artaxerxes. Ein historischer Kommentar*. Göttinger Forum für Altertumswissenschaften Beihefte Band 1. Berlin and New York: De Gruyter

Black, J., N. Hashimzade and G. Myles 2009[3] *A Dictionary of Economics*. Oxford University Press

Boiy, T. 2000 'Dating methods during the early Hellenistic period', *JCS* 52: 115–21

2001 'Dating problems in cuneiform tablets concerning the reign of Antigonus Monophthalmus', *JAOS* 121: 645–49

2002 'Royal titulature in Hellenistic Babylonia', *ZA* 92: 241–57

2004 *Late Achaemenid and Hellenistic Babylon*. OLA 136. Leuven: Peeters

2007a *Between High and Low. A Chronology of the Early Hellenistic Period*. Oikumene Studien zur antiken Weltgeschichte 5. Frankfurt/Main: Verlag Antike

2007b 'Cuneiform tablets and Aramaic ostraca. Between high and low chronologies for the early Diadoch period', in Heckel, Tritle and Wheatley (eds.): 199–207

2010 'Royal and satrapal armies in Babylonia during the second Diadoch War. The chronicle of the successors on the events during the seventh year of Philip Arrhidaeus (= 317/316 BC)', *Journal of Hellenic Studies* 120: 1–13

Bongenaar, A. C. V. M. 1997 *The Neo-Babylonian Ebabbar Temple at Sippar. Its Administration and its Prosopography*. PIHANS 80. Istanbul: NINO

Bosworth, A. B. 1988 *Conquest and Empire. The Reign of Alexander the Great*. Cambridge University Press

2002 *The Legacy of Alexander: Politics, Warfare, and Propaganda under the Successors*. Oxford University Press

Bresson, A. 2005 'Coinage and money supply in the Hellenistic age', in Archibald, Davies and Gabrielsen (eds.): 44–72

2016 *The Making of the Ancient Greek Economy. Institutions, Markets and, Growth in the City-States*. Princeton University Press

Briant, P. 1982 *Rois, tributs, et paysans. Études sur les formations tributaries du Moyen-Orient ancient*. Paris: Les Belles Lettres

1996 *Histoire de l'empire perse de Cyrus à Alexandre*. Paris: Fayard

1997 'Bulletin d'histoire achéménide I', *Topoi* Suppl. 1: 5–127

2001 *Bulletin d'histoire achéménide II*. Persika 1. Paris: De Boccard

Briant, P. and F. Joannès (eds.) 2006 *La transition entre l'empire achéménide et les royaumes hellénistiques (vers 350–300 BC)*. Persika 9. Paris: De Boccard

Briant, P., W. Henkelman and M. Stolper (eds.) 2008 *L'archive des fortifications de Persépolis. État des questions et perspectives de recherché*. Persika 12. Paris: De Boccard

Bringmann, K. 2005 'Königliche Ökonomie im Spiegel des Euergetismus der Seleukiden', *Klio* 87: 102–15

Brinkman, J. A. 1968 *A Political History of Post-Kassite Babylonia, 1158–722 B.C.* An.Or. 43. Rome: Pontificum Institutum Biblicum

1973 'Sennacherib's Babylonian problem: an interpretation', *JCS* 25: 89–95

1984a *Prelude to Empire. Babylonian Society and Politics, 747–626 B.C.* Philadelphia University Museum

1984b 'Settlement survey and documentary evidence: regional variation and secular trend in Mesopotamian demography', *JNES* 43.2: 168–80

Brosius, M. and A. Kuhrt (eds.) 1998 *Studies in Persian History. Essays in Memory of David M. Lewis*. Ach. Hist. XI. Leiden: NINO

Brown, D. 2000 *Mesopotamian Planetary Astronomy-Astrology*. CM 18. Groningen: Styx

2002 'The level of the Euphrates', in Wunsch (ed.): 37–56

Bunge, J. G. 1976 'Die Feiern Antiochos' IV. Epiphanes in Daphne im Herbst 166. v. Chr. Zu einem umstrittenen Kapitel syrischer und jüdischer Geschichte', *Chiron* 6: 53–71

Butzer, K. 1995 'Environmental change in the Near East and the human impact on the land', in J. Sasson (ed.), *Civilizations of the Ancient Near East*, vol. I. New York: Scribner: 123–51

Capdetrey, L. 2007 *Le pouvoir séleucide. Territoire, administration, finances d'un royaume hellénistique (312–129 av. J.-C.)*. Presses Universitaires Rennes

Cardascia, G. 1951 *Les archives des Murašû. Une famille d'hommes d'affaires babylo-niens à l'époque perse (455–403 av. J.-C.)*. Paris: Imprimerie nationale

Chaniotis, A. 2005 *War in the Hellenistic World. A Social and Cultural History*. Oxford: Wiley-Blackwell

Chankowski, V. and F. Duyrat (eds.) 2004 *Le roi et l'économie. Autonomies locales et structures royales dans l'économie de l'empire séleucide*. Topoi Suppl. 6. Paris: De Boccard

Charles, M. P. 1984 'Introductory remarks on the cereals', *BSA* 1: 17–44

    1985 'An introduction to the legumes and oil plants of Mesopotamia', *BSA* 2: 39–61

Clancier, P. 2009 *Les bibliothèques en Babylonie dans la deuxième moitié du Ier millènaire av. J.-C.* AOAT 363. Münster: Ugarit Verlag

    2012a ' "Le *rab sikkati*" de Babylone contre "l'homme de renom venu d'Égypte": le troisième guerre syrienne dans les rues de Babylone', in P. Goukowksy and C. Feyel (eds.), *Folia Greca in honorem É. Will*. Paris: De Boccard: 9–31

    2012b ' "Le *satammu*, l'assemblée de l'Esagil et les Babyloniens". Les notables de Babylone: du relais locale à la marginalisation', in C. Feyel, J. Fournier, L. Graslin-Thomé and F. Kirbihler (eds.): 297–325

Clancier P. and J. Monerie 2014 'Les sanctuaires babyloniens à l'époque hellénis-tique. Évolution d'un relais de pouvoir', *Topoi* 19.1: 181–237

Clancier, P., F. Joannès, P. Ruoillard and A. Tenu (eds.) 2005 *Autour de Polanyi. Vocabulaires, théories et modalités des échanges*. Paris: De Boccard

Cocquerillat, D. 1968 *Palmeraies et cultures de l'Eanna d'Uruk (559–520)*. ADFU 8. Berlin: Mann

Cohen, G. 1978 *The Seleucid Colonies. Studies in Founding, Administration and Organization*. Historia Einzelschriften 30. Wiesbaden: Harrassowitz

    2013 *The Hellenistic Settlements in the East from Armenia and Mesopotamia to Bactria and India*. Berkeley: University of California Press

Cooper, J. S. 1983 *The Curse of Agade*. Baltimore and London: The Johns Hopkins University Press

Corò, P. 2005 *Prebende tempari in età seleucide*. HANEM VIII. Padua: SARGON

Crow, B. and K. A. S. Murshid 1994 'Economic returns to social power: mer-chants' finance and interlinkage in the grain markets of Bangladesh', *World Development* 22.7: 1011–30

Dandamaev, M. 1984 *Slavery in Babylonia from Nabopolassar to Alexander the Great (626–331 BC)*. DeKalb: Northern Illinois University Press

    1994 'The Neo-Babylonian *zazakku*', *AoF* 21: 34–40

de Callataÿ, F. 1989 'Les trésors achéménides et les monnayages d'Alexan-dre: espèces immobilisées et espèces circulantes?', *Revue des Études Antiques* 91: 259–74

    2000 'Guerres et monnayage à l'époque hellénistique. Essai de mise en per-spective suivi d'une annexe sur le monnayage de Mithridate VI Eupator', in Andreau, Briant and Descat (eds.): 337–64

2005 'A quantitative survey of Hellenistic coinages: recent achievements', in Archibald, Davies and Gabrielsen (eds.): 73–91

2011 'Quantifying monetary production in Greco-Roman times: a general frame', in F. de Callataÿ (ed.), *Quantifying Monetary Production in Greco-Roman Times*. Bari: Edipuglia: 7–29

Del Monte, G. 1997 *Testi dalla Babilonia Ellenistica*, vol. I, *Testi cronografici*. Pisa and Rome: Istituto Editoriali e Poligrafici Internazionali

Depuydt, L. 1997 'The time of death of Alexander the Great: 11 June 323 BC (-322), ca. 4:00–5:00 PM', *WdO* 28: 117–35

Dercksen, J. G. 2004a *Old Assyrian Institutions*. MOS Studies 4 = PIHANS 122. Istanbul: NINO

(ed.) 2004b *Assyria and Beyond. Studies Presented to Mogens T. Larsen*. PIHANS 100. Leiden: NINO

De Zorzi, N. 2014 *La serie teratomantica šumma izbu. Test, tradizione, orizzonti culturali*, 2 vols. HANE/M 15. Padua: SARGON

Doty, L. T. 1977 *Cuneiform Archives from Hellenistic Uruk*. Ann Arbor, MI: University Microfilms International

Duyrat, F. 2005 *Arados hellénistique. Étude historique et monétaire*. Beirut: Institut français du proche-orient

Ebeling, E. 1949 *Neubabylonische Briefe*. Munich: Verlag der Bayerischen Akademie derWissenschaften

Eckstein, A. 2008 *Rome Enters the Greek East. From Anarchy to Hierarchy in the Hellenistic Mediterranean, 230–170 BC*. Berkeley: University of California Press

Ehling, K. 2008 *Untersuchungen zur Geschichte der späten Seleukiden (164–63 v.Chr.). Vom Tode des Antiochos IV. bis zur Einrichtung der Provinz Syria unter Pompeius*. Historia Einzelschriften 196. Stuttgart: Franz Steiner

Eph'al, I. 2009 *The City Besieged. Siege and Its Manifestations in the Ancient Near East*. CHANE 36. Leiden and Boston: Brill

Erdkamp, P. 2005 *The Grain Market in the Roman Empire. A Social, Political and Economic Study*. Cambridge University Press

Erickson, K. and G. Ramsey (eds.) 2011 *Seleucid Dissolution. The Sinking of the Anchor*. Wiesbaden: Harrassowitz

Esty, F. 1986 'Estimation of the size of a coinage: a survey and comparison of methods', *Numismatic Chronicle* 146: 185–215

Fanselow, F. 1990 'The bazaar economy, or How bizarre is the bazaar really?', *Man* (NS) 25.2: 250–65

Feinstein, C. and M. Thomas 2002 *Making History Count. A Primer in Quantitative Methods for Historians*. Cambridge University Press

Feyel, C., J. Fournier, L. Graslin-Thomé and F. Kirbihler (eds.) 2012 *Communautés locales et pouvoir centrale dans l'Orient hellénistique et romain*. Collection études anciennes 47. Paris: De Boccard

Fischer, T. 1980 *Seleukiden und Makkabäer. Beiträge zur Seleukidengeschichte und zu den politischen Ereignissen in Judäa während der 1. Hälfte des 2. Jahrhunderts v. Chr.* Bochum: Brockmayer

Flynn, D. and A. Gíraldez 2002 'Cycles of silver: global economic unity through the mid-eighteenth century', *Journal of World History* 13.2: 391–427

Földvári, P. and B. van Leeuwen 2011 'What can price volatility tell us about market efficiency? Conditional heteroscedasticity in historical commodity price series', *Cliometrica* 5.2: 165–86

Földvári, P., B. van Leeuwen and R. Pirngruber 2011 'Markets in pre-industrial societies: storage in Hellenistic Babylonia in the medieval English mirror', *Journal of Global History* 6: 169–93

Földvári, P., B. van Leeuwen and J.-L. van Zanden 2011 'Long-run patterns in market efficiency and the genesis of the market economy: markets around the Mediterranean from Nebuchadnezzar to Napoleon (580 BC and 1800 AD)'. CEPR Discussion Paper Series 8521. London: Centre for Economic Policy Research

Foster, B. 2005³ *Before the Muses. An Anthology of Akkadian Literature*, 2 vols. Bethesda, MD: CDL Press

2007 *Akkadian Literature of the Late Period*. GMTR 2. Münster: Ugarit Verlag

Frame, G. 1992 *Babylonia, 689–627 BC. A Political History*. PIHANS 69. Leiden: NINO

Freedman, S. M. 1998 *If a City is Set on a Height*, vol. I, *The Omen Series* šumma ālu ina melê šakin, *Tablets 1–21*. OPSNKF 17. Philadelphia University Museum

Fuchs, A. 2014 'Die unglaubliche Geburt des neubabylonischen Reiches, oder: Die Vernichtung einer Weltmacht durch den Sohn eines Niemand', in M. Krebernik and H. Neumann (eds.), *Babylonien und seine Nachbarn in neu- und spätbabylonischer Zeit. Wissenschaftliches Kolloquium aus Anlass des 75. Geburtstags von Joachim Oelsner. Jena, 2. und 3. März 2007*. AOAT 369. Münster: Ugarit Verlag: 25–71

Furubotn, E. and R. Richter 2005² *Institutions and Economic Theory. The Contribution of the New Institutional Economics*. Ann Arbor: University of Michigan Press

Garfinkle, S. 2012 *Entrepreneurs and Enterprise in Early Mesopotamia. A Study of Three Archives from the Third Dynasty of Ur (2112–2004 BC)*. CUSAS 22. Bethesda, MD: CDL Press

Gehlken, E. 2005 'Childhood and youth, work and old age in Babylonia – a statistical analysis', in Baker and Jursa (eds.): 89–120

Geller, M. 2000 Review of Slotsky 1997a, *OLZ* 95: 409–12

Gera, D. and W. Horowitz 1997 'Antiochus IV in life and death: evidence from the Babylonian Astronomical Diaries', *JAOS* 117: 240–52

Glassner, J.-J. 2004 *Mesopotamian Chronicles*. Writings from the Ancient World 19. Atlanta, GA: SBL

Golenko, V. K. 1993 'Notes on the coinage and currency of the early Seleucid state, I. The reign of Seleucus I', *Mesopotamia* 28: 71–167

Grainger, J. D. 1999 'Prices in Hellenistic Babylonia', *JESHO* 42.3: 303–25

2002 *The Roman War of Antiochus III*. Mnemosyne Supplements 239. Leiden and Boston: Brill

2010 *The Syrian Wars*. Mnemosyne Supplements 320. Leiden and Boston: Brill

Graslin-Thomé, L. 2009 *Les échanges à longue distance en Mésopotamie au Ier millénaire. Une approche économique*. Orient et Méditerranée 5. Paris: De Boccard

Graßhoff, G. 2010 'Babylonian meteorological observations and the empirical basis of ancient science', in G. Selz and K. Wagensonner (eds.), *The Empirical Dimension of Ancient Near Eastern Studies*. WOO 6. Vienna: LIT Verlag: 33–48

Grayson, A. K. 1975 *Assyrian and Babylonian Chronicles*. TCS V. New York: Eisenbrauns

Green, P. 1990 *Alexander to Actium. The Historical Evolution of the Hellenistic Age*. Berkeley: University of California Press

Hackl, J. 2013 'Materialien zur Urkundenlehre und Archivkunde der spätzeitlichen Texte aus Nordbabylonien', 2 vols. Unpublished PhD thesis, University of Vienna.
forthcoming 'The Esangila temple during the Late Achaemenid Period and the impact of Xerxes' reprisals on the Northern Babylonian temple households', in Waerzeggers (ed.)

Hackl, J. and R. Pirngruber 2015 'Prices and related data from Northern Babylonia in the Late Achaemenid and Hellenistic periods, ca. 480–300 BC', in Van der Spek, Van Leeuwen and van Zanden (eds): 107–27

Harrison, T. 2011 *Writing Ancient Persia*. Duckworth Classical Essays. London: Duckworth

Hatcher, J. and M. Bailey 2001 *Modelling the Middle Ages. The History and Theory of England's Economic Development*. Oxford University Press

Hauser, S. 1999 'Babylon in arsakidischer Zeit', in J. Renger (ed.) *Babylon: Focusmesopotamischer Geschichte, Wiege früher Gelehrsamkeit, Mythos der Moderne*. Berlin: SDV: 207–39

Heckel, W. 2008 *The Conquests of Alexander the Great*. Cambridge University Press

Heckel, W. and J. C. Yardley 1997 *Justin's Epitome of the Philippic History of Pompeius Trogus*. Oxford University Press

Heckel, W., L. Tritle and P. Wheatley (eds.) 2007 *Alexander's Empire. Formulation to Decay*. Claremont, CA: Regina Books

Henkelman, W. and A. Kuhrt (eds.) 2003 *A Persian Perspective. Essays in Memory of H. Sancisi-Weerdenburg*. Ach. Hist. XIII. Leiden: NINO

Hölbl, G. 1994 *Geschichte des Ptolemäerreichs. Politik, Ideologie und religiöse Kultur von Alexander dem Grossen bis zur römischen Eroberung*. Darmstadt: Wissenschaftliche Buchgesellschaft

Hollander, D. 2008 'The demand for money in the Late Roman Republic', in W. V. Harris (ed.), *The Monetary Systems of the Greeks and Romans*. Oxford University Press: 112–36

Honigman, S. 2014 *Tales of High Priests and Taxes. The Books of the Maccabees and the Judean Rebellion Against Antiochos IV*. Oakland: University of California Press

Houghton, A. 2004 'Seleucid coinage and monetary policy of the 2nd century BC. Reflections on the monetization of the Seleucid economy', in Chankowski and Duyrat (eds.): 49–79

Houghton, A. and C. Lorber 2002 *Seleucid Coins. A Comprehensive Catalogue, Part I: Seleucus I through Antiochus IV*, vol. I, *Introduction, Maps, and Catalogue*; vol. II, *Appendices, Indices, and Plates* (with a contribution by B. Kritt). Lancaster, NY: American Numismatic Society

Houghton, A., C. Lorber and O. Hoover 2008 *Seleucid Coins. A Comprehensive Catalogue, Part II: Seleucus IV through Antiochus XII*, vol. I, *Introduction, Maps, and Catalogue*; vol. II, *Appendices, Indices, and Plates*. Lancaster, NY: American Numismatic Society

Hudson, M. and M. van de Mieroop (eds.) 2002 *Debt and Economic Renewal in the Ancient Near East*. Bethesda, MD: CDL Press

Huijs, J., R. Pirngruber and B. van Leeuwen 2015 'Climate, war and economic development: the case of Babylon', in van der Spek, van Leeuwen and van Zanden (eds.): 128–48

Hunger, H. and D. Pingree 1999 *Astral Sciences in Mesopotamia*. HdO I/XLIV. Leiden and Boston: Brill

Hunger, H. and A. Sachs 1988 *Astronomical Diaries and Related Texts from Babylonia*, vol. I, *652–262 BC*. Vienna: Verlag der Akademie der Wissenschaften

1989 *Astronomical Diaries and Related Texts from Babylonia*, vol. II, *261–165 BC*. Vienna: Verlag der Akademie der Wissenschaften

1996 *Astronomical Diaries and Related Texts from Babylonia*, vol. III, *164–61 BC*. Vienna: Verlag der Akademie der Wissenschaften

Hunger, H. and R. J. van der Spek 2006 'An astronomical diary concerning Artaxerxes II: military operations in Babylonia', *ARTA* 2006.002: 1–16

Janković, B. 2008 'Travel provisions in Babylonia in the first millennium BC', in Briant, Henkelman and Stolper (eds.): 429–64

2013 'Aspects of Urukean agriculture in the first millennium BC.' Unpublished PhD thesis, University of Vienna

Joannès, F. 1982 *Textes économiques de la Babylonie récente*. Paris: Éditions Recherche sur les Civilisations

1997 'Prix et salaire en Babylonie du VIIe au IIIe siècle avant notre ère', in Andreau, Briant and Descat (eds.): 313–33

2000a *La Mésopotamie au 1er millénaire avant J.-C*. Paris: De Boccard

2000b 'Une chronique judiciaire d' époque hellénistique et le châtiment des sacrilèges à Babylone', in Marzahn and Neumann (eds.): 193–211

2006 'La Babylonie mériodionale: continuité, déclin ou rupture?', in Briant and Joannès (eds.): 101–35

2008 'Place et rôle des femmes dans le personnel des grands organismes néo-babyloniens', in Briant, Henkelman and Stolper (eds.): 465–80

Johnstone, S. 2011 *A History of Trust in Ancient Greece*. University of Chicago Press

Jursa, M. 1995 *Die Landwirtschaft in Sippar in neubabylonischer Zeit*. AfO Beiheft 25. Vienna: Archiv für Orientforschung

1997 'Neu- und spätbabylonische Texte aus den Sammlungen der Birmingham Museums and Art Gallery', *Iraq* 59: 97–174

1998 *Der Tempelzehnt in Babylonien vom siebenten bis zum dritten Jahrhundert v. Chr.* AOAT 254. Münster: Ugarit Verlag

2002 'Florilegium babyloniacum: Neue Texte aus hellenistischer und spätachämenidischer Zeit', in Wunsch (ed.): 107–30

2004a 'Grundzüge der Wirtschaftsformen Babyloniens im ersten Jahrtausend v. Chr.', in Rollinger and Ulf (eds.): 115–32

2004b 'Accounting in Neo-Babylonian institutional archives', in M. Hudson and C. Wunsch (eds.) *Creating Economic Order. Record Keeping, Standardization, and the Development of Accounting in the Ancient Near East.* Bethesda, MD: CDL Press: 145–98

2005a *Neo-Babylonian Legal and Administrative Documents. Typology, Contents and Archives.* GMTR 1. Münster: Ugarit Verlag

2005b 'Money-based exchange and redistribution: the transformation of the institutional economy in first millennium Babylonia', in Clancier, Joannès, Ruoillard and Tenu (eds.): 171–86

2006 'Agricultural managing, tax farming, and banking: aspects of entrepreneurial activity in Babylonia in the Late Achaemenid and Hellenistic periods', in Briant and Joannès (eds.): 137–222

2007a 'The transition of Babylonia from the Neo-Babylonian Empire to Achaemenid rule', *Proceedings of the British Academy* 136: *Regime Change in the Ancient Near East and Egypt: From Sargon of Agade to Saddam Hussein*: 73–94

2007b 'Die Söhne Kudurrus und die Herkunft der neubabylonischen Dynastie', *RA* 101: 125–36

2008 'The remuneration of institutional labourers in an urban context in Babylonia in the first millennium BC', in Briant, Henkelman and Stolper (eds.): 387–427

2009 with contributions by C. Waerzeggers 'On aspects of taxation in Achaemenid Babylonia: new evidence from Borsippa', in P. Briant and M. Chauveau (eds.), *Organisation des pouvoirs et contacts culturels dans les pays de l'empire achéménide.* Persika 14. Paris: De Boccard: 237–69

2010 with contributions by J. Hackl, B. Janković, K. Kleber, E. E. Payne, C. Waerzeggers and M. Weszeli *Aspects of the Economic History of Babylonia in the First Millennium BC. Economic Geography, Economic Mentalities, Agriculture, the Use of Money and the Problem of Economic Growth.* AOAT 377 = Veröffentlichungen zur Wirtschaftsgeschichte Babyloniens im 1. Jahrtausend v. Chr., Band 4. Münster: Ugarit Verlag

2011 'Taxation and service obligations in Babylonia from Nebuchadnezzar to Darius and the evidence for Darius' tax reform', in R. Rollinger, B. Truschnegg and J. Wiesehöfer (eds.), *Herodot und das Persische Weltreich. Akten des 3. Internationalen Kolloquiums zum Thema 'Vorderasien im Spannungsfeld klassischer und altorientalischer Überlieferungen', Innsbruck, 24.–28. November 2008.* Wiesbaden: Harrassowitz: 431–48

2011/13 'Steuer D. Spätbabylonisch', *RlA* 13: 168–75

2014a 'On the existence of factor markets in Babylonia from the long sixth century to the end of Achaemenid rule', *JESHO* 57: 173–202

2014b 'Babylonia in the first millennium BCE – economic growth in times of empire', in L. Neal and J. Williamson (eds.), *The Cambridge History of Capitalism*, vol. I, *The Rise of Capitalism from Ancient Origins to 1848*. Cambridge University Press: 24–42

Jursa, M. and M. Stolper 2007 'From the Tattannu archive fragment', *WZKM* 97: 243–81

Kessler, K. 2000 'Hellenistische Tempelverwaltungstexte. Eine Nachlese zu CT 49', in Marzahn and Neumann (eds.): 213–41

2004 'Urukäische Familien versus babylonische Familien. Die Namengebung in Uruk, die Degradierung der Kulte von Eanna und der Aufstieg des Gottes Anu', *AoF* 31: 237–62

2005 'Zu den ökonomischen Verhältnissen von Uruk in neu- und spätbabylonischer Zeit', in Baker and Jursa (eds.): 269–87

2006 Review of Boiy 2004 and Linssen 2005, *ZA* 96: 278–80

Kleber, K. 2008 *Tempel und Palast. Die Beziehungen zwischen dem König und dem Eanna-Tempel im spätbabylonischen Uruk*. AOAT 358 = Veröffentlichungen zur Wirtschaftsgeschichte Babyloniens im 1. Jahrtausend v. Chr., Band 3. Münster: Ugarit Verlag

2012 'Famine in Babylonia. A microhistorical approach to an agricultural crisis in 528–526 BC', *ZA* 102: 219–44

Kleber, K. and E. Frahm 2006 'A not-so-great escape: crime and punishment according to a document from Neo-Babylonian Uruk', *JCS* 58: 109–22

Kosmin, P. 2014a *The Land of the Elephant Kings: Space, Territory, and Ideology in the Seleucid Empire*. Cambridge, MA and London: Harvard University Press

2014b 'Seeing double in Seleucid Babylonia: rereading the Borsippa Cylinder of Antiochus I', in A. Moreno and R. Thomas (eds.), *Patterns of the Past: Epitēdeumata in the Greek Tradition*. Oxford University Press: 173–98

Kuhrt, A. 1990 'Alexander and Babylon', in H. Sancisi-Weerdenburg and W. Drijvers (eds.), *The Roots of the European Tradition*. Ach. Hist. V. Leiden: NINO: 121–30

Leichty, E. 1970 *The Omen Series šumma izbu*. TCS IV. Locust Valley, NY: Eisenbrauns

Leisten, B. 1986 'Die Münzen von Uruk-Warka', *BaM* 17: 309–67

Lendle, O. 1995 *Kommentar zu Xenophons Anabasis (Bücher 1–7)*. Darmstadt: Wissenschaftliche Buchgesellschaft

Le Rider, G. 1992 'Les clauses financières des traités de 189 et de 188', *Bulletin de correspondance héllenique* 116: 267–77

1993 'Les ressources financières de Séleucos IV (187–175) et le paiement de l'indemnité aux Romains', in M. Price, A. Burnett and R. Bland (eds.), *Essays in Honour of Robert Carson and Kenneth Jenkins*. London: Spink: 49–67

1994 'Antiochos IV (175–164) et le monnayage de bronze séleucide', *Bulletin de correspondance héllenique* 118: 17–34

2003 *Alexandre le Grand. Monnaie, finances et politique*. Paris: Presses Universitaires Françaises

Le Rider, G. and F. de Callataÿ 2006 *Les Séleucides et les Ptolémées. L'héritage monétaire et financier d'Alexandre le Grand*. Paris: Éditions du Rocher

Lerner, J. 1999 *The Impact of Seleucid Decline on the Eastern Iranian Plateau. The Foundations of Arsacid Parthia and Graeco-Bactria*. Historia Einzelschriften 123. Stuttgart: Franz Steiner

Lewis, D. 1977 *Sparta and Persia*. Cincinnati Classical Studies 1. Leiden: Brill

Liddell, H. G. and R. Scott 1968⁹ *A Greek–English Lexicon*. Oxford University Press

Linssen, M. J. H. 2005 *The Cults of Uruk and Babylon. The Temple Ritual Texts as Evidence for Hellenistic Cult Practices*. CM 25. Leiden: Brill-Styx

Liverani, M. 1988 *Antico Oriente. Storia società economia*. Bari: Edipuglia

Luther, A. 1999 'Überlegungen zur *defectio* der östlichen Satrapien vom Seleukidenreich', *Göttinger Forum für Altertumswissenschaft* 2: 5–15

Ma, J. 2000 *Antiochus III and the Cities of Western Asia Minor*. Oxford University Press

McCloskey, D. and J. Nash 1984 'Corn at interest: the extent and cost of grain storage in Medieval England', *American Economic Review* 74.1: 174–87

Marzahn, J. and H. Neumann (eds.) 2000 *Assyriologica et Semitica. Festschrift für Joachim Oelsner anlässlich seines 65. Geburtstages am 18. Februar 1997*. AOAT 252. Münster: Ugarit Verlag

Manning, J. 2003 *Land and Power in Ptolemaic Egypt. The Structure of Land Tenure*. Cambridge University Press

2007 'Egypt', in Scheidel, Morris and Saller (eds.): 434–59

Mayhew, N. 1995a 'Population, money supply, and the velocity of circulation in England, 1300–1700', *Economic History Review* (NS) 48.2: 238–57

1995b 'Modelling medieval monetisation', in B. Campbell and R. H. Britnell (eds.), *A Commercializing Economy: England, 1086–1300*. Manchester University Press: 55–77

Ménard, C. and M. Shirley 2008 'Introduction', in C. Ménard and M. Shirley (eds.), *Handbook of Neo-Institutional Economics*. Berlin: Springer: 1–18

Migeotte, L. 2007 *The Economy of the Greek Cities from the Archaic Age to the Early Roman Empire*. Berkeley: University of California Press

Mileta, C. 2008 *Der König und sein Land. Untersuchungen zur Herrschaft der hellenistischen Monarchen über das königliche Gebiet Kleinasiens und seine Bevölkerung*. Klio – Beiträge zur Alten Geschichte, NF 14. Berlin: Oldenbourg Akademieverlag

Mittag, P. F. 2006 *Antiochus IV Epiphanes: eine politische Biographie*. Klio – Beiträge zur Alten Geschichte, NF 11. Berlin: Oldenbourg Akademieverlag

Mollo, P. 1996 'Il problema dell' ἁλική seleucide alla luce die materiali degli archivi di Seleucia sul Tigri', in M.-F. Boussac and A. Invernizzi (eds.), *Archives et sceaux du monde hellénistique, Turin 13–16 January 1993*. Bulletin de correspondence hellénique Supplement 29. Athens: École français: 145–56

Monerie, J. 2013 'Aspects de l'économie de la Babylonie aux époques hellénistique et parthe (IVe s. av. J.-C.–1er s. av. J.-C.).' Unpublished PhD thesis, Université Paris I – Panthéon-Sorbonne. Paris

Monson, A. 2012 *From the Ptolemies to the Romans. Political and Economic Change in Egypt.* Cambridge University Press

    2015 'Hellenistic empires', in A. Monson and W. Scheidel (eds.), *Fiscal Regimes and the Political Economy of Premodern States.* Cambridge University Press: 169–207

Morris, I. and J. Manning 2005 'Introduction' in I.Morris and J. Manning (eds.), *The Ancient Economy. Evidence and Models.* Stanford University Press: 1–44

Morris, I., R. Saller and W. Scheidel 2007 'Introduction', in Scheidel, Morris and Saller (eds.): 1–12

Müller, G. W. 1995/6 'Die Teuerung in Babylon im 6. Jh. v. Chr.', *AfO* 42–43: 163–75
    1999/2000 'Preise, Kurse, Wasserstände', *AfO* 46–47: 201–7

Newell, E. T. 1938 *The Coinage of the Eastern Seleucid Mints. From Seleucus I to Antiochus III.* Numismatic Studies 1. New York: American Numismatic Society

Neumann, J. and S. Parpola 1987 'Climatic change and the eleventh–tenth-century eclipse of Assyria and Babylonia', *JNES* 46.2: 161–82

North, D. C. 1977 'Markets and other allocation systems in history: the challenge of Karl Polanyi', *Journal of European Economic History* 6: 703–16

    1978 'Structure and performance: the task of economic history', *Journal of Economic Literature* 16.3: 963–78

    1990 *Institutions, Institutional Change and Economic Performance.* Cambridge University Press

    2005 *Understanding the Process of Economic Change.* Oxford and Princeton: Princeton University Press

North, D. C., J. J. Wallis and B. Weingast 2009 *Violence and Social Orders. A Conceptual Framework for Interpreting Recorded Human History.* Cambridge University Press

Oelsner, J. 1971 'Review of CT 49', *ZA* 61: 159–70

Ogilvie, S. 2007 ' "Whatever is, is right"? Economic institutions in pre-industrial Europe', *Economic History Review* 60.4: 649–84

    2011 *Institutions and European Trade. Merchant Guilds, 1000–1800.* Cambridge University Press

Oppenheim, A. L. 1955 ' "Siege documents" from Nippur', *Iraq* 17: 69–89

Ossendrijver, M. 2015 'Babylonian mathematical astronomy', in C. N. L. Ruggles (ed.), *Handbook of Archaeoastronomy and Ethnoastronomy.* New York: Springer: 1863–70

Persson, K. G. 1999 *Grain Markets in Europe, 1500–1900: Integration and Deregulation.* Cambridge Studies in Modern Economic History. Cambridge University Press

Pirngruber, R. 2010 'Seleukidischer Herrscherkult in Babylon?', in R. Rollinger, B. Gufler, M. Land and I. Madreiter (eds.), *Interkulturalität in der Alten*

Welt. Vorderasien, Hellas, Ägypten und die vielfältigen Ebenen des Kontakts. Philippika. Marburger altertumskundliche Abhandlungen 34. Wiesbaden: Harrasowitz: 533–49

2013 'The historical sections of the Astronomical Diaries in context: developments in a Late Babylonian scientific text corpus', *Iraq* 75: 197–210

2014 'Plagues and prices: locusts', in Baker and Jursa (eds.): 163–86

2016 'The value of silver: wages as guides to the standard of living in first millennium BC Babylonia', in K. Kleber and R. Pirngruber (eds.), *Studies in Silver, Money and Credit. Festschrift for Robartus J. van der Spek on the Occasion of his 65th Birthday on 18th September 2014*. PIHANS 128. Leiden: NINO: 218–28

forthcoming A 'Land and power in a Northian perspective: state building and its reflection in private archives from first millennium BC Babylonia', in S. Prochazka and S. Tost (eds.), *Land and Power in the Ancient and Post-Ancient World. Proceedings of the 3rd International Conference of the Research Network Imperium and Officium*. Vienna: Institut für Orientalistik. Preliminary version available online at: http://iowp.univie.ac.at/?q=node/340 (accessed 24 October 2016)

forthcoming B 'Towards a framework for interpreting social and economic change in Babylonia during the long 6th Century BC', in Waerzeggers (ed.). Preliminary version available on-line at: http://iowp.univie.ac.at/?q=node/342 (accessed 24 October 2016)

Pirngruber, R. and C. Waerzeggers 2011 'Prebend prices in first millennium BC Babylonia', *JCS* 63: 111–44

Poyck, A. G. P. 1962 *Farm Studies in Iraq. An Agro-Economic Study of the Agriculture inthe Hilla-Diwaniya Area in Iraq*. Wageningen: Veenman

Rathbone D. 2014 'Mediterranean and Near Eastern grain prices. Some preliminary conclusions', in Baker and Jursa (eds): 313–21

Reade, J. 1986 'A hoard of silver currency from Achaemenid Babylon', *Iran* 24: 79–89.

Reger, G. 1993 'The public purchase of grain on independent Delos', *Classical Antiquity* 12.2: 300–34

1994 *Regionalism and Change in the Economy of Independent Delos, 314–167 BC*. Berkeley, Los Angeles and Oxford: University of California Press

Ries, G. 1976 *Die neubabylonischen Bodenpachtformulare*. Berlin: J. Schweitzer

Rochberg F. 1988 *Aspects of Babylonian Celestial Divination. The Lunar Eclipse Tablets of* Enūma Anu Enlil. AfO-Beiheft 22. Vienna: Institut für Orientalistik

2004 *The Heavenly Writing. Divination, Horoscopy, and Astronomy in Mesopotamian Culture*. Cambridge University Press

Rollinger, R. and C. Ulf 2004 *Commerce and Monetary Systems in the Ancient World. Means of Transmission and Cultural Interaction*. Oriens et Occidens 6. Stuttgart: Franz Steiner Verlag

Roth, M. T. 1995 *Law Collections from Mesopotamia and Asia Minor*. Writings from the Ancient World 6. Atlanta: SBL

Ruzicka, S. 2012 *Trouble in the West. Egypt and the Persian Empire 525–332 BCE*. Oxford University Press

Sachs, A. 1948 'A classification of the Babylonian astronomical tablets of the Seleucid period', *JCS* 2: 271–90

Sachs, A. and D. J. Wiseman 1954 'A Babylonian king list from the Hellenistic period', *Iraq* 16: 202–11

San Nicolò, M. 1951 *Babylonische Rechtsurkunden des ausgehenden 8. und des 7. Jahrhundert v. Chr*. Munich: Verlag der Bayerischen Akademie der Wissenschaften

Sarkisian, G. 1969 'City Land in Seleucid Babylonia (1953)', in I. Diakonoff (ed.), *Ancient Mesopotamia. Socio-Economic History*. Moscow: Nauka: 312–31
    1974 'New cuneiform texts from Uruk of the Seleucid period in the Staatliche Museen zu Berlin', *FuB* 16: 15–76

Scheidel, W. 2007 'Demography', in Scheidel, Morris and Saller (eds.): 38–86

Scheidel, W. and S. von Reden (eds.) 2002 *The Ancient Economy*. Edinburgh Readings on the Ancient World. New York: Routledge

Scheidel, W., I. Morris and R. Saller (eds.) 2007 *The Cambridge Economic History of the Greco-Roman World*. Cambridge University Press

Schmitt, H. H. 1964 *Untersuchungen zur Geschichte Antiochos' des Großen und seiner Zeit*. Historia Einzelschriften 6. Wiesbaden: Harrassowitz

Schober, L. 1981 *Untersuchungen zur Geschichte Babyloniens und der Oberen Satrapien von 323–303 v. Chr*. Europäische Hochschulschriften III/147. Frankfurt/Main and Bern: Peter Lang

Schuler, C. 2004 'Landwirtschaft und königliche Verwaltung im hellenistischen Kleinasien', in Chankowski and Duyrat (eds.): 509–43

Sherwin-White A. N. 1984 *Roman Foreign Policy in the East*. London: Duckworth

Sherwin-White, S. and A. Kuhrt 1991 'Aspects of Seleucid royal ideology: the cylinder of Antiochus I from Borsippa', *Journal of Hellenic Studies* 111: 71–86
    1993 *From Samarkhand to Sardis. A New Approach to the Seleucid Empire*. London: Duckworth

Shipley, G. 2000 *The Greek World after Alexander 323–30 BC*. London and New York: Taylor and Francis

Silver, M. 2004 'Modern ancients', in Rollinger and Ulf (eds.): 63–87

Slotsky, A. L. 1997a *The Bourse of Babylon. Market Quotations in the Astronomical Diaries of Babylonia*. Bethesda, MD: CDL Press
    1997b 'You CAN teach an old dog new tricks: computer age analysis of ancient data (prices in the Astronomical Diaries of -463 to -72)', in Andreau, Briant and Descat (eds.): 355–60

Slotsky, A. and R. Wallenfels 2009 *Tallies and Trends. The Late Babylonian Commodity Price Lists*. Bethesda, MD: CDL Press

Söderberg, J. 2004 'Prices in the medieval Near East and Europe', Paper read at the Towards a Global History of Prices and Wages conference, Utrecht,

19–21 August 2004. Available at www.iisg.nl/hpw/papers/soderberg.pdf (last accessed September 2015)

Steinkeller, P. 2002 'Money lending practices in Ur III Babylonia. The issue of economic motivation', in Hudson and van de Mieroop (eds.): 109–37

Stevens, K. 2014 'The Antiochos cylinder, Babylonian scholarship and Seleucid imperial ideology', *Journal of Hellenic Studies* 134: 66–88

Stol, M. 1983/4 'Cress and its mustard', *JEOL* 28: 24–32

    1985 'Remarks on the cultivation of sesame and the extraction of its oil', *BSA* 2: 119–26

    1994 'Beer in Neo-Babylonian times', in L. Milano (ed.), *Drinking in Ancient Societies: History and Culture of Drinks in the Ancient Near East*. Padua: SARGON: 156–83

Stolper, M. 1985 *Entrepreneurs and Empire. The Murašû Archive, the Murašû Firm, and Persian Rule in Babylonia*. PIHANS 54. Istanbul: NINO

    1987 'Bēlšunu the satrap', in F. Rochberg (ed.), *Language, Literature and History. Philological and Historical Studies Presented to Erica Reiner*. AOS 67. New Haven: Eisenbrauns: 389–402

    1993a *Late Achaemenid, Early Macedonian, and Early Seleucid Records of Deposit and Related Texts*. AION Supplement 77. Naples.

    1993b 'Militärkolonisten', *RLA* 8: 205–7

    1995 'The Babylonian enterprise of Belesys', in P. Briant (ed.), *Dans les pas des Dix-Mille*. Pallas 43. Toulouse: Presses Universitaires du Mirail: 217–38.

    2000 'No harm done: on Late Achaemenid *pirku* guarantess', in Marzahn and Neumann (eds.): 467–77

    2001/2 'Texts of the Murašûs and from their surroundings', *JCS* 53.4: 83–132

    2003 ' "No-one has exact information except for you": communication between Babylon and Uruk in the first Achaemenid reigns', in Henkelman and Kuhrt (eds.): 265–87

    2004 'The Kasr texts, the Rich collection, the Bellino copies and the Grotefend Nachlass', in Dercksen (ed.): 511–49

    2007 'Kasr texts: excavated – but not in Berlin', in M. Roth, W. Farber, M. Stolper and P. van Bechtolsheim (eds.), *Studies Presented to R. D. Biggs, June 4 2004*. Oriental Institute of the University of Chicago: 243–83

Stolper, M. and V. Donbaz 1997 *Istanbul Murašû Texts*. PIHANS 79. Istanbul: NINO

Streck, M. 2004 'Dattelpalme und Tamariske in Mesopotamien nach dem akkadischen Streitgespräch', *ZA* 94, 250–90

Studer, R. 2008 'India and the Great Divergence: assessing the efficiency of grain markets in eighteenth- and nineteenth- century India', *Journal of Economic History* 68.2: 393–437

Temin, P. 2002 'Price behaviour in ancient Babylon', *Explorations in Economic History* 39: 46–60

Thoneman, P. 2009 'Estates and the land in early Hellenistic Asia Minor: the estate of Krateuas', *Klio* 39, 363–93

Tolini, G. 2011 'La Babylonie et l'Iran. Les relations d'une province avec le cœur de l'empire achéménide (539–331 avant notre ère).' Unpublished PhD thesis, Université Paris I – Panthéon-Sorbonne

　2012 'Le discours de domination de Cyrus, de Darius Ier et d'Alexandre le Grand sur la Babylonie (539–323)', in Feyel, Fournier, Graslin-Thomé and. Kirbihler (eds.): 259–96

Tuplin, C. 1998 'The seasonal migration of Achaemenid kings: a report on old and new evidence', in Brosius and Kuhrt (eds.): 63–114

van de Mieroop, M. 1997 *The Ancient Mesopotamian City*. Oxford University Press

　1999 *Cuneiform Texts and the Writing of History*. London and New York: Routledge

　2005 *King Hammurapi of Babylon. A Biography*. Oxford. Blackwell

van der Spek, R. J. 1986 'Grondbezit in het Seleucidische rijk.' Unpublished PhD thesis, VU Unversity Amsterdam

　1987 'The Babylonian city', in S. Sherwin-White and A. Kuhrt (eds.), *Hellenism in the East. The Interaction of Greek and Non-Greek Civilizations from Syria to Central Asia after Alexander*. Berkeley: University of California Press: 57–74

　1993a 'The Astronomical Diaries as a source for Achaemenid and Seleucid history', *Bi.Or.* 50: 91–101

　1993b 'New evidence on Seleucid land policy', in H. Sancisi-Weerdenburg, R. J. van der Spek, H. C. Teitler and H. T. Wallinga (eds.), *De Agricultura. In memoriam Pieter W. De Neevem*. Amsterdam: J. C. Gieben: 61–77

　1995 'Land ownership in Babylonian cuneiform documents', in M. Geller and H. Maehler (eds.), *Legal Documents from the Hellenistic World*. London: The Warburg Institute: 173–245

　1997/8 'New evidence from the Babylonian Astronomical Diaries concerning Seleucid and Arsacid history', *AfO* 44–45, 167–75

　1998a 'The chronology of the wars of Artaxerxes II in the Babylonian Astronomical Diaries', in Brosius and Kuhrt (eds.): 239–56

　1998b 'Cuneiform documents on Parthian history: the Rahimesu archive. Materials for the study of the standard of living', in Wiesehöfer (ed.): 205–58

　2000a 'The effect of war on the prices of barley and agricultural land in Hellenistic Babylonia', in Andreau, Briant and Descat (eds.): 293–313

　2000b Review of G. Del Monte 1997, *Or* 69: 433–38

　2003 'Darius III, Alexander the Great and Babylonian scholarship', in Henkelman and Kuhrt (eds.): 289–346

　2005 'Ethnic segregation in Hellenistic Babylon', in R. Kalvelagen, D. Katz and W. van Soldt (eds.), *Ethnicity in Ancient Mesopotamia. Papers read at the 48th Rencontre Assyriologique Internationale, Leiden, 1–4 July 2002*. Leiden: NINO: 393–408

2006a 'The size and significance of the Babylonian temples under the successors', in Briant and Joannès (eds.): 261–307

2006b 'How to measure prosperity? The case of Hellenistic Babylonia', in A. Bresson and R. Descat (eds.), *Approches de l'économie hellénistique*. EAHSBC 7. St.-Bertrand-des-Comminges: Musée archéologique départemental: 287–310

2007 'The Hellenistic Near East', in Scheidel, Morris and Saller (eds.): 409–33

2009 'Multi-ethnicity and ethnic segregation in Hellenistic Babylon', in T. Derks and N. Roymans (eds.), *Ethnic Constructs in Antiquity. The Role of Power and Tradition*. Amsterdam University Press: 101–15

2010 'Seleukiden, Seleukidenreich', *RlA* 12: 369–83

2012 Review of Capdetrey 2007, *Klio* 94.2: 527–9

2014a 'Seleukos, self-appointed general (*strategos*) of Asia (311–305 B.C.) and the satrapy of Babylonia', in H. Hauben and A. Meeus (eds.), *The Age of the Successors and the Creation of the Hellenistic Kingdoms (323–276 B.C.)*. Studia Hellenistica 53 . Leuven: Peeters: 323–44

2014b 'The volatility of prices of barley and dates in Babylon in the third and second centuries BC', in Baker and Jursa (eds.): 234–59

2014c 'Factor markets in Hellenistic and Parthian Babylonia (331 BC–224 AD)', *JESHO* 57.2: 203–30

van der Spek, R. J. and B. van Leeuwen 2014 'Quantifying the integration of the Babylonian economy in the Mediterranean world using a new corpus of price data, 400–50 BC', in F. de Callataÿ (ed.) *Quantifying the Greco-Roman Economy and Beyond*. Pragmateiai 27. Bari: Edipuglia: 79–101

van der Spek, R. J. and C. Mandemakers 2003 'Sense and nonsense in the statistical approach of Babylonian prices', *Bi.Or.* 60: 521–37

van der Spek, R. J., P. Földvári and B. van Leeuwen 2015 'Growing silver and changing prices: the development of the money stock in ancient Babylonia and medieval England', in Van der Spek, Van Leeuwen and van Zanden (eds.): 489–505

van der Spek, R. J., B. van Leeuwen and J.-L. van Zanden (eds.) 2015a *A History of Market Performance from Ancient Babylonia to the Modern World*. London: Routledge

2015b 'Introduction', in van der Spek, van Leeuwen and van Zanden (eds.): 1–16

van Driel, G. 1989 'The Murašûs in context' (Review of Stolper 1985), *JESHO* 32: 203–29

1999 'Agricultural entrepreneurs in Mesopotamia', in H. Klengel and J. Renger (eds.), *Landwirtschaft im Alten Orient*. BBVO 18. Berlin: Reimer: 213–23

2002 *Elusive Silver. In Search for a Market in an Agrarian Environment. Aspects of Mesopotamia's Society*. PIHANS 95. Istanbul: NINO

van Zanden, J.-L. 2004 'On the efficiency of markets for agricultural products: rice prices and capital markets in Java, 1823–1853', *Journal of Economic History* 64.4: 1028–55

Vargyas, P. 1997 'Les prix des denrées alimentaires de première nécessité en Babylonie à l'époque achéménide et hellénistique', in Andreau, Briant and Descat (eds.): 335–54

    2001 *A History of Babylonian Prices in the First Millennium BC*, vol. I, *Prices of Basic Commodities*. HSAO 10. Heidelberger Orientverlag

Veenhof, K. 1972 *Aspects of Old Assyrian Trade and its Terminology*. Leiden: NINO

Verboven, K. 2014 'Like bait on a hook. Ethics, etics and emics of gift exchange in the Roman world', in F. Carlà and M. Gori (eds.), *Gift Giving and the 'Embedded' Economy in the Ancient World*. Universitätsverlag Heidelberg: 135–53

Volk, K. 2003–5 'Palme', *RlA* 10: 283–92

von Reden, S. 2007 *Money in Ptolemaic Egypt*. Cambridge University Press

    2010 *Money in Classical Antiquity*. Key Themes in Ancient History. Cambridge University Press

    2014 'Wheat prices in Ptolemaic Egypt', in Baker and Jursa (eds): 206–86

von Reden, S. and D. Rathbone 2015 'Mediterranean grain prices in classical antiquity', in Van der Spek, Van Leeuwen and van Zanden (eds.): 149–235

Waerzeggers, C. 2003/4 'The Babylonian revolts against Xerxes and the "end of archives"', *AfO* 50: 150–73

    2006 'The Carians of Borsippa', *Iraq* 68, 1–22

    2010 *The Ezida Temple of Borsippa. Prieshood, Cult, Archives*. Ach. Hist. XV. Leiden: NINO

    2012 'The Babylonian chronicles: classification and provenance', *JNES* 71: 285–98

    2014 *Marduk-rēmanni. Local Networks and Imperial Politics in Achaemenid Babylonia*. OLA 233. Leuven: Peeters

    (ed.) forthcoming *Proceedings of the International Workshop 'Xerxes and Babylonia: The Cuneiform Evidence'*, Leiden, 16–17 January 2014

Walbank, F., A. Astin, M. Frederiksen and R. Ogilvie (eds.) 1984 *The Cambridge Ancient History*, vol. VII.i, *The Hellenistic World*. Cambridge University Press

Warburton, D. 2003 *Macroeconomics from the Beginning. The General Theory, Ancient Markets, and the Rate of Interest*. Neuchâtel: Recherches et publications

Weber, M. 1978 *Economy and Society. An Outline of Interpretive Sociology*, ed. G. Roth and C. Wittich. Berkeley, Los Angeles and London: University of California Press

Weiskopf, D. 1989 *The So-Called 'Great Satrap's Revolt', 366–360 BC. Concerning Local Instability in the Achaemenid Far West*. Historia Einzelschriften 63. Stuttgart: Franz Steiner

Wheatley, P. 2007 'An introduction to the chronological problems in the early Diadoch sources and scholarship', in Heckel, Tritle and Wheatley (eds.): 179–92

Wiesehöfer, J. 1993 *Das antike Persien: von 550 v. Chr. bis 650 n. Chr.* Munich: Becks

    (ed.) 1998 *Das Partherreich und seine Zeugnisse*. Historia Einzelschriften 122. Stuttgart: Franz Steiner

    2003 'Tarkumuwa und das Farnah', in Henkelman and Kuhrt (eds.): 173–87

2007 'The Achaemenid Empire in the fourth century B.C.E.: a period of decline?', in O. Lipschits, G. Knoppers and R. Albertz (eds.), *Judah and the Judeans in the Fourth Century B.C.E.* Winona Lake, IN: Eisenbrauns: 11–30

Wilcke, C. 2007 'Markt und Arbeit im Alten Orient am Ende des 3. Jahrtausends v. Chr.', in W. Reinhard and J. Stagl (eds.), *Menschen und Märkte. Studien zur historischen Wirtschaftsanthropologie.* Historische Anthropologie 9. Vienna: Böhlau: 71–132

Will, É. 1979² *Histoire politique du monde hellénistique, 323–30 av. J.-C.*, vol. I, *De la mort d'Alexandre aux avènements d'Antiochos III et de Philippe V.* Presses universitaires de Nancy

1982² *Histoire politique du monde hellénistique, 323–30 av. J.-C.*, vol. II, *Des avènements d'Antiochos III et de Philippe V à la fin des Lagides.* Presses universitaires de Nancy

Wunsch, C. 1993 *Die Urkunde des babylonsichen Geschäftsmannes Iddin-Marduk. Zum Handel mit Naturalien im 6. Jahrhundert v. Chr.* Groningen: Styx

2000 *Das Egibi-Archiv I. Die Felder und Gärten.* CM 20A and B. Groningen: Styx

2002a 'Debt, interest, pledge, and forfeiture in the Neo-Babylonian and early Achaemenid period: the evidence from the private archives', in Hudson and van de Mieroop (eds.): 221–55

(ed.) 2002b *Mining the Archives. Festschrift for Christopher Walker on the Occasion of his 60th Birthday, 4 October 2002.* Babylonische Archive 1. Dresden: Islet

Zaccagnini, C. 1997 'Price and price formation in the Ancient Near East. A methodological approach', in Andreau, Briant and Descat (eds.): 361–84

Index